SIGNIFICANT PRISONER RIGHTS CASES

SIGNIFICANT PRISONER RIGHTS CASES

James F. Anderson

Nancie J. Mangels

Laronistine Dyson

CAROLINA ACADEMIC PRESS

Durham, North Carolina

Library of Congress Cataloging-in-Publication Data

Anderson, James F.
  Significant prisoner rights cases / James F. Anderson, Nancie J. Mangels, and
Laronistine Dyson.
     p. cm.
  Includes index.
  ISBN 978-1-59460-415-7 (alk. paper)
  1. Prisoners--Legal status, laws, etc.--United States--Cases. 2. Correctional
law--United States--Cases. I. Mangels, Nancie J. II. Dyson, Laronistine. III.
Title.

  KF9731.A962 2010
  344.7303'56--dc22

                        2009051499

CAROLINA ACADEMIC PRESS
700 Kent Street
Durham, North Carolina 27701
Telephone (919) 489-7486
Fax (919) 493-5668
www.cap-press.com

Printed in the United States of America

This book is dedicated to everyone in the struggle for social justice.
JFA

Dedicated to the memory of my father, Jack Mangels, and my companion, Zeffar, both of whom were committed to championing the causes of the less fortunate.
NJM

Contents

Acknowledgments

Any work of this magnitude owes a great deal to a number of people who unselfishly provided assistance when called upon. In fact, this book could not have been accomplished were it not for the help of others who devoted their time and energy by providing us with invaluable criticisms throughout the process. As such, we express our sincere appreciation to several colleagues and a mentor.

We thank the faculty in the Department of Criminal Justice at East Carolina University for providing the encouragement for us to start and finish this book. More specifically, we appreciate the warm discussions they provided on the subject matter and the commitment they displayed by providing positive criticisms on how to strengthen the quality of the work. We would like to offer sincere appreciation to Gary Kowaluk for his invaluable contribution to this work. We also appreciate the assistance rendered by Dr. Adam H. Langsam, Associate Professor of Sociology at Northeastern State University, who spent an extensive amount of time discussing the work and providing suggestions used in several rewrites.

Dr. Anderson thanks Dr. Rolando V. del Carmen, Distinguished Professor of Criminal Justice at Sam Houston State University (SHSU), for his encouragement over the years. He is a national scholar in matters of the law and how it relates to the legal aspects of the criminal justice system. As one of his former students at SHSU, I was fascinated by his intelligence and his capacity to take complex legal concepts and effortlessly explain them to students who were untrained in the law. His understanding of the law seemed endless. What impressed me the most was his commitment to teaching doctoral students to research the legal aspects of the criminal justice system even if it meant he had to accomplish it with many of us yelling and screaming every step of the way. He has devoted his career to teaching his students to engage in legal research and work toward reforming the justice system. He greatly influenced my commitment to contribute to the body of criminal justice scholarship. For that, I am eternally grateful.

With the benefit of many selfless contributions, the authors assume complete responsibility for any weaknesses that are found in the finished work.

Introduction

Prior to the 1960s, U.S. courts generally practiced a "hands-off" approach to matters related to the corrections system. During this time, inmate complaints went unheard by the courts. Judicial officials believed that decisions on issues related to corrections were better left to penal administrators since they were familiar with prisoners and inmates (Dilulio, 1987). This belief was best captured in 1958 by Justice Felix Frankfurter in *Gore v. United States* (357 U.S. 386, 1958), when he stated, "in effect, we are asked to enter the domain of penology ... [T]his Court has no such powers." The philosophy of nonintervention from the judiciary meant that correctional administrators decided every facet of life within prisons, because there was no judicial oversight that would challenge the legality of their practices and policies.

Penologists and historians reported that nearly every penal institution in the country subjected inmates to insufferable conditions. Physical abuse such as corporal punishment by guards and elite cons, such as "building tenders" and "floorwalkers," was common. In addition, inmate lease systems allowed prison officials to lease prisoners to outside contractors, who often failed to provide adequate food, clothing, shelter, and medical care, which resulted in the deaths of many prisoners (see Walker, 1988). Moreover, the prison experience for many inmates, especially those in southern and western states, was tantamount to slavery, since forced labor was the norm in correctional institutions that were reported to be self-sufficient (Dilulio, 1987). In some prisons, rapes, suicides, and murders were common. Yet the courts did not intervene holding that prisoners were not entitled to any rights or redress because they were merely "slaves of the State" (see *Ruffin v. Commonwealth*, 62 Va. 790, 1871 and *Stroud v. Swope*, 187 F.2d 850, 9th Circuit, 1951).

However, during the 1960s, America experienced a number of social and political changes that challenged institutions and traditional ways of thinking. Many of the proponents for change questioned the existing social order. Minority groups and other oppressed people started to demand inclusion in all areas of mainstream society. Young Americans protested U.S. involvement in the Vietnam War and fought for equality and access to public education, housing, voting rights, employment opportunities, and the full protection of the U.S. Constitution for all citizens. Those arrested and imprisoned for engaging in antigovernment demonstrations and other crimes took with them into the nation's jails and prisons the philosophy of penal reform and human dignity, and fought to rid themselves and others of institutional oppression that ran counter to rights guaranteed by the Constitution.

Though there were several riots that resulted from prisoners' struggles for equal rights and justice, the 1971 riot that occurred in upstate New York at Attica, which resulted in the deaths of forty-three people, dramatized the inhumanity that was widespread in the corrections system and galvanized the prison rights movement of the 1970s. The Attica riot was televised for four days into the homes of Americans. The aftermath of the riot revealed that the inhumane conditions the inmates were protesting had reached a boiling point with no remedy in place for negotiation or mediation. Adler, Mueller, and Laufer (2006) report that the tragic events at Attica occurred because inmates were denied basic human rights and constitutional guarantees, such as religious freedom, adequate nutrition, procedures to resolve complaints, recreation, medical treatment, humane discipline, and contact with the outside world. Prison riots and other violent incidents exposed the problems within the correctional system, and forced prison officials and the justice system to address the issue of prisoners' rights.

The shift from a "hands-off" to "hands-on" philosophy in the courts can be traced to one particular case, *Cooper v. Pate* (378 U.S. 546, 1964). In *Cooper*, the petitioner brought an action under the Civil Rights Act of 1871, alleging that Illinois prison officials denied him the right to purchase certain religious publications so that he could worship in a manner consistent with his religion. He argued that this right was afforded to other inmates. The U.S. Supreme Court reversed the judgment of the District Court and agreed with the prisoner. *Cooper* signaled that a prisoner could sue a warden for a violation of his or her civil rights. Prisoners now had rights guaranteed by the Constitution and could therefore seek assistance from the courts to challenge the conditions of their confinement. As such, *Cooper* opened the door to other issues that inmates faced as consequences of their incarceration. These issues include the rights to freedom of communication; correspond with counsel; access the courts; political expression; freedom of religion, right to marry, reasonable expectation to privacy, right to be free from strip searches, right to have access to law libraries, right to be free from cruel and unusual punishment, right to due process in prison disciplinary hearings, and right to recourse when property is damaged. Despite being a prisoner, one does not surrender the constitutional protections guaranteed to citizens.

As a result of *Cooper*, prisoners are protected by the Constitution, but not to the same extent as citizens in free society. Prisoners' rights are limited because the conditions and circumstances of confinement require correctional officials to conduct a balancing act between ensuring the safety and security of employees and prisoners and preserving prisoners' constitutional rights. Issues where rights and security and/or safety must be balanced include denial of contact visits; cell searches; the right to engage in non-Christian worship; access to court; equal treatment for homosexual inmates; disciplinary hearings for prison rule infractions; the right of unmarried inmates to participate in Family Reunion Programs; freedom from inmate violence; and denial of medical care. Some other issues may include denial of Family Reunion Programs because of AIDS status; mandatory blood tests for AIDS; freedom from corporal punishment committed by correctional guards; freedom from sexual harassment by prison guards; freedom from the infliction of the death penalty; journalists interviewing prisoners; the right to possess nude photos of a spouse; access to clergy; mandatory body cavity searches; wrongful death in suicides; administrative segregation without a hearing; denial of special diets; conversations between inmate and visitors electronically recorded; denial of law libraries; prison transfer; segregation of inmates diagnosed with the AIDS virus; free association in prison; revocation of good time credit; and more.

Correctional experts argue that the majority of lawsuits filed by prisoners that involve correctional officials (i.e., line officers, wardens, directors, and superintendents) are brought under federal statute, Title 42 U.S. Code Section 1983 or the Civil Rights Act. The Civil Rights Act was passed by Congress in 1871. It states the following:

> Every person who, under color of any statute, ordinance, regulation, custom, or usage, of any State or Territory, subjects or causes to be subjected, any citizens of the United States or other persons within the jurisdiction thereof to the deprivation of any rights, privileges, or immunities secured by the Constitution and laws, shall be liable to the party injured in an action at law, suit in equity, or other proper proceeding for redress.

Though the Act was created to correct the injustices committed by the Ku Klux Klan in the post-Civil War South, it was rarely used until rediscovered by the prisoners' rights movement during the 1950s and 1960s (see del Carmen, 1991; Collins, 2001). Section 1983 protects against violations of individuals' constitutional rights and specific rights protected by federal statute. Some experts argue the latter is rare because very few federal statutes protect prisoners (see Collins, 2001). Prisoners prefer to use Section 1983 lawsuits for several reasons. First, they can bring declaratory and injunctive relief along with requiring a defendant to pay damages to plaintiffs. Second, these civil rights lawsuits are typically filed in the federal court system (yet they can be filed in state courts), where the judiciary has historically been more receptive to hearing inmate complaints. The same cannot be said for inmate claims filed in the state court system. Third, because these cases are usually filed in federal court, these lawsuits do not have to exhaust the range of state remedies that could delay justice for prisoners seeking relief. Finally, successful civil rights cases allow plaintiffs to recover attorney fees under the Attorney Fees Act (Cripe, 1997).

When prisoners file a Section 1983 claim, they must establish two basic requirements. First, the defendant must have been *acting under color of law*. Second, there must be a violation of a constitutional or federally protected right (see Chemerinsky, 2007; del Carmen, 1991; Collins, 2001). Where the first requirement is concerned, the prisoner needs to demonstrate that the person who deprived him or her of a constitutional or federally protected right was an official employed at a correctional institution and misused his or her authority. The phrase "acting under color of law" means that the official engaged in the constitutional violation while working within the scope of his or her employment with the state. These suits target governmental employees. However, Section 1983 claims do not apply to federal officers. Where the second requirement is concerned, the prisoner has to demonstrate that he or she was deprived of a right given by the Constitution or by federal law. Therefore, prisoners who allege a violation of the First, Fourth, Fifth, Sixth, Eighth, or Fourteenth Amendments or several of these amendments typically file lawsuits under Section 1983 for relief. If the prisoner (plaintiff) is successful in the lawsuit, the violator (defendant) can be liable for either having to pay damages to the offended party, grant other forms of court-ordered relief, or a combination of these (Collins, 2001). Although prisoners can bring a number of issues before the court, they usually claim that correctional employees violated either their First, Fourth, Eighth, or Fourteenth Amendment right or a combination of them. A brief discussion of these amendments and the likely challenges that inmates could bring from them follows.

The First Amendment

The First Amendment states in part that "Congress shall make no law respecting an establishment of religion, or prohibiting the free exercise thereof." Inmates who bring claims under the First Amendment often allege that they were prohibited from worshipping in a manner consistent with their religious beliefs. They contend that if they do not have traditional Christian beliefs shared by penal administrators, and they are discriminated against by not being afforded the same opportunities and resources as Christian prisoners. They argue that prison officials violate the First Amendment by respecting Christianity yet preventing non-Christians from freely engaging in the religion of their choice. When inmates argue for relief under the First Amendment, they also attach the Fourteenth Amendment, which extends equal protection to the state level.

The argument of discrimination and religious freedom is complex in an institutional setting. For example, prisoners' claims often include the denial of religious practices or observance, access to clergy members, proper dietary needs, and required grooming or personal appearance (Cripe and Pearlman, 2005). Inmates who challenge religious discrimination contend that the tenets of their beliefs often require that they engage in rituals that are essential to their faith. For example, their religion may require them to worship several times a day, which conflicts with a penal schedule that prohibits the slightest deviation. Inmates also may argue that their religion requires diets that are not provided at some institutions. For example, Muslim and Jewish inmates may not eat pork, and depending on their beliefs, may be required by their religion to adhere to a special diet.

Another common claim in complaints that allege religious discrimination is that correctional institutions do not allow prisoners to observe their particular religious practices related to personal grooming. For example, some religious practices of Native Americans require them to wear long hair, and some Jews are required to grow a beard, which can create security problems, according to correctional officials. Because of these types of complaints filed under the First Amendment, the courts must do a balancing test between the inmate's freedom to worship in a manner consistent with his or her "true" religious beliefs and correctional policies that promote legitimate penological interests.

The Fourth Amendment

The Fourth Amendment states in part that "The right of the people to be secure in their persons, houses, papers, and effects, against unreasonable searches and seizures shall not be violated." Inmates who bring challenges under the Fourth Amendment believe that even within the prison setting, they should be afforded some level of privacy. Inmates differ from the courts as to what they feel is reasonable within the context of a search in prison. Prisoners do not enjoy the same level of protection as citizens in the free community, who could argue that a warrant is needed to make a legal search. This could never be the case for jail or prison inmates. Rather, the courts are concerned with the following issues where searches are conducted in penal setting: (1) Is the area of the search protected by the Constitution? and (2) Was the search conducted in a reasonable or unreasonable manner?

According to Cripe and Pearlman (2005), there are two types of searches in places of confinement: those of an inmate's cell and those of the inmate's person. Where the latter is concerned, the method can be performed in a number of ways that include frisk search, strip searches, digital instrument searches, urine testing, x-ray examination, and even blood tests. Moreover, searches are also made in recreation areas, work areas, and in all areas that surround an institution (Cripe and Pearlman, 2005). Where the former is concerned, the Supreme Court has ruled that inmates do not enjoy any reasonable expectations to privacy in their prison cells. Therefore, searches of cells and their contents cannot be deemed unreasonable or off-limits. When inmates bring lawsuits in which the Fourth Amendment is at issue, the courts must consider the type of search and balance the interest of the inmate to be free from unreasonable searches and seizures, and the correctional institution's need to enforce legitimate penological interests, such as safety, stopping the flow of contraband, and preventing escapes. Essentially, the courts have said that prison officials must have the freedom and latitude to search prisoners, prison cells, guards, and visitors and to seize items that may be used to harm inmates, correctional guards, penal administrators, or items designed to undermine legitimate institutional interests.

The Eighth Amendment

The Eighth Amendment states in part that "Excessive bail should not be required, nor excessive fines imposed, nor cruel and unusual punishments inflicted." Inmates who bring an Eighth Amendment challenge allege that their punishment is excessive and is disproportionate to the offense they have committed. For example, inmates who are denied access to health care and treatment for injuries, pain, or AIDS often bring this challenge. Other inmates who were physically beaten with whips and those subjected to sexual harassment by correctional guards have initiated claims of cruel and unusual punishment. When such claims are filed, the courts have to determine whether prisoners are being treated in a manner that does not reflect the standards of an evolving society. At the same time, prison officials may be required to demonstrate that they have not acted in a manner that is "deliberately indifferent" to the plight of offenders in their custody. This is especially true in suicides or attempted suicide cases, when surviving family members or the inmate alleged that the warning signs were there, but no efforts were made to prevent the suicide or its attempt. This issue is more complicated in cases where inmates challenge the total conditions of their confinement.

The Fourteenth Amendment

The Fourteenth Amendment states in part that "nor shall any State deprive any person of life, liberty, or property, without due process of law; nor deny to any person on this its jurisdiction the equal protection of the law."

This amendment has a twofold purpose: due process and equal protection under the law. The amendment was created to protect newly freed slaves. It was adopted after the Civil War to ensure that every citizen of the United States would be afforded the same constitutional protections and safeguards. The amendment requires that every citizen of the United States receives due process and equal protection on the state level. Citizens were already given due process protection on the federal level by the Fifth Amendment, but states were not legally compelled to extend constitutional protection until the passage of the Fourteenth Amendment. Essentially, the amendment requires that before any citizen can be deprived of life, liberty or property, he or she must be afforded due process. That is to say, before a U.S. citizen can be put to death, imprisoned, or have property taken, there must be a trial or legal proceeding so that his or her legal interests are safeguarded every step of the way. Usually, a host of other amendments attach, such as the Fourth, Fifth, and Sixth Amendments (i.e., search/arrest warrant, right to remain silent or not self-incriminate, and the right to have legal assistance). Where the equal protection clause is concerned, it states that all citizens of the United States, regardless of race, ethnicity, place of natural origin, or gender, must be afforded equal or the same treatment. It is highly unusual for an inmate to bring a Fourteenth Amendment challenge alone. It is usually filed along with another alleged constitutional violation. For example, when prisoners allege that they have been denied the right to the First Amendment free exercise of religion, they also will include the Fourteenth Amendment. In doing so, they allege that other inmates who practice traditional religions are allowed to exercise their religious faith, while they are subjected to unequal treatment in violation of the Fourteenth Amendment guarantee to equal protection under the law. Similarly, same-sex married inmates who are not allowed to participate in conjugal visitation programs may argue that such a penal policy violates their First and Fourteenth Amendment rights to enter into and maintain association. They would have to argue that because the practice is extended to one group, heterosexual married couples, but denied to homosexual married couples, the practice constitutes disparate treatment in violation of the equal protection clause. Furthermore, prisoners often claim that when they are accused of rule infraction and face the prospect of losing accumulated good time, there should be a procedure in place to ensure that their due process interest (the loss of good time) is protected. When these issues emerge, courts must weigh the balance of the inmates' interest and the need for correctional institutions to enforce certain policies. Because the federal courts have historically been more receptive to hearing complaints from prisoners than state courts, a brief discussion of the federal court system is warranted.

The Structure of the Federal Judicial System

The federal system derives its power from Article III, Section I, of the U.S. Constitution, where it states in part: "Congress shall establish one Supreme Court and inferior courts as the Congress may from time to time establish." Therefore, the federal court system represents the culmination of a series of congressional mandates that can be characterized as a three-tier system: district courts, courts of appeals, and one Supreme Court. They are referred to as constitutional courts because they are authorized by Article III of the Constitution (Goldman and Jahnige, 1985; Schmalleger, 2001).

District Courts

District courts are the federal judicial trial courts. They are the lowest of the federal courts. There are approximately ninety-four district courts that geographically serve fifty states. Each state has at least one district court. However, some of the larger states, such as California and New York, have as many as four district courts. These courts address federal cases that could be presided over by a jury or a judge, if a bench trial takes place. These courts can hear civil or criminal matters (Scheb and Scheb, 1999). Their subject matter jurisdiction can include a broad range of civil and criminal offenses, including tort suits, commerce, contracts, antitrusts, and others (Wasby, 1989). In a district court, the decision of a case is made by one judge. However, in special situations, these courts have used three judges to preside over hearings. When this occurs, a district court can have two district judges and one from a court of appeals. Most decisions made by district courts are final. These decisions are typically not appealed. If they are appealed, they go to one of the U.S. Circuit Courts of Appeals. District court judges are appointed by the President, confirmed by the Senate, and serve a life term.

Courts of Appeals

Courts of Appeals are also referred to as Circuit Courts. They are intermediate federal appellant courts. They review matters from the district courts of their geographic regions, tax courts, and federal administrative agencies (Goldman and Jahnige, 1985). There are approximately twelve Circuit Courts of Appeals and one federal circuit encompassing the United States (Scheb and Scheb, 1999). The First Circuit contains the states of Maine, Massachusetts, New Hampshire, Puerto Rico, and Rhode Island, and is located in Boston. The Second Circuit contains the states of Connecticut, New York, and Vermont, and is located in New York. The Third Circuit contains the states of Delaware, New Jersey, Pennsylvania, and the U.S. Virgin Islands, and is located in Philadelphia. The Fourth Circuit is composed of the states of Maryland, North Carolina, South Carolina, Virginia, and West Virginia, and is located in Richmond. The Fifth Circuit is composed of the states of Louisiana, Mississippi, and Texas, and is located in New Orleans. The Sixth Circuit is composed of the states of Kentucky, Michigan, Ohio, and Tennessee, and is located in Cincinnati. The Seventh Circuit is composed of the states of Illinois, Indiana, and Wisconsin, and is located in Chicago. The Eighth Circuit is composed of Arkansas, Iowa, Minnesota, Missouri, Nebraska, North Dakota, and

South Dakota, and is located in St. Louis. The Ninth Circuit is composed of the states of Alaska, Arizona, California, Guam, Hawaii, Idaho, Montana, Nevada, Northern Mariana Islands, Oregon, and Washington, and is located in San Francisco. The Tenth Circuit is composed of the states of Colorado, Kansas, New Mexico, Oklahoma, Utah, and Wyoming, and is located in Denver. The Eleventh Circuit is composed of the states of Alabama, Florida, and Georgia, and is located in Atlanta. The Twelfth Circuit hears cases arising in the District of Columbia and has appellate jurisdiction over legislation concerning many departments of the federal government. The Thirteenth Circuit is composed of the U.S. Court of Appeals for the federal circuit. The court includes the U.S. Court of Claims and the U.S. Court of Customs and Patent Appeals. Both the Twelfth and Thirteenth Circuits are located in Washington, D.C.

By law, federal circuit courts are required to hear cases brought to them. They have what is referred to as mandatory jurisdiction. Their primary purpose is to correct errors of laws. They handle federal laws. These courts emerged in response to increasing federal court caseload and the fact that it was impractical to have Supreme Court Justices sit on circuit (Wasby, 1989). Circuit courts have significant input in the judicial system because they bring uniformity to regional laws. Unlike the federal district courts, which typically rely on a single judge to hear a case (except in special situations), appeals courts use panels of three judges who vote to affirm, reverse, or modify decisions under review from the lower court. However, there are times when all judges assigned to the court may participate in a decision. This process is referred to as an *en banc* hearing (Scheb and Scheb, 1999). Circuit court judges are appointed by the President, and confirmed by the Senate. They serve a life term.

The Supreme Court

The U.S. Supreme Court is the highest appellate court in the federal structure. Its rulings are the final say on matters of the law, and it is known as the highest court in the land. There is only one Supreme Court and it has nine members: one Chief Justice and eight Associate Justices. Supreme Court Justices are appointed by the President, confirmed by the Senate, and serve a life term. The Court is located in Washington, D.C. Unlike the other courts in the system, the Supreme Court has both original and appellate jurisdictions. As a result, the Court can hear any case it chooses to hear. Its original jurisdiction is derived from the Constitution and is found in Article III, Section II. Original jurisdictions refer to cases that are brought directly to the Court. They account for a small amount of the Court's workload. As illustrated in *Marbury v. Madison* (5 U.S. 137, 1803), the Court has historically limited its jurisdiction. Legal experts argue that because the Court has avoided using its original jurisdiction to hear cases, original jurisdiction is primarily used to hear matters between two states. Unlike its original jurisdiction, the Constitution makes the Court's appellate jurisdiction open and only subject to change by Congress (Wasby, 1989). It is important to note that when the Court had to hear all the cases within its appellate jurisdiction, cases came to the Court on a writ of error, which allowed only review of the law and not the facts in a case (Wasby, 1989). Today, almost all cases come to the Court in one of two ways: appeal and certiorari (Scheb and Scheb, 1999). Historians report that after the courts of appeals were created, the Court was given the authority to select the cases it wanted to hear—essentially, its certiorari jurisdiction. Cases are also brought to the Court on appeal. Though theoretically a mandatory action in that the Court is obliged to hear all cases in this category of jurisdiction, the reality is that the Court has made this jurisdiction a matter of discretion. Mandatory jurisdiction creates problems because it could force the Court to deal with an issue when it is not ready or prefers not to hear cases. Cases that are eligible for appeal to the Court include the following:

- The highest state court invalidates a federal law or treaty as unconstitutional or upholds a state law or state constitutional provision against a challenge that it violates a federal law, treaty, or the U.S. Constitution.
- A court of appeals declares a state law or state constitution provision as unconstitutional or declares a federal law constitutional when the federal government is a party to a case.
- A federal district court declares a federal law unconstitutional when the United States is a party.
- A three-judge district court has granted or denied an injunction in cases required to be brought before such a court (Wasby, 1989, p. 74).

Another avenue by which cases can reach the Supreme Court (though rare) is called certification. When this occurs, a lower court faced with a new legal question certifies (rather than resolves the matter) the question for answer by the Supreme Court. When this action is taken, the Court has three options: (1) It can refuse the certificate, thus forcing the lower court to decide the question; (2) It can provide an answer, which the lower court applies; or (3) It can take the case and render a decision directly without returning it to the lower court (see also Wasby, 1989).

Writ of Certiorari

The writ of certiorari is the most popular means for a case to reach the Supreme Court. In fact, the majority of state and federal cases that reach the Court are heard on certiorari (Wasby, 1989). However, the overwhelming majority of cases that are petitioned to the Court for review are rejected. The Court has the power to either grant or deny certiorari due to its discretionary power (Scheb and Scheb, 1999). This power has led some to wonder if the Court is political because it has the authority and power to hear what it wants to hear. Certiorari is granted when at least four Justices vote to hear a case. This is referred to as the "rule of four." Even when the rule of four has been exercised, those same Justices can decide later not to hear the case. They can simply change their minds. This process is referred to as the DIG "escape" or disposing of the writ by dismissing it as "improvidently granted" (Wasby, 1989). The Court has been known to engage in such action, for example, when briefs or legal arguments present a different picture from the one painted in the petition for certiorari, which contained less information. However, when certiorari is granted as a matter of discretion, the Court does not have to give any reasons for granting, denying, or dismissing review. Nevertheless, the Supreme Court is inclined to grant the writ of certiorari when:

1. A federal court of appeals has rendered a decision in conflict with the decision of another federal court of appeals on the same matter; has decided a federal question in a way that is in conflict with a state court of last resort; or has so far departed from the accepted and usual course of judicial proceedings or so far sanctioned such a departure by a lower court as to call for an exercise of this Court's power of supervision.
2. A state court of last resort has decided a federal question in a way that conflicts with the decision of another state court of last resort or a federal court of appeals.
3. A state court or federal court of appeals has decided an important question of federal law that has not been, but should be, settled by this Court, or has decided a federal question in a way that is in conflict with applicable decisions of this Court.

References

Adler, F., Mueller, G.O.W., & Laufer, W.S. (2006). *Criminal justice: An introduction.* New York,: McGraw-Hill.

Chemerinsky, E. (2007). *Federal jurisdiction* (5th Ed.). New York: Aspen Publishers.

Collins, W.C. (2001). *Correctional law for the correctional officer* (3rd Ed.). Lanham, MD: American Correctional Association.

Cripe, C.A. (1997). *Legal aspects of corrections management.* Gaithersburg, MD: An Aspen Publication.

Cripe, C.A., & Pearlman, M.G. (2005). *Legal aspects of corrections management* (2nd Ed.). Sudbury, MA: Jones and Bartlett Publishers.

del Carmen, R.V. (1991). *Civil liabilities in American policing: A text for law enforcement personnel.* Englewood Cliffs, NJ: Prentice Hall.

Dilulio, J.J. (1987). *Governing prisons: A cooperative study of correctional management.* New York: Free Press.

Goldman, S., & Jahnige, T.P. (1985). *The federal courts as a political system* (3rd Ed.). New York: Harper & Row Publishers.

Scheb, J.M., & Scheb, J.M. (1999). *Criminal law and procedure* (3rd Ed.). Belmont, CA: West/Wadsworth.

Schmalleger, F. (2001). *Criminal justice today: An introductory text for the 21st century.* Upper Saddle River, NJ: Prentice Hall.

Walker, D.R. (1988). *Penology for profit: A history of the Texas prison system 1867–1912.* College Station: Texas A&M University Press.

Wasby, S.L. (1989). *The Supreme Court in the federal judicial system* (3rd Ed.). Chicago: Nelson-Hall Publishers.

SIGNIFICANT PRISONER RIGHTS CASES

Bell v. Wolfish

441 U.S. 520 (1979)

Facts

Inmates brought a class action suit in the U.S. District Court of the Southern District of New York challenging the constitutionality of several conditions of confinement and practices occurring in the Metropolitan Correctional Center (MCC), a federally operated short-term facility in New York City used to house pretrial detainees. The pretrial detainees challenged: (1) The "double bunking" practice of assigning two inmates to rooms originally designed for single occupancy by replacing single bunks with double bunk beds; (2) A rule that prevented inmates from receiving hardcover books unless they were mailed directly from the publishers, book clubs, or book stores; (3) A rule prohibiting inmates from receiving food or personal property packages from outside the MCC except for one package of food at Christmas; (4) Inspections by officials of inmates' rooms during which inmates were not allowed to be present; and (5) Strip or body cavity searches conducted on inmates after contact visits with someone from outside the institution. The District Court of Appeals for the Second District affirmed the District Court rulings in regard to pretrial detainees, holding that with respect to the double bunking practice, the MCC had failed to make a showing of "compelling necessity" sufficient to justify such practices.

Issue

Do jail officials violate pretrial detainees' First, Fourth, Fifth, and Eighth Amendment rights by treating them the same as convicted prisoners?

U.S. Supreme Court Holding

Reversed and remanded the decision of the U.S. Court of Appeals. MCC rules regarding double bunking, hardcover books, receiving outside packages, room searches, and body cavity searches were rationally related to legitimate institutional security interests and thus did not violate the pretrial detainees' First, Fourth, Fifth, and Eighth Amendment rights of due process or the pretrial detainees' rights.

Reason

There is no source in the U.S. Constitution for the Court of Appeals to consider which requests requires a compelling necessity standard. Nor should due process be extended to a pretrial detainee who is subjected to double-bunking. There is no Fifth Amendment violation. While the Constitution prohibits the punishment of pretrial detainees, historically pretrial detainees have been subject to the rules and restrictions of detention facilities. In regard to pretrial detainee constitutional claims, the proper inquiry is to determine whether institutional rules and restrictions amount to punishment. Absent an expressed intent to punish, institutional rules and restrictions do not amount to punishment if they are rationally related to a legitimate non-punitive government security interest or objective. Punishment and unconstitutionality can be inferred from arbitrary and purposeless institutional rules that are not rationally related to legitimate security interests.

Case Significance

A typical constitutional law case involves government rules and regulations that conflict with the constitutional rights of citizens. Such cases are resolved by weighing the interests of each party. To weigh the government's interest in the case, the Court requires that the government must demonstrate one of three levels of justification to maintain the conflicting government regulation or law. The federal court agreed that pretrial detainees, by virtue of not having been found guilty, should be treated differently from offenders who have been officially convicted. For fundamental rights such as freedom of speech, the Court frequently requires that the government regulation pass the highest level test, or the government must show a "compelling interest" before it can regulate in this area of the First Amendment. The highest level compelling interest test is difficult to pass, and frequently government regulations fail to pass constitutional muster and are struck down under this test. In this case, however, although worded slightly differently, the lower federal courts used the highest level compelling necessity test to weigh the justification for the MCC regulations in regard to the pretrial detainees' claims, and subsequently struck down the MCC regulations. The federal courts also used a medium level test where the government must show its regulation is advancing a "substantial government interest in the least restrictive way," or that the regulation is "reasonably related" to a legitimate government interest. It is somewhat difficult for the government to show that its regulation or law is rationally related to some government interest. In regard to constitutional law cases, one of the most important issues involves what level of test to use in weighing the government regulations and laws against the rights at issue. In this case, the Court decided that the prison regulation must be rationally related to advancing a legitimate government security interest and that prison regulations are only subject to the lowest level "rational relation" test. This set precedence for future cases involving prison regulations that conflicted with the liberty interests of either pretrial detainees or convicted prisoners, and after *Bell v. Wolfish*, the federal courts have used the lowest level rational relation test in deciding whether prison regulations infringe on the rights of prisoners. It is also one of the few cases involving pretrial detainees that the Court has decided.

Benjamin v. Coughlin
905 F. 2d 571 (1990)

Facts

Plaintiffs, a group of Rastafarian prisoners in the New York prison system, sued various New York State prison administrators in 1979 claiming that four prison regulations violated their First Amendment right to free exercise of religion and their Fourteenth Amendment right to equal protection of the law. The Rastafarian prisoners sought constitutional protection from: (1) New York's prison haircut regulations requiring every prisoner on admittance to the prison to obtain a haircut; (2) Prison regulations preventing them from wearing a religious "crown" cap; (3) Prison regulations preventing them from holding a weekly service; and (4) Regulations forbidding them their special vegetarian diet known as Ital. No action was taken on the lawsuit from 1980 until 1985 while a settlement was unsuccessfully dismissed. In May 1986, the lawsuit resumed with the U.S. District Court for the Southern District of New York granting the Rastafarians a preliminary injunction to prohibit prison authorities from cutting their hair on initial entry to the prison system. The case was appealed to the Second Circuit Court of Appeals.

Issues

Whether Rastafarian prisoners' First Amendment religious rights protected them from New York's prison regulations regarding (1) initial entry haircuts, (2) prohibiting the Rastafarian's from wearing their religious crowns, (3) preventing the Rastafarians from holding a weekly service, and (4) forbidding the Rastafarians special dietary privileges to eat their Ital diet.

Holding by the Second Circuit Court of Appeals

The Second Circuit Court of Appeals affirmed the decision of the U.S. District Court holding that prison authorities were permanently enjoined from enforcing the initial entry haircut regulation on newly admitted Rastafarian prisoners. The Circuit Court also found that the other three prison regulations were constitutionally permissible.

Reason

In this case, the Second Circuit Court of Appeals cited *Turner v. Safely* and its four-part test to each prison regulation. *Turner* requires a standard of reasonableness where prison regulations affect constitutional rights asserted by prisoners. It also requires that prison regulations be reasonably related to legitimate penological interests. Under *Turner*, prison authorities must show (1) the regulation rationally advances legitimate security interests; (2) alternative means of exercising the right available to prisoners; (3) accommodations to allow prisoners to exercise the right would negatively affect prison staff and other prisoners; and (4) there are no easy alternatives to the restriction. In deciding for the prisoners regarding the initial entry haircut regulation, the District Court first found that prison authorities advanced legitimate security interests in the initial haircut regulations because they allowed for identifying escaped prisoners, who could easily mask their identity by cutting their hair. In the alternative, however, the court recognized that the haircut regulation was a severe violation of the Rastafarian rights to which no alternative means of exercising the rights were available. In addition, the court did not find that accommodations that exempted the Rastafarians from the haircut regulations would negatively impact the prison staff or other prisoners, and an easy alternative in the form of the Rastafarians tying their hair in a ponytail for the initial identification photographs existed. Applying *Turner*, the District Court had no trouble finding the other three regulations were rationally related to legitimate security interests, that alternative means to exercising the right existed, that accommodating the right would negatively impact prison staff and or other prisoners, and that easy alternatives were not available.

Where the Fourteenth Amendment violation of equal protection was concerned, petitioners argued that they were treated differently from other religious groups. The court argued that the reasonableness of the prison rules and policies must be examined to determine whether distinctions made between religious groups in prison are reasonably related to legitimate penological interest. In this case, the Department of Corrections, pursuant to Section 610 of the New York Correctional Law, required a "free-world" sponsor or someone from the outside to supervise religious observances held by inmates. Because the Rastafarians could not find anyone from the outside to serve as a spiritual leader, prison officials, pursuant to the second *Turner* prong, denied them the use of an in-house inmate leader. Reasoning is known for being a part of Rastafarian services. The Second Circuit Court argued that it was not convinced that the free-world sponsor requirement violated the equal protection clause. The court went on to say that consistent with *Turner*, the defendants expressed a national basis for requiring outside sponsors. The Rastafarians' inability to find an authority willing to serve as a sponsor is not the fault of the department. Moreover, there is no violation of equal protection because the free-world sponsor policy has a legitimate basis and is imposed on all religious groups.

Case Significance

This case reveals that the First Amendment is fundamental and as such, it cannot be easily discounted or denied. However, in this case, the court weighed the right of prisoners to engage in religious worship with the needs of prison administrators to safely run their institutions. By relying on the *Turner* decision, the court engaged in a four-prong analysis of what places of confinement could do to accommodate or offer alternatives to inmates whose religious beliefs run counter to correctional policy. In the end, as long as prisons can demonstrate the legitimate need to curtail or limit rights, the court has given them leeway.

Block v. Rutherford

486 U.S. 576 (1984)

Facts

Pretrial detainees at the Los Angeles County Central Jail brought a class action suit under 42 U.S.C. 1983 to the U.S. District Court for the Central District of California against the County Sheriff and County Board of Supervisors claiming a deprivation of liberty without due process. In their complaint, the detainees alleged that the jail had a policy that denied them contact visits with their spouses, relatives, children, and friends. They also contended that the jail had a practice of conducting random irregular "shakedown" searches of cells while detainees were away at meals, recreation, and other activities. The District Court, in weighing the balance between the jail's safety interest and permitting low-security risk inmates to have physical contact visits with loved ones, decided there was not enough security risk to warrant the deprivation of contact. Therefore, the District Court sustained the challenges and ordered jail officials to allow low-risk detainees incarcerated for more than one month to have contact visits and to allow all inmates to observe searches of their cells if they were in the area when their cell was being searched. The Court of Appeals affirmed the District Court ruling.

Issue

Does denying pretrial detainees contact visits with outsiders and searching their cells in their absence constitute a due process violation?

U.S. Supreme Court Holding

When a pretrial detainee has been deprived of liberty without due process, the constitutional question is whether the challenged practice amounts to punishment or is reasonably related to a legitimate governmental interest. The practices of both denying pretrial detainees contact visits with outsiders and conducting cell searches without them present are reasonable responses by jail officials to legitimate security interests. Therefore, the U.S. Supreme Court reversed the Court of Appeals for the Ninth Circuit.

Reason

In weighing the liberty interests of pretrial detainees against the jail officials' security concerns, the District Court used a medium level balancing test in finding that jail officials could advance their security interests in the less restrictive ways of allowing low-risk detainees confined for at least one month to have contact visits and by allowing the inmates to be present during cell searches if they were in the area when their cell was being searched. In this case, the Court reversed the District Court's citing in *Bell v. Wolfish* as the Court held that the proper level of inquiry when weighing the liberty interest of pretrial detainees against the jail officials' security concerns was the minimum level "reasonable relation" balancing test. Under the "reasonable relation" balancing test, jail officials need only to show that regulations are reasonably related to legitimate security interests to pass constitutional muster. The Court stressed that the "reasonable relation" test provided maximum deference to jail officials on matters related to running a jail. Regarding suits involving pretrial detainees, if the jail officials' security interests are not reasonably related to legitimate security interests, the regulations are assumed to be punishment and unconstitutional, because pretrial detainees are still assumed innocent, which bars the state from punishing them. However, the Court did not reach the punishment issue, finding that the jail officials' contact visit policy was a reasonable response to the legitimate security goals of stopping the flow of contraband, such as drugs, weapons, or escape plans, into the jail and preventing violent disturbances between inmates and outsiders. In regard to not allowing the pretrial detainees to view searches of their cells, the Court decided that jail officials' concerns about preventing friction between the guards and inmates as a result of the cell searches, and concerns about inmates interfering with the cell searches if present, were reasonable measures related to legitimate security concerns.

Case Significance

This case is part of a series of cases favoring the use of the minimum level reasonable relation balancing test over the medium level least restrictive means balancing test when weighing the liberty interests of prisoners against the security interests of prison and jail officials. The minimum level reasonable relation test maximizes deference to prison and jail officials on matters concerning the running of the prisons and jails and minimizes the ability of the federal judges to engage in judicial activism. This case clearly indicates that the Court is more likely to decide issues regarding prison safety and regulations in favor of prison administrators because some of the language used by the Court signals this course of action. For example, in this case, the Court stated, "courts should play a very limited role since considerations are peculiarly within the province and professional expertise of corrections officials." The language can be inferred to mean that the Court is likely to give prison administrators great discretion to manage their inmate populations, especially if their decisions are related to security interests.

Blumhagen v. Sabes

834 F. Supp. 1347 (1993)

Facts

Plaintiffs, Wyoming State Penitentiary prisoners, brought a class action Section 1983 claim to the U.S. District Court for the District of Wyoming alleging that Wyoming prison officials, the Wyoming Department of Health, and several members of the medical staff of the prison violated their Eighth Amendment right to be free from cruel and unusual punishment as applied to the states through the Due Process Clause of the Fourteenth Amendment. The prisoners reported that one of the Wyoming prisoners was diagnosed with active tuberculosis and was never quarantined or isolated from the rest of the prison population. Although Wyoming prison officials initially screened all

prisoners for tuberculosis, the prisoners claimed that follow-up tests to identify inmates with the disease were never performed, the prison medical staff failed
to implement procedures to prevent the spread of the disease, and no monitoring of the prison population was ever conducted. In all, the prisoners alleged
that the Wyoming prison officials' failure to provide follow-up amounted to acting with "deliberate indifference" to their serious medical needs because they
had been exposed to the risk of contracting tuberculosis. The plaintiffs sought
a declaratory judgment, an injunction ordering the prison to implement new
medical procedures, and compensatory and punitive damages totaling $40
million. Wyoming prison officials filed a motion in the District Court to dismiss the complaint for failure to state a claim, or a motion for a more definite
statement.

Issue

Whether a court could find that the Wyoming prison officials acted with
deliberate indifference to prisoners' serious medical needs in their handling of
the tuberculosis problem in the Wyoming State Penitentiary.

Holding by the Tenth Circuit Court of Appeals

The Tenth Circuit Court of Appeals affirmed the decision of the U.S. District Court of the District of Wyoming, holding that the District Court did
not abuse its discretion by denying plaintiffs' motion for appointment of counsel, injunctive relief or discovery, or by failure to hold a hearing.

Reason

In this case, the District Court relied on the U.S. Supreme Court case of
Estelle v. Gamble, the leading case on Eighth Amendment medical claims, as
standing for the idea that deliberate indifference is a culpability standard that
stands for something more than negligence in the treatment of prisoners' serious medical problems. The District Court noted that while prison officials have
a duty to fulfill the serious medical needs of prisoners, the prisoners have no
Eighth Amendment claim when officials act with an "ordinary lack of due care"
to their medical needs, and that the Eighth Amendment ban against cruel and
unusual punishment applies to a level of "wanton disregard of the prisoners'
medical needs." In finding that the Wyoming prison officials' actions in the
treatment of the tuberculosis problem amounted to negligence at best, the
District Court granted the prison officials summary judgment, but encouraged the prisoners to bring a medical malpractice action against the prison of-

ficials in state court. The District Court ruled that plaintiffs failed to allege specific facts that would satisfy the legal standard of deliberate indifference under *Estelle v. Gamble*. The plaintiffs' allegations were conclusory and failed to establish a genuine dispute of material fact on the issue. The District Court closed by commenting that this case is a classic example of where medical judgment should be addressed by a state court because the case presented no constitutional cause of action to grant relief.

Case Significance

The case was decided by the District Court and later appealed, and the Tenth Circuit Court of Appeals affirmed the District Court decision that the plaintiffs did not establish that the defendants acted with deliberate indifference in violation of the Eighth Amendment prohibition against cruel and unusual punishment. The decision would only affect prisoners in Wyoming and within the Tenth Circuit. The decision reveals that prisoners simply cannot allege the claim exists; they must demonstrate the action occurred to prevail at trial. The District Court commented that this case is a classic prison medical treatment case for the state to rule on. Taking action to identify and prevent the spread of tuberculosis among prisoners, state prison officials did not act with the subjective state of mind of wantonly disregarding the prisoners' medical needs, necessary for Eighth Amendment relief against cruel and unusual punishment. But questions regarding whether the prison officials were negligent in regard to preventing the spread of tuberculosis among the state prisoners still exists.

Bounds v. Smith
430 U.S. 817 (1977)

Facts

Prisoners incarcerated by the Division of Prisons of the North Carolina Department of Corrections filed an action under 42 U.S.C. 1983 in the District Court for the Eastern District of North Carolina, claiming that the state's sole prison library was "severely inadequate," and with no other legal assistance available they were being denied access to the courts in violation of their Fourteenth Amendment rights. The District Court granted the respondents summary judgment, agreeing that the prison library in the state was "severely inadequate" and that the state failed to provide legal assistance to prisoners. In citing *Younger v. Gilmore* (404 U.S. 15 1971), the court held that by not assisting prisoners with accessing the court, the prison system had denied them their due process rights because prisoners were not assisted with writing petitions or writs. However, the court did not attempt to determine the "appropriate relief to order" because the North Carolina prison system is decentralized. Rather, the court left the remedy to the Department of Corrections and charged it with creating a constitutionally-correct program that would provide prisoners access to court. North Carolina proposed creating seven institutions across the state to serve all prison units. The respondents rejected the proposal, contending it was inadequate. They argued for a law library at every prison institution in the state. The District Court disagreed, holding that what the state had proposed was fair and could meet the prisoners' needs to access the courts. The inmates also argued that the state was required to provide independent legal advisors for inmates. The District Court held that no such constitutional requirement existed, and the plans for building a library was enough to provide inmates reasonable access to court. The Court of Appeals largely affirmed the lower court's decision.

Issue

Whether states must protect the rights of prisoners to access the courts by providing them with adequate law libraries or alternative sources of legal knowledge.

U.S. Supreme Court Holding

Prisoners have a fundamental right of access to the courts; which places affirmative obligations on the part of prison authorities to assist prisoners in the preparation and filing of meaningful legal papers by providing adequate law libraries or adequate assistance from persons trained in law. Maintaining adequate prison law libraries is one way for states to fulfill their obligation to provide prisoners with access to the courts. Other ways include the use of professional or paraprofessional assistance. Alternative means of providing prisoners with access to the courts could include (1) training prisoners to work as paralegals under the supervision of attorneys; (2) the use of paraprofessionals and law students in formal or volunteer programs; (3) using volunteer attorneys through bar associations; (4) hiring attorneys on a part-time basis; or (5) the use of full-time staff attorneys working in newly established prison legal assistance programs, or as part of their legal aid or public defender duties.

Reason

The Court noted that their holding was consistent with *Younger v. Gilmore* when it recognized a prisoner's right to access the courts. The holding also clarifies the obligation of the state to ensure that prisoners can effectively exercise their right to access the courts, which have been expressed in past decisions.

Case Significance

In this case, the Court is clear in reiterating its previous decisions in prisoners' access to court. However, the Court is careful to accept what prison officials are willing to offer to help prisons operate in a constitutionally correct manner by assisting prisoners with the right to access the courts. The Court noticed that at this time, half of the states and the District of Columbia provided some degree of professional or quasi-professional legal assistance to prisoners. In addition to providing a law library, alternatives to helping inmates access the courts may include training prisoners as paralegals to assist lawyers, the use of paraprofessionals and law students (either as volunteers or in informal clinical programs), the organization of volunteer attorneys through bar associations or other groups, and legal services. The Court never implied in this decision that correctional departments were required to provide law libraries or defend prisoners; it simply stated that their access to courts must not be denied.

Brown v. Johnson

743 F. 2d 408 (1984)

Facts

State prisoners at Michigan's Jackson State Prison appealed to the Sixth Circuit Court of Appeals the decision of the U.S. District Court for the Eastern District of Michigan's ruling that state prison officials were not acting unreasonably when they prohibited the Detroit Metropolitan Community Church from conducting congregate worship services at the prison. The Detroit Metropolitan Community Church is a member of the Universal Fellowship of Metropolitan Community Churches, which ministers to the spiritual needs of homosexuals in and out of prisons. Prison authorities denied church officials and inmate members the privilege of conducting worship services because they linked homosexuality with prison violence. Officials argued that the presence of worship services by the church would result in the increased identification of homosexuals in prison who otherwise would not be identified as homosexual. For prison officials, the increased identification of homosexuals could lead to an increased victimization of the homosexual prisoners identified as such by predators, and an increase in other prison violence among others who would compete with each other to form relationships with the homosexual prisoners. As an alternative to worship services, prison authorities allowed the church to conduct individual counseling sessions with prisoners and made religious ministry sessions available. The prisoners and church officials maintained that they had the First Amendment's free exercise of religion right to conduct worship services because other churches were allowed to conduct services with inmates of other faiths. The prisoners also argued they were denied the Fourteenth Amendment's equal protection of the law.

Issue

Whether state prison officials can deny inmates their First and Fourteenth Amendment affiliation with the Universal Fellowship of Metropolitan Community Churches, which ministers to the special religious needs of homosexuals, while allowing other churches to hold worship service.

Court of Appeals Holding

The Court of Appeals affirmed the decision of the District Court after finding that prison officials expressed a reasonable security concern in preventing prison violence by denying the Universal Fellowship of Metropolitan Community Churches the privilege of conducting congregate worship services while allowing other churches to conduct similar services.

Reason

The Court of Appeals found a reasonable security interest in the prison authorities' argument that allowing the Universal Fellowship of Metropolitan Community Churches worship services would result in the increased identification of prison homosexuals and would invariably lead to increased prison violence. In deferring to correctional experts, the court noted that to allow members to congregate would put them at risk along with innocent inmates who might attend the church's meetings. Predatory and violent inmates may use such gatherings as an opportunity to compete for the affection of homosexual inmates or those who are passive or physically nonaggressive. The court felt that prison officials offered reasonable accommodations to the needs of those inmates by offering them individual counseling and religious ministry sessions.

Case Significance

This case addressed two prison issues related to the First and Fourteenth Amendments. The appeals court ruled that prison officials were not unreasonable in their decision to refuse this church (unlike other churches in the prison) the opportunity to have congregate worship services. Prison officials argued that to do so would expose homosexual, passive, and innocent inmates and open them up to attack, thereby creating a security risk. The court agreed and went a step further by indicating that when faced with balancing the security interest of their penal institution and inmates' rights, officials are not required to demonstrate actual danger; they only need to show that a potential danger exists. Moreover, where the Fourteenth Amendment is concerned, it is within the discretion of prison officials to determine which groups should be allowed to operate within the prison walls. This is not the job for the courts to decide. This case reaffirms that prison officials are empowered to curb prisoners' rights if their policy is justified by legitimate penological interests.

City of Revere v. Massachusetts General Hospital
463 U.S. 239 (1983)

Facts

On September 20, 1978, Revere, Massachusetts, police officers shot and wounded Patrick M. Kivlin after he was ordered to stop fleeing from the scene of a breaking and entering. The officers summoned a private ambulance and accompanied Kivlin to Massachusetts General Hospital (MGH) in Boston, where Kivlin was treated for his injuries. He remained hospitalized until September 29. He was issued an arrest warrant, arraigned, and released on his own recognizance. On October 18, MGH sent the Chief of Police of Revere a bill in the amount of $7,948.50 to cover Kivlin's hospitalization costs. On October 27, Kivlin returned to MGH for further treatment and stayed until November 10, incurring a bill of $5,360.41. In January 1979, MGH sued the City of Revere to recover the full cost of its hospitalization services to Kivlin. The Superior Court for the County of Suffolk dismissed the complaint. MGH appealed the case to the Supreme Judicial Court of Massachusetts. MGH argued that the Eighth Amendment prohibition against deliberate indifference to the medical needs of prisoners compels a government agency or division responsible for those needs to pay for them. The court held that the Eighth Amendment's prohibition against cruel and unusual punishment required that Revere be held liable to MGH for Kivlin's first stay at the hospital. The City of Revere appealed to the U.S. Supreme Court.

Issue

Whether a state or municipality has a constitutional duty under the Eighth Amendment to pay for medical treatment received by an individual in police custody.

U.S. Supreme Court Holding

The Supreme Judicial Court of Massachusetts was reversed. The U.S. Supreme Court held that a municipality is not constitutionally required to reimburse a hospital for treatment given to a suspect wounded by its city police. Police do not owe pretrial detainees or other people in their care medical treatment. However, in this case, police fulfilled their constitutional obligation by promptly seeking medical help at a hospital for Kivlin. Governmental agencies needed only to ensure that medical care was provided. The Constitution does not mandate that the agency must pay the cost. The Court held this was a matter of state law.

Reason

The Court ruled that the Eighth Amendment did not apply to this case because Kivlin had not been convicted of a crime. The Court ruled that a state is only subject to Eighth Amendment scrutiny after a criminal prosecution has occurred and punishment is the issue. The Court, however, determined that the Due Process Clause required the City of Revere, or any responsible government agency, to provide medical care to persons, such as Kivlin, who have been injured while being apprehended by the police, and that the Due Process Clause protections for Kivlin were as great as the Eighth Amendment protections to a convicted prisoner. In its ruling, the Court specifically noted that it did not define in this case the state's obligation to pretrial detainees and others in its care who require medical attention. To resolve the payment for the medical costs issue, the Court ruled that the Constitution only ensures that medical treatment be provided to those detainees in need of it. Payment for providing such medical services is a matter of state law.

Case Significance

This case demonstrates the Court's limited interpretation of the Eighth Amendment where pretrial detainees are concerned. In this case, the Court reversed the Massachusetts Judicial Court decision to hold the Revere Police Department liable for medical services that a wounded suspect in their custody received from MGH. In fact, the Court stated that an injured detainee's constitutional right to receive needed medical treatment is not a federal constitutional question and perhaps patients should seek to have medical treatment paid by other channels, such as by hospitals who receive federal monies.

Cleavinger v. Saxner
474 U.S. 193 (1985)

Facts

David Saxner and Alfred Cain were inmates at the Federal Correctional Institution at Terre Haute, Indiana, serving four- and five-year sentences, respectively. Each was within eighteen months of release and soon to appear before the parole board. On January 6, 1975, Lowe, another inmate at Terre Haute, died in the prison hospital. To protest Lowe's death, a prison work stoppage occurred at the prison on January 7 and 8. Saxner, a "jailhouse lawyer," and Cain, who was the librarian for the African and New World Cultural Society, were active in gathering information about Lowe's death and conditions at the prison hospital. They passed that information to members of the press, members of Congress, prison officials, and Saxner's attorney, but both inmates denied participating in the work stoppage. On February 14, each inmate was placed in administrative segregation and given a written copy of the charges against them. Each received a hearing before the Prison Disciplinary Committee, where each was allowed to call and cross-examine witnesses on their behalf; each was represented by a member of the prison staff. Saxner was found guilty of encouraging the work stoppage, possessing illegal materials advocating a prisoner union (which were found in his cell during a search), and sentenced to serve time in administrative segregation. He was also stripped of eighty-four days of good time and a transfer to another institution was recommended. Cain was found guilty of encouraging the work stoppage, possessing illegal materials, and advocating a prisoners' union. He was placed in administrative segregation, forfeited ninety-six days of good time, and was recommended to be transferred to another institution. Through appeals to the Warden at Terre Haute and the Regional Director of the Bureau of Prisons, each prisoner was granted relief from all sanctions administered by the Prison Disciplinary Board. However, to recover damages because of the time each prisoner spent in ad-

ministrative detention, both prisoners filed a suit against the Prison Disciplinary Board with the U.S. District Court for the Southern District of Indiana
in March 1975. Both prisoners were paroled by June 1975 and released in December. The District Court dismissed the prisoners' complaint on the ground
that the Prison Disciplinary Board members were entitled to absolute immunity in their function as hearing officers. In April 1981, the District Court re-
considered the case on appeal based on a recent ruling suggesting that prison
disciplinary members in their function as hearing officers were only entitled to
qualified immunity. The case went to jury, and each prisoner was awarded a
total of $4,500 to be paid by members of the Prison Disciplinary Board. The
U.S. Court of Appeals for the Seventh Circuit affirmed the District Court's ruling and the jury award.

Issue

Whether a prison's disciplinary committee members responsible for hearing cases of inmates charged with prison rule violations are entitled to absolute
immunity.

U.S. Supreme Court Holding

Members of a prison disciplinary committee are responsible for hearing cases
of inmates charged with prison rule infractions. They are not adjudicators of
the law or judges who enjoy absolute immunity. Unlike disciplinary board members, judges are involved in the judicial process which, on occasion, requires
absolute immunity. Disciplinary committee members are correctional workers
who have contact with inmates and, therefore, should enjoy the same level of
protection afforded to members on school boards. The Court held that the
prison disciplinary committee was only entitled to qualified immunity.

Reason

In recognizing that judges, administrative law judges, prosecutors, and parole board members enjoy absolute immunity, the Court commented that the
line between granting judicial decision makers absolute or qualified immunity
is often difficult to determine. However, the Court commented that qualified
immunity was the norm, and it was relatively easy to determine that Prison
Disciplinary Board members were not entitled to absolute immunity to properly perform their jobs as administrators of justice. Citing the facts that prisoners were not entitled to an attorney at such proceedings, that there was no
right to compel witnesses or to cross-examine witnesses, no right to discovery,
no standard of proof, no transcripts of the proceedings were required, infor-

mation was often hearsay, and the committee members were not independent but members of the prison staff, the Court easily found that prison disciplinary members could not be identified with other members of the judicial process who have been granted absolute immunity and were thus only entitled to qualified immunity. The Court also held that qualified immunity was enough protection to address in substantial lawsuits and ensure that "federal officials are not harassed by frivolous lawsuits." In fact, the Court stated that qualified immunity has been widely imposed on executive officials who possess greater responsibilities.

Case Significance

In this case, the Court's holding is clear that prison disciplinary board members are not on equal par or footage with judges, federal hearing examiners or administrative law judges, or federal and state prosecutors. Its rationale is that the latter deals with judicial matters that typically occur within the context of a courtroom, in the company of a defense attorney and legal procedures. Moreover, the job of these officials would be subverted if they had to deal with the threat of a lawsuit. However, members of prison disciplinary committees are not independent; they are prison officials who are directly accountable to the warden. They work directly with correctional guards to resolve disciplinary disputes in favor of the institution. The Court suggests that it is not prudent to give correctional officers who are a rank removed from line officers absolute immunity from legal recourse. The Court is also not convinced that disciplinary committees will be flooded with inmate litigation or challenges because prisons have a number of mechanisms to address inmates' concerns about this treatment.

Cromwell v. Coughlin

773 F. Supp. 606 (1991)

Facts

William Cromwell, a prisoner at New York's Sing Sing Correctional Facility, brought action to the U.S. District Court in the Southern District of New York claiming that by not establishing a Family Reunion Program at Sing Sing, New York prison authorities violated his procedural and substantive Fourteenth Amendment due process rights. Authorities previously denied Cromwell, a married prisoner, conjugal visits with his wife that allow for spending a certain amount of time in privacy. Prison officials only allowed the conjugal visits with privacy through its Family Reunion Program, which operated in thirteen of its sixty prisons. Cromwell claims (1) the state regulations that created the Family Reunion Program also created a liberty interest in conjugal visits for all inmates for which a denial would be a violation of his procedural rights under the Fourteenth Amendment; and (2) he has a substantive and fundamental right to privacy in marital relations, which prevents officials from denying him conjugal visits with privacy time. The case at hand involves the District Court's answer to New York prison officials' motion for summary judgment, where the officials claimed that Cromwell did not plead any issue of material fact.

Issue

Whether the decision not to implement the Family Reunion Program at Sing Sing, while establishing the program at a number of other correctional facilities, violates Cromwell's Fourteenth Amendment procedural and substantive due process rights.

District Court Holding

The District Court dismissed Cromwell's procedural due process claim but refused to grant New York prison officials summary judgment on his substantial law claim that the denial of conjugal visits by New York officials violated his fundamental right to privacy.

Reason

By using the U.S. Supreme Court's ruling in *Hewitt v. Helms* that a prison regulation creates a liberty interest for prisoners only if the regulation places substantial limitations on official discretion in regard to participation in the program, the District Court determined that the regulations authorizing the Family Reunion Program does not create a liberty interest for Cromwell because the regulations give the Commissioner of Corrections broad discretion in the establishment of prison visitation programs, including the conjugal visits. The District Court then refused to dismiss Cromwell's substantive law claim that his constitutional rights to privacy in marriage forbade officials from denying conjugal visits with privacy time because they failed to satisfy the requirements set by the Supreme Court's four-prong test set forth in *Turner v. Safley*. The District Court determined that Cromwell had retained limited privacy rights in marriage and that under *Turner,* officials had to show that the regulations were reasonably related to legitimate security interests before they could deny Cromwell admission to the program. The District Court pointed out that

Cromwell maintained that several companies were willing to donate trailers and services for conjugal visits with privacy privileges, and that such could be considered a reasonable alternative to the regulations. One prong of the four-prong *Turner* test required that officials demonstrate that no reasonable alternatives to the regulations existed, and since the officials failed to address the "reasonable alternative" issued required by *Turner*, the District Court could not grant them summary judgment on Cromwell's substantive law claim. The District Court referred the case to the Pro Se Law Clerk to act as an attorney for Cromwell.

Case Significance

In dismissing Cromwell's procedural law complaint, the District Court clearly articulates the complicated Supreme Court rule on when prison regulations create liberty interests for prisoners. Also, critics maintain that the *Turner* standard represents a "hands-off" approach to ruling on prison matters, whereas the Supreme Court maintains that the *Turner* standard had "teeth." This case provides a good demonstration on how *Turner* can work in favor of establishing prisoner rights.

Cruz v. Beto

405 U.S. 319 (1972)

Facts

Cruz was an inmate of the Texas Department of Corrections (TDC), and one of a number of prisoners there who either practiced Buddhism or had an interest in Buddhism. TDC repeatedly refused to allow Buddhist inmates the right to hold religious services and even punished prisoners who borrowed and loaned Buddhist religious materials and books to other prisoners. Cruz was placed in solitary confinement and given a diet of bread and water for two weeks for sharing his Buddhist materials with other prisoners. While TDC maintained rules prohibiting the practice of Buddhism, it (1) hired Protestant, Jewish, and Roman Catholic chaplains to work at various prisons; (2) distributed free copies of the Bible to prisoners at the state's expense; (3) allowed religious services and classes for inmates with the Protestant, Jewish, or Roman Catholic faiths; and (4) encouraged religious participation in the Protestant, Jewish, and Roman Catholic faiths by awarding good merit points to prisoners for religious participation, which could help prisoners with class promotions within the Texas prison system, job assignments, and parole. Cruz and other Buddhists in the system filed a class action suit in the U.S. District Court for the Southern District of Texas alleging they were subject to arbitrary and unreasonable exclusion from practicing Buddhism without any lawful justification, which violated their First Amendment right to religious freedom. The federal District Court denied Cruz relief without a hearing because it considered the matter within the discretion of prison administration. The Court of Appeals affirmed the District Court opinion.

Issue

Whether denying Cruz and other Buddhists the same opportunity to worship in a manner consistent with traditional religions constitutes a violation of the First and Fourteenth Amendments.

U.S. Supreme Court Holding

The U.S. Supreme Court vacated and remanded holding that the First Amendment is applicable to the states through the Fourteenth Amendment, which prohibits government from making a law or regulation that prohibits the free exercise of religion. The Court ruled that Texas violated Cruz's and other Buddhists First and Fourteenth Amendment rights to practice Buddhism.

Reason

The First and Fourteenth Amendments to the U.S. Constitution require that states not promote a religion and discourage others, but rather, prison officials should provide reasonable opportunities for prisoners to practice religion, regardless of faith and without fear of penalty. The Court specifically mentioned that this does not mean that every religious sect must be provided with identical facilities or personnel. Special chapels, places of worship, and chaplains, priests, or ministers need not be provided for every faith; however, prisoners must be afforded similar or reasonable opportunities to practice their respective faiths.

Case Significance

This is the U.S. Supreme Court's first prison case that involves an inmate's challenge of a policy or practice that prohibits the free exercise of religion. In this case, the Court is clear in its announcement that prisoners do not forfeit this fundamental right as a consequence of their status as inmates. It is also clear that the Court does not at this time view the right to practice one's chosen religion as a safety or security risk to places of confinement. Prior to this case, inmates were not very likely to challenge the notion of practicing a religion that was not traditional since it had not occurred before. This case sends the message that religious freedom is fundamental. What is also apparent in this case is that the Court is careful not to judge the worth of different religions by stating or suggesting that one is better than another. The Court does, however, indicate that Buddhism is a legitimate religion that has existed since 600 B.C., long before Christianity. The Court is also careful not to create excessive demands on penal institutions as the Court does not require prisons to provide each religion with identical facilities and access to religious leaders.

Daniels v. Williams

474 U.S. 327 (1986)

Facts

An inmate at the city jail in Richmond, Virginia, slipped on a pillowcase left on the stairs by a sheriff's deputy and filed a Section 1983 action in the U.S. District Court for the Eastern District of Virginia to recover damages for back and ankle injuries sustained from the fall. The inmate claimed that the deputy's negligence deprived him of his "liberty" interest in freedom from bodily injury "without due process of law" within the meaning of the Fourth Amendment. The District Court granted the deputy's motion for summary judgment. The Court of Appeals for the Fourth District affirmed.

Issue

Whether an inmate's Fourteenth Amendment right to due process is violated if a state official's negligence causes him the unintentional loss of or injury to life, liberty, or property.

U.S. Supreme Court Holding

The U.S. Supreme Court affirmed the decision of the Appeals Court, ruling that the Fourteenth Amendment's Due Process Clause is not implicated by a state official's negligent act causing unintended loss of or injury to life, liberty, or property.

Reason

The Court cited its decision in *Parratt v. Taylor*, where it held that a mere lack of due care by a state official does not equal a deprivation within the meaning of the Fourteenth Amendment. In this case, the Court held that the Due Process Clause was intended to protect individuals from abuse at the hands of governmental officials, not serve as a mechanism to punish state officials for acts of negligence that may occur when they fail to take due care of duties owed to prisoners. To do so would be to trivialize and distort the meaning and intent of the Constitution. More specifically, the Court indicated in this case that where jailers fail to execute a special duty that they owe to inmates, liability for injuries should be sought under a tort law action and not a Section 1983 claim, because a negligence claim does not rise to the level of a due process violation.

Case Significance

In overruling *Parratt*, the Court states that the new standard for Fourteenth Amendment due process claims by a prisoner is that it must be shown that a prison official "deliberately" deprived them of life, liberty, or property for which there is no adequate remedy in state law to allow them full compensation for their loss. As such, the case sends several messages. First, every case of negligence does not constitute a civil rights claim or can be construed as a constitutional law violation. Second, such cases can be directed from the federal courts and be settled on the state level,perhaps in civil law, because they represent a tort action. Third, *Daniels* was decided the same day as *Davidson v. Cannon*.

Davidson v. Cannon
474 U.S. 344 (1986)

Facts

On December 19, 1980, Davidson, a prisoner at the New Jersey State Prison at Leesburg, was attacked by McMillian, another prisoner at the same institution. Earlier in the day on December 19, Davidson sent a note to Cannon, the Assistant Superintendent of the prison, notifying him that he had been threatened by McMillian. Cannon read the note and passed it on to James, a Corrections Sergeant, who left the note on his desk unread while he attended to what he called "other emergencies" that night and forgot about the note. Since James had the next two days off, the officers on duty were not informed of the threat McMillian had made to Davidson on December 19. Davidson filed a Section 1983 claim in the U.S. District Court for the District of New Jersey against Cannon and prison officials under the Eighth and Fourteenth Amendments for injuries he sustained when they negligently failed to protect him. After a bench trial, the District Court awarded damages, holding Davidson had been deprived of his liberty interest in personal security as a result of the respondent's negligence and that such negligence was without due process because of a new statute that protects prison officials from liability for injuries caused by one prisoner to another. The Court of Appeals for the Third Circuit reversed the District Court.

Issue

Whether an inmate who is attacked by another inmate is afforded due process protection under the Fourteenth Amendment when a prison administrator's negligence fails to prevent the attack.

U.S. Supreme Court Holding

In this case, the U.S. Supreme Court affirmed the Court of Appeals decision by holding that the protections of the Due Process Clause, whether procedural or substantive, are not triggered by negligence of prison officials.

Reason

The Court decided *Davidson v. Cannon* on the same day it heard the argument in *Daniels v. Williams*. In both cases, the Court held that the Fourteenth Amendment's Due Process Clause was not intended to address the lack of due care of an official that causes unintended injury or injuries that are caused by negligence. However, the Due Process Clause was intended to be invoked where there has been a deprivation of a protected interest, such as the loss of or injury to life, liberty, or property. The Due Process Clause was designed to prevent abusive governmental conduct. In the current case, the prison administrator thought the threat was nonserious, and the correctional guard forgot to read and share the threat with other guards. This act of negligence does not rise to the level of a due process violation. Whereas *Davidson* asks for a remedy from New Jersey, the Court held the Fourteenth Amendment does not require a remedy where there has not been a deprivation of a liberty interest. The Court also held that similar to *Daniels*, the protections of the Due Process Clause, whether procedural or substantive, are not triggered by lack of due care by prison officials.

Case Significance

This case parallels the Court's decision in *Daniels,* and together the cases are to be interpreted to mean that negligence and the lack of due care by a prison official are not enough to rise to the level of invoking the Fourteenth Amendment Due Process Clause. The Court is stating that the Due Process Clause protects against deliberate deprivation to life, liberty, and property. This case is also important because both decisions from *Daniels* and *Davidson* are essentially informing detainees and prison inmates that they would perhaps be better served when these types of cases emerge to look for some other remedy via state law or civil tort action instead of trying to invoke a suit via the Fourteenth Amendment.

Doe v. Coughlin

518 N.E.2d 536 (1987)

Facts

On June 6, 1985, John Doe, a New York State inmate serving a five-and-a-half- to eleven-year sentence at Auburn Correctional Facility married Jane Doe. The Does qualified for participation in the Auburn Prison Family Reunion Program and were allowed two-day conjugal visits in a trailer on prison grounds. In December, John Doe was diagnosed with AIDS, prompting correctional officials to deny the couple further conjugal visits. John Doe filed a lawsuit alleging that by denying him participation in the Family Reunion Program because of his AIDS status, New York State correctional officials violated his Fourth and Fourteenth Amendment rights. He contends that his fundamental rights to marital privacy, due process, and equal protection were violated. The New York Supreme Court dismissed his lawsuit ruling that the actions of correctional officials did not violate the U.S. Constitution, New York's constitution, or any New York state law. The case was appealed to the Second Circuit Court.

Issue

Whether New York correctional officials violated John Doe's Fourteenth Amendment rights to due process and equal protection by denying him continued participation in the Auburn Prison Family Reunion Program after he was diagnosed with AIDS.

Holding

The Second Circuit Court affirmed the decision of the New York Supreme Court, holding that in denying John Doe continued conjugal visits because he was diagnosed with AIDS, New York correctional officials did not violate his

Fourth and Fourteenth Amendment rights or any of his rights under New York's constitution.

Reason

In making a ruling in this case, the Court of Appeals relied on previous decisions made by the court regarding its decisions that marital privacy rights can be retained by an inmate when they are not inconsistent with his status as a prisoner or when they do not conflict with the legitimate penological objectives of the correctional system. The appeals court dismissed Doe's claim that the Fourth Amendment entitled him to marital privacy and conjugal visits. The court reasoned that neither a prisoner nor his spouse has a constitutional right to marital relations as a condition of confinement. The state of New York has an obligation to make such arrangement for married inmates. The Appeals Court also disagreed with the assertion that since the correctional facility has established the Family Reunion Program, he has (because of his marital status) a constitutional interest that is protected by due process. The court noted that being married did not automatically qualify an inmate for participation in the program; rather, an inmate had to be approved, which required an evaluation by state officials. Inmates had no legitimate expectation of participation or even continued participation in the program, so there could be no due process rights attached to the program. The Appeals Court also rejected the contention that being denied further participation in the program constituted an equal protection violation. In this case, Doe asserted that if other inmates are allowed to participate and his participation is terminated because he has been diagnosed with AIDS, it constitutes an equal protection violation. The Court of Appeals noted that to be successful in an equal protection claim, a prisoner must show he was excluded from participation in a correctional program without a rational reason. The Court of Appeals held that denying Doe's participation in the conjugal visits program, because he was diagnosed with AIDS, rationally advances New York's interest in preventing the spread of infectious and contagious diseases and that Doe does not have an equal protection claim. The Appeals Court held that the decision to deny an inmate participation in the Family Reunion Program is a discretionary matter and will not be disturbed if supported on a rational basis.

Case Significance

This case is important for several reasons. First, it is the first prisoner AIDS case that empowered prison officials to protect individuals in the free community. Second, it prevents married prisoners from trying to establish a right to have conjugal visits with a spouse. More specifically, it enables prison officials to engage in public health care by keeping the AIDS virus contained within the prisons. At the same time, the case clearly established that conjugal visitation is a discretionary matter to be determined by prison officials. Conjugal visits are not a constitutionally-protected right; therefore, there can be no deprivation of a right that does not exist, nor is there any claim to due process or an equal protection violation. Despite the latitude given to prison administrators in this case, it is very difficult to determine its impact because the case is not a U.S. Supreme Court decision. It was decided by a circuit court, so its decision will only affect the courts and prisons in the circuit where the case was decided.

Dunn v. White

880 F.2d 1188 (1989)

Facts

Terry Dunn, an Oklahoma state prisoner, filed a Section 1983 claim asserting that Oklahoma prison officials violated his Fourth Amendment right to privacy and to be free from an unreasonable search and seizure. Dunn alleged that prison officials assaulted and threatened him with disciplinary segregation when he refused to submit to a blood test for AIDS. Dunn contended that he refused to submit to the test for religious reasons. However, he took the test to avoid governmental abuse. Dunn claimed that the threats and test violated his constitutional rights. Moreover, he asserted that statutory exemption from such tests should apply under religious objections. The U.S. District Court in the Northern District dismissed the complaint. The case was reviewed by the Court of Appeals in the Tenth Circuit.

Issue

Whether a nonconsensual blood test for AIDS violates an inmate's right to privacy guaranteed by the Fourth Amendment.

Tenth Circuit Court of Appeals Holding

Nonconsensual blood tests for AIDS are reasonably related to the legitimate penological objectives of reducing the spread of AIDS within a prison and does not constitute an unreasonable search and seizure within the meaning of the Fourth Amendment.

Reason

Commenting that no federal court ruled on whether mandatory testing for AIDS violated a prisoner's Fourth Amendment rights, the Court of Appeals first assumed that a prisoner had a diminished expectation of privacy in searches of their person. The court reasoned that the prisoner's constant subjugation to searches did not completely destroy their expectation of privacy in searches of the person, distinguishing searches of the person from searches of places, such as cells or rooms. The court then compared the mandatory AIDS blood tests with involuntary urine tests for drugs given to prisoners, which the federal courts have determined to be within the scope of the Fourth Amendment because of security concerns related to illegal drug use. The Court of Appeals then reasoned that prison officials' concern in preventing AIDS from spreading in prison was a substantial security concern reasonably related to the mandatory blood tests, and those interests outweighed any privacy interest against searches involving blood tests that a prisoner might have.

Case Significance

This case is significant for several reasons. The case is the first to rule that mandatory AIDS testing does not constitute an unreasonable search within the meaning of the Fourth Amendment. In fact, the Court of Appeals balances the interest of the prisoner not wanting his status revealed and the interest of the prison administration's need to know who among its population has HIV/AIDS. In the end, the court ruled that the prison's need to know outweighed the inmate's right to privacy.

Estelle v. Gamble
429 U.S. 97 (1976)

Facts

Gamble, an inmate of the Texas Department of Corrections, filed a Section 1983 claim against the state corrections department's medical director and two correctional officials alleging he was injured when a bale of cotton fell on him as he was unloading a truck in November 1973. He continued to work, but after four hours he became stiff and was granted a pass to the unit hospital, where he was checked and sent back to work. Within two hours, Gamble's pain became so intense that he was taken back to the hospital where he received pain pills. The next day he saw a doctor who described his injury as a "lower back strain," prescribed pain pills, and medically excused him from work. Gamble was excused from work and prescribed pain pills until December 3, when prison doctors certified him to be capable of light work. He maintained that he was in too much pain to work and soon was sent to administrative segregation for refusing to work. Gamble remained in administrative segregation until he filed a lawsuit on February 11, 1974. Over the course of the three months between his injury and the lawsuit, Gamble saw Texas prison medical personnel seventeen times for his back ailment. Gamble alleged that Texas prison authorities subjected him to cruel and unusual punishment in violation of the Eighth and Fourteenth Amendments to the U.S. Constitution because they inadequately treated his back injury. The District Court dismissed the complaint for failure to state a claim on which relief could be granted. The Court of Appeals held that the alleged insufficiency of medical treatment required reinstatement of the complaint. This case was appealed to the U.S. Supreme Court.

Issue

Did the Texas Department of Corrections violate Gamble's Eighth and Fourteenth Amendment rights to be free from cruel and unusual punishment by not providing him with adequate medical treatment?

U.S. Supreme Court Holding

The U.S. Supreme Court reversed and remanded the decision of the appeals court. In this case, the Court held that deliberate indifference by prison personnel to a prisoner's serious illness or injury constitutes cruel and unusual punishment in violation of the Eighth and the Fourteenth Amendments, but Gamble's claim does not suggest such indifference, because the defendant saw medical personnel seventeen times over three months.

Reason

In this case, the Court reasoned that this was not a cruel and unusual punishment case, relying on its prior decision in *Trop v. Dulles* (356 U.S. 86, 1958) where the Court held that the Eighth Amendment prohibits punishments that are incompatible with "evolving standards of decency," and in *Gregg v. Georgia* where the Court held that punishment repugnant to the Eighth Amendment involves the "unnecessary and wanton infliction of pain." The Court then commented on how the infliction of pain and suffering on a prisoner because of inadequate medical care serves no penological purpose and that such suffering is inconsistent with evolving standards of decency that are manifested in current state legislation producing health standards for prisoners. These standards are designed to codify the common law principle that the public be required to care for the prisoner because the prisoner cannot care for himself by reason of his confinement. The Court concluded that deliberate indifference to the serious medical needs of a prisoner constitutes unnecessary and wanton infliction of pain in violation of the Eighth Amendment's ban against cruel and unusual punishment. The Court finished its analysis by distinguishing a deliberate indifference claim from a medical malpractice claim that results in negligent medical treatment. The Court commented that an Eighth Amendment medical claim involves more than negligence; it involves deliberate indifference on the part of the prison staff to a prisoner's medical claim that results in unnecessary and wanton suffering. Moreover, the Court stated that in the present case, there can be no claim of deliberate indifference because Gamble had seen doctors on seventeen different occasions over a three month period. However, if Gamble was seeking a malpractice claim under the Texas Tort Claims Act, the case would have had merit.

Case Significance

This case is important because it distinguishes between deliberate indifference and medical malpractice within the context of a correctional setting. Moreover, it clearly defines what constitutes a violation of the Eighth Amendment protection against cruel and unusual punishment. It also advises prisoners on what might be an appropriate remedy for relief if doctors misdiagnose their medical status. At the same time, the case can be taken as a warning to prison officials, because the U.S. Supreme Court ruled that prison authorities ignoring a prisoner's serious medical needs or complaints constitutes deliberate indifference and rises to the level of cruel and unusual punishment. As such, the prison, doctors, and correctional guards could face litigation if they knowingly allow prisoners to suffer with untreated medical needs.

Farmer v. Brennan
511 U.S. 825 (1984)

Facts

Inmate Dee Farmer, a preoperative transsexual who projected feminine characteristics, was incarcerated with other male inmates in the federal prison system at times in the general population, but mostly in segregation. He claimed to have been beaten and raped by another inmate after being transferred to a high-security facility with more troublesome prisoners and being placed in the general population. In filing a Bivens action, he alleged that federal prison officials violated his Eighth Amendment right to be free from "cruel and unusual" punishment by acting with deliberate indifference in regard to his personal safety. Farmer had been diagnosed by prison medical personnel as a transsexual. Before his incarceration at age eighteen for credit card fraud, he had worn women's clothing, undergone estrogen therapy, received silicone breast implants, and submitted to unsuccessful "black market" testicle removal surgery. While in prison, he claimed to have continued hormonal treatment using smuggled drugs and wore his clothing in a feminine manner. For disciplinary reasons, federal prison officials transferred Farmer from the Federal Correctional Institute in Oxford, Wisconsin, to the U.S. Penitentiary in Terre Haute, Indiana (USP-Terre Haute), a higher security prison that houses more dangerous prisoners. Within two weeks at USP-Terre Haute, Farmer was assaulted by his cellmate. Farmer alleged that federal prison officials acted with deliberate indifference to his personal safety when they transferred him to USP-Terre Haute and placed him in the general population despite knowledge that he would be particularly vulnerable to sexual attacks by some of its inmates. The District Court granted the federal prison officials summary judgment concluding that there had been no "deliberate indifference" to Farmer's safety because he never expressed to them concerns about his safety. The Seventh Circuit Court of Appeals affirmed. Farmer appealed to the U.S. Supreme Court, and it granted certiorari.

Issue

Whether prison officials acted with deliberate indifference, which violates the Eighth Amendment's protection against cruel and unusual punishment, when they transferred Farmer to a high-security prison.

U.S. Supreme Court Holding

The U.S. Supreme Court vacated and remanded the decision. It held that a prison official may be held liable under the Eighth Amendment for acting with deliberate indifference to an inmate's health or safety only if the official knows that the inmate faces a substantial risk of serious harm and disregards the risk by failing to take reasonable measures to abate it. The official must be aware of facts from which the inference could be drawn that a substantial risk of serious harm exists, and he or she must also draw this inference. Moreover, prison officials have a duty under the Eighth Amendment to provide humane conditions of confinement. They must ensure that inmates receive adequate food, clothing, shelter, and medical care and must protect prisoners from violence at the hands of other prisoners.

Reason

The Court recognizes that incarceration strips prisoners of virtually every means of self-protection and prevents their access to outside aid. The Court further acknowledges that prison rape is not constitutionally tolerable, and it clearly states that prisoners can obtain relief before being victimized. Finally, under the Court's holding, prison officials may be held liable for failure to remedy a risk of harm so obvious and substantial that the prison officials must have known about it. Prison officials must fulfill this affirmative duty under the Constitution to prevent inmate assault, including prison rape, or otherwise face a serious risk of being held liable for damages.

Case Significance

With its holding in this case, the U.S. Supreme Court clarified the deliberate indifference standard used by inmates alleging an Eighth Amendment violation when attacked by other inmates. The case is important for two reasons. First, the idea of acting in a manner that is deliberately indifferent goes beyond merely being negligent. Second, the case is clear concerning when a prison official is in violation of the Eighth Amendment. It states that officials owe inmates an affirmative duty to provide them with adequate food, clothing, shelter, medical care, and protection from violence at the hands of other inmates.

Forts v. Ward
621 F.2d 1210 (1980)

Facts

In 1977, pursuant to a change in New York state policy, male correctional officers were assigned to duties within the sleeping and living quarters of the Bedford Hills Correctional Facility, a women's prison operated by the state of New York. Several months later, ten female inmates at Bedford Hills filed a Section 1983 claim against the New York prison officials and the correctional officers' union with the U.S. District Court for the Southern District of New York. Their claim asserted that the assignment of male guards to areas of the prison where partially or fully unclothed female prisoners were involuntarily exposed to them violated the female prisoners' constitutional right to privacy. Bedford Hills defended its policy, contending that to deny male officers an opportunity to supervise female inmates would constitute a violation of Title VII of the Civil Rights Act of 1964. The District Court granted the plaintiffs' motion for a preliminary injunction against assigning male correctional officers to parts of the housing and hospital units. The case was appealed by defendants to the Second Circuit Court of Appeals.

Issues

Does the assignment of male guards to female inmate housing quarters, where female inmates may be exposed to them, violate female inmates' Fourth Amendment privacy rights? Does denying male officers the assignment of guarding female inmates constitute discrimination under Title VII?

Holding

The U.S. Court of Appeals for the Second Circuit vacated and remanded the decision of the District Court.

Reason

In this case, the Court of Appeals held that an individual's normal right of privacy must necessarily be abridged on incarceration in the interest of prison security. However, inmates do retain some residual privacy rights. With respect to the guards' interest in equal job opportunity, the court found no dispute that the job of a corrections officer at Bedford Hills can be equally well performed by any qualified and trained man or woman but concluded that "equal job opportunity must in some measure give way to the right of privacy." The court ruled that the female inmates were entitled to protection from being viewed by male guards when they were partially or completely unclothed while receiving medical treatment at the prison hospital or while showering, using toilet facilities, or sleeping in the housing units. The Court of Appeals balanced the interests of both parties and stated there is no reason to bar male guards from assignment to the housing corridors during the daytime hours, because prison rules permitted an inmate to protect her privacy during these hours by covering the cell door window for up to fifteen-minute intervals while dressing or attending to personal needs. However, assignment during the nighttime violated females' right to privacy. The court determined that an invasion of privacy typically occurred while inmates were showering or changing into and out of their clothes. As such, this could be corrected by installing a shower screen.

Case Significance

This case is significant for several reasons. First, the case demonstrates that the court respects the inmates' right to privacy, especially in cases where female offenders may be partially clothed or completely nude. The case established that female inmates were entitled to be protected from being viewed by male officers while they slept, received medical treatment, showered, and used toilet facilities. Second, it is important because it could serve to prevent reported cases of sexual exploitation, coercion, and rape that typically occur in prisons where male guards have access to female offenders. Third, the case also demonstrates the court's concern about male officers and Title VII of the Equal Employment Act. In realizing that male guards have the right to be employed in female correctional facilities, the court sought to accommodate all parties concerned by endorsing a plan that changed the supervision and living arrangements. The appeals court also agreed to a plan by the state to allow female inmates to cover their windows when they were changing clothes and using the toilets. The court also allowed the women to explore the kind of sleepwear they could use to hide their bodies from guards. These simple remedies would allow female inmates a degree of protection against being viewed and allow for male correctional guards to work in areas with female offenders.

Fullwood v. Clemmer
206 F. Supp. 370 (D.D.C. 1962)

Facts

Fullwood, a District of Columbia jail inmate, alleged that jail policies forbidding Muslims from holding religious services and wearing religious medals violated his First Amendment right to practice the religious belief of his choice. At the time of the lawsuit, District of Columbia jail officials funded Catholic, Protestant, and Jewish religious services at their facilities and allowed Lutherans, Unitarians, and Christian Scientists to voluntarily conduct religious services. The jail authorities considered the Muslims under their control to be a hate group because of their depiction of the white race as evil. They denied Muslims permission to hold religious services because of what they considered to be the inflammatory nature of Muslim teachings.

Issue'

Is the Muslim faith, as practiced by black prisoners, a legitimate religion, and if so, what First Amendment religious rights do Muslims have?

Holding

The Muslim prisoners' concept of religion is legitimate and they are to be recognized by the federal courts as a religious group. Furthermore, allowing some religious groups privileges while denying others the same privileges amounts to religious discrimination. The Muslims are to be allowed to hold religious services and wear medals because the District of Columbia jail authorities allow other religious groups to do so.

Reason

In regard to whether the Muslim faith is legitimate, the District Court noted that the U.S. Constitution does not define religion and that it is not a function of the federal courts to judge religions according to their tenants, however fanatical or preposterous they may be. The District of Columbia commented that the belief that there is a supreme being that controls the destiny of humanity is the only requirement the courts use to determine what constitutes a religion. Muslims believe that Allah is a supreme being and the one true God who controls their destiny, and this belief qualifies them as a religious group. As a religious group, they have a right to be treated the same as other religious groups by jail officials.

Case Significance

This decision is consistent with historical rulings by federal courts that have avoided controversies over what constitutes a religion by broadly defining the concept of religion. Also, federal courts' decisions granting Muslim prisoners a right to equal treatment regarding religious privileges is consistent with the way federal courts treat the rights of prison religious groups today.

Furman v. Georgia
408 U.S. 238 (1972)

Facts

In *Furman*, the Supreme Court consolidated three death penalty cases: *Jackson v. Georgia*, *Branch v. Texas*, and *Furman v. Georgia*. The first petitioner was convicted of murder in Georgia and was sentenced to death pursuant to Ga. Code Ann. 26-1005. The second petitioner was convicted of rape in Georgia and was sentenced to death pursuant to Ga. Code Ann. 26-1302. The third petitioner was convicted of rape in Texas and was sentenced to death pursuant to Tex. Penal Code, Art. 1189. The U.S. Supreme Court granted certiorari.

Issue

Does the imposition of the death penalty constitute cruel and unusual punishment in violation of the Eighth and Fourteenth Amendments?

U.S. Supreme Court Holding

The case was reversed and remanded. The U.S. Supreme Court held that the imposition and carrying out of the death penalty constitute cruel and unusual punishment in violation of Eighth and Fourteenth Amendments.

Reason

In this case, the Court was concerned with whether the imposition of the death penalty constituted cruel and unusual punishment within the meaning of the U.S. Constitution and whether the Fourteenth Amendment's equal protection clause was applicable to the state in this case. It reasoned that although cruel and unusual punishment include penalties that are barbaric, it is also cruel and unusual to apply the penalty selectively to minorities, whose members are few, who are outcasts of society, and who are unpopular, but whom society is willing to see suffer, though it would not impose this general application of the same penalty across the board. In this case, the Court defined "unusual" punishment as that which discriminates against a person because of his or her race, religion, wealth, social position, or class, or if it is imposed under procedures that give rise to such prejudices. The Court also noted that all of the defendants in these cases were black. Two of them were mentally deficient. Two had committed the act of rape, and one had committed a murder. All defendants were given the death penalty. The Court stated that in examining how the sentences were handed down, the states involved had no standard to govern the selection of the death penalty. The sentence was left to the whim of a judge or jury. The Court determined that race and class biases existed in the administration of the death sentence. It commented that the current system resulted in the arbitrary application of the death penalty. The Court found that the way the death penalty was imposed discriminated and violated the equal protection clause of the Fourteenth Amendment.

Case Significance

The case is important because it was the first time the U.S. Supreme Court ruled that the manner in which the death penalty was being imposed violated the Fourteenth Amendment's equal protection clause. More specifically, the Court held that the manner in which courts in Georgia and Texas applied the death penalty constituted cruel and unusual punishment because it was disproportionately applied in cases in which the defendants were poor minorities and suffered poor mental health. *Furman* is also important because this case required that all states desist from imposing the death penalty in a racially-discriminatory manner. Because of this ruling, many states refrained from imposing the death sentence at all. The case forced states that wanted to keep this sentencing option to revise their sentencing process to address concerns about fairness because the Court ruled that the death penalty had "no meaningful basis for distinguishing the few cases in which it is imposed from the many cases in which it is not." Judges arbitrarily imposed the sentence like any other.

Garrett v. Estelle
556 F. 2d 1274 (1977)

Facts

Tony Garrett, a TV news cameraman, sought an injunction in the U.S. District Court for the Northern District of Texas to prohibit Texas prison authorities from preventing him from filming executions in state prisons. The District Court ordered Texas to allow Garrett to attend and film executions of prisoners. The court stated that the prison regulation violated Garrett's First and Fourteenth Amendments. On appeal, the state argued that the First Amendment does not impose an affirmative duty to make executions available for mechanical recording or photographing. Garrett argued that to prevent him from filming executions deprived him of rights as a newsman guaranteed under the First and Fourteenth Amendments.

Issue

Whether a news cameraperson has First and Fourteenth Amendment rights to film executions that take place in a state prison.

Holding

The Fifth Circuit Court of Appeals reversed the decision of the District Court.

Reason

In this case, the appeals court held that the press has no greater right of access to information than does the public at large and that the First Amendment does not require the government to make available to the press information not available to the public. The court relied on recently decided U.S. Supreme Court rulings that held that the press has no greater right of access to prisons or prisoners than the general public. Therefore, because the public has no right under the First Amendment to film executions, a member of the press has no such right. The Court of Appeals cited *Pell v. Procunier* and *Saxbe v. Washington Post* in their holding that the U.S. Constitution does not require government to accord the press special access to information not shared by members of the public generally. Where the Fourteenth Amendment is concerned, Garrett argued an equal protection of law violation. The court indicated that the claim was without merit. Garrett argued that to prevent him from filming executions denies him equal protection because other members of the press are allowed free use of their usual reporting tools. The court held that while Texas denies Garrett the right to film executions, it also denied the print reporter use of a camera and the radio reporter use of a tape recorder. However, Garrett is free to make his report by anchor desk or stand-up delivery on the TV screen or even by simulations.

Case Significance

The case is important because it reaffirms the U.S. Supreme Court's earlier holdings in *Pell* and *Saxbe*. The case sends a clear message that the media or press does not have a First Amendment right that goes beyond that which is enjoyed by every other U.S. citizen. It also states that there can be no televised public executions.

Gates v. Rowland

39 F. 3d 1439 (9th Cir. 1994)

Facts

Inmates at the California Medical Facility (CMF) in Vacaville brought a Section 1983 class action suit challenging the conditions of their confinement. Inmates argued that conditions at the main and Northern Reception Center were overcrowded and understaffed. They alleged that these conditions exposed them to an unconstitutional risk of harm in violation of the Eighth and Fourteenth Amendments. As a remedy, the District Court proposed limits on the number of inmates who could be housed at CMF and an increase in the correctional staff to provide "adequate supervision" for inmates. The District Court stated that the denial of access to medical and mental health care and to attorneys, and the segregation of HIV-positive inmates violated inmates' constitutional rights. A subclass of HIV-positive inmates made claims under Section 504 of the Rehabilitation Act of 1973, 29 U.S.C. Section 794. The Section 504 claims of mobility-impaired inmates confined to wheelchairs and mentally ill inmates were also included in the action. After two months of trial, settlement negotiations began and the defendants agreed to an alternative dispute resolution procedure that used a mediator with correctional experience to assist with negotiations. A consent decree was agreed on by both parties to guide the dispute resolution process and negotiate findings and recommendations with the District Court. California state officials appealed two of the District Courts orders that resulted from the dispute resolution process: (1) that state officials increase staffing at the CMF by adding twelve additional employees to provide adequate supervision of the inmates, and (2) to allow HIV-positive inmates to work in food service employment at CMF if qualified, and to reasonably accommodate the inmates to enable them to perform their jobs.

Issue

Whether the District Court had the authority to (1) order California officials to increase staff by twelve additional employees to provide adequate supervision to CMF inmates, and (2) mandate that California authorities allow qualified HIV-positive inmates to work in food service jobs at CMF.

Holding

In this case, the Ninth Circuit Court of Appeals affirmed the ruling of the U.S. District Court for the Eastern District of California that officials increase staff by twelve additional employees and reversed the court's order requiring authorities to allow qualified HIV-positive inmates to work food service jobs at CMF.

Reason

In its ruling, the Appeals Court stated that when the parties concerned could not agree on the consent decree regarding the total number of custodial staff members that were needed to provide adequate supervision and escorts to inmates in the unit, a mediator was asked to review a report by a consultant and correctional staffing expert. After reviewing the report, the mediator concluded that twelve additional positions were necessary. Despite this, the defendants argued that the mediator had not used the constitutional standard of whether inmates were exposed to an unreasonable risk of harm to measure "adequate custodial staffing." The mediator felt the consent decree was ambiguous, as it was not clear whether it was establishing a standard based on whether staffing was adequate from a correctional perspective or if it was adequate "to properly supervise prisoners and to provide escorts and other services." The Court of Appeals stated the language of the consent decree was not ambiguous. Regarding the District Court's decision to allow HIV-positive inmates to work in food service, the court of appeals reversed. In this case, defendants and HIV-positive inmates disagreed with the prison policy that segregated them from other inmates and denied them access to jobs and programs open to other inmates. Through the mediator, the parties mediated three issues. Issues concerning the defendant's policy regarding the HIV-positive inmates in the CMF population were agreed to with the exception of their participation in food preparation. The defendants created a blanket policy excluding all HIV-positive inmates from food service programs. After negotiations proved unsuccessful, the mediator recommended that the court enjoin defendants from denying food service employment to HIV-positive inmates absent a written determination that an individual inmate is not otherwise qualified to perform the job and that efforts to reasonably accommodate the inmate failed to assist in the essential functions of the job. The appeals court disagreed and reversed citing *Turner v. Safley*. The court stated that in *Turner*, deference was extended to the prison authorities' policy not to open food service jobs to HIV-infected inmates.

Case Significance

The case is significant for several reasons. First, it demonstrates the power of a consent decree and the deference that the court places in the hands of mediators. In the current case, inmates who challenged the conditions of confinement claiming they faced an Eighth Amendment violation because of the potential risk associated with a shortage of custodial staff and overcrowding were successfully able to get twelve additional correctional guards to provide them more protection, escort, and service. Second, the case also demonstrates that when it comes to HIV-positive inmates and job assignments, courts show a tremendous amount of deference to prison administrators. The *Turner* decision essentially upholds penal policies if they are used to accomplish a particular penal interest. In this case, perhaps the issue is inmate safety that could potentially stem from inmates being afraid of contracting HIV/AIDS if infected inmates are allowed to work in food preparation.

Giano v. Senkowski

54 F. 3d 1050 (1995)

Facts

In July 1991, inmate Julio Giano, received an envelope from his girlfriend containing two seminude photographs of herself. Pursuant to prison policy, a mailroom employee confiscated the photographs. Giano filed a Section 1983 claim in the U.S. District Court for the Northern District of New York against two high-ranking prison officials. He argued that the prison policy banning sexually explicit photographs of inmates' wives and girlfriends constituted a violation of his First Amendment right to free speech and a violation of his Fourteenth Amendment right to equal protection, and that the policy was also constitutionally vague. He alleged that the Clinton Correctional Center's policy was unfair because it allowed prisoners to possess commercially produced erotic literature, such as *Playboy Magazine*. In his claim, Giano sought injunctive and declaratory relief as well as monetary damages. After both sides moved for summary judgment, the action was assigned to a magistrate judge who recommended granting the defendant's motion for summary judgment. The district court adopted the recommendation without opinion. Giano appealed.

Issue

Do New York prison policies that prohibit prisoners from possessing nude and seminude photographs of their wives or girlfriends but allow inmates possession of commercially produced erotic literature, such as *Playboy Magazine*, violate inmates' First and Fourteenth Amendment rights?

Holding

The Second Circuit Court of New York affirmed the District Court's decision that the prison policy that prohibited prisoners from possessing nude and seminude photographs of their wives and girlfriends does not violate the First and Fourteenth Amendment rights.

Reason

In reviewing *Giano*, the Court of Appeals cited the *Turner v. Safley* Court of 1987. In doing so, it applied the four-prong test set forth in *Turner*. The U.S. Supreme Court ruled in *Turner* that if prison policies are to pass constitutional muster, there must be: (1) a rational connection between the prison regulation and the reason put forward to justify it; (2) alternative means of exercising the right must be open to prisoners; (3) a situation wherein accommodating the right would have a negative impact on guards and other inmates; and (4) an absence of reasonable alternatives to the regulation. First, the court accepted the government's reasons why allowing nude or seminude photographs of inmates' wives or girlfriends would precipitate violence against inmates and guards, thus justifying the prohibition against such actions because a rational connection can be made. Second, the court believed that Clinton provided an alternative to inmates to exercise their First Amendment right by allowing them to have access to commercially produced erotica and sexually graphic written notes, conventional photographs, and romantic letters. Third, the court concluded that accommodating the inmates and allowing them to exercise their First Amendment right in the manner they chose would have an adverse impact on guards, other inmates, and prison resources. Citing *Turner*, the court held that to allow inmates to have such photographs would have a "ripple effect" throughout the institution and drain prison resources. Finally, the court found that no easy alternatives to the policy existed despite Giano's suggestion of allowing inmates to possess but not display or distribute the photos. The court ruled that this would be extremely difficult to enforce and create great cost on the state's valid penological concerns. In regard to the Fourteenth Amendment challenge, the court ruled that the claimant must prove purposeful discrimination that is directed at an identifiable or suspect class, and in his claim, he failed to present evidence supporting that contention. Moreover, the court found that Clinton's policy on the prohibition of semi-nude and nude photos of wives and girlfriends applied to all inmates. The court rejected Giano's argument that the prison policy was unconstitutionally vague because a statute is unconstitutionally vague if persons of common intelligence must guess at its meaning and differ as to its application, or if it fails to give a person of ordinary intelligence fair notice of conduct prescribed or required by the regulation and encourages arbitrary and erratic behavior on the part of officials charged with enforcing the rule. The court found the policy to be plainly and clearly stated.

Case Significance

This case is important for several reasons. First, it demonstrates the seriousness that the circuit court gives to First Amendment claims and the deference it gives to prison administrators who are charged with day-to-day overseeing of the inmate population. The court does a balancing act between the constitutional rights of the inmate and the interests of prison officials to properly run their facilities. Circuit court judges are aware that "prison walls are not a barrier separating inmates from the protections of the Constitution." However, "the fact of confinement and the needs of the penal institution impose limitations on constitutional rights, including those derived from the First Amendment." Essentially, in citing *Turner*, the court concluded that even if a First Amendment right is at issue, prison policies can curtail that right if they can be justified as being rationally related to a legitimate penological interest. This case was concerned with security and order. Second, this case is also important because it shows consistency in the application of laws and prison policies, because the same issue had been addressed and settled in like fashion in other circuits involving other prisons. Third, the *Turner* decision is consistently cited by circuit courts and the U.S. Supreme Court to empower correctional officials to have the final voice on how prisons are to operate.

Gittlemacker v. Prosse

428 F. 2d. 1 (3rd Cir. 1970)

Facts

Gittlemacker, an inmate at the State Correctional Institute at Dallas, Pennsylvania, filed a Section 1983 claim against the State Commissioner of Corrections and the Dallas superintendent. In the claim, Gittlemacker alleged that prison authorities had denied him proper medical treatment by transferring him to an institution where adequate care was unavailable. He also alleged that the prison had discriminated against him because he is Jewish when it failed to provide the service of a rabbi, and that prison regulations relating to the preparation of legal papers denied him due process. The Dallas superintendent responded with a motion for summary judgment supported by affidavits, and on finding no genuine issue of any material fact, the District Court dismissed the complaint.

Issue

If the state hires a prison chaplain of a specific faith but fails to provide a rabbi for Jewish inmates, does the free exercise clause require the state to provide every prisoner with a clergy member of his or her choice?

Holding

The Third Circuit Court of Appeals affirmed the District Court's decision holding that the Dallas prisoners were not discriminated against in the free exercise of their religion as a result of policies by the Dallas superintendent regarding the hiring of prison chaplains.

Reason

In *Gittlemacker*, the Court of Appeals argued that the requirement that a state interpose no unreasonable barriers to the free exercise of an inmate's religion cannot be equated with the suggestion that the state has an affirmative duty to provide, furnish, or supply every inmate with a clergy member or religious services of his or her choice. Moreover, it stated that it is one thing to provide facilities for worship and the opportunity for any clergy to visit the institution, but in this case, the Court of Appeals found that the Dallas superintendent did not discriminate against Jewish prisoners because he had unsuccessfully tried to hire a Jewish rabbi on a part-time basis to provide services for the prisoners and was in the process of making an offer to another rabbi. The Third Circuit Court judge thought that requiring a state to provide each prisoner with a clergyperson of their choice would conflict with the establishment clause, which guarantees the separation of church and state.

Where the issue of inadequate or inappropriate medical care is concerned, the court held that summary judgment was an appropriate disposition because the complainant failed to show or establish a constitutional deprivation. More specifically, the court held that without a proper allegation of constitutional deprivation, an action requesting damages for personal injuries found only in common law or statutory tort, and because no federal interest is involved, is triable only under state law or in a state court. Only when an inmate's complaint of improper or inadequate medical treatment rises to the level of cruel and unusual punishment does a violation of the Eighth Amendment attach. These actions constitute claims under Section 1983. The appellant also alleged the prison rules that prohibited an inmate from maintaining a private law library in his cell and the failure to provide a typewriter constituted a deprivation. In his affidavit, the superintendent stated the policy of the Bureau of Corrections and the State Correctional Institute at Dallas was that no inmate could maintain a law library in his cell. The policy is based on the necessity for prevention of the accumulation of vast quantities of paper materials in the cells of inmates, which creates fire hazards. The plaintiff has adequate legal materials in the prison library and may order legal materials as needed. The court agreed that the Due Process Clause of the Fourteenth Amendment provides the inmate access to the courts, but prison regulations can place reasonable limits on the time, place, and manner in which inmates may engage in legal research and the preparation of legal papers.

Case Significance

The case demonstrates the Appeals Court's unwillingness to require penal administrators to hire clergy for every religious denomination found in the prison setting. (This could create a financial burden on prisons because there are many types of religion.) The court states that as long as the prison has created a place or facility for inmates to partake in religious worship, it has satisfied the conditions of the Free Exercise Clause of the First Amendment. The Appeals Court appeared to be generally satisfied with the effort made by the penal administrator in this case because he had taken reasonable steps to secure a Jewish rabbi for the few inmates of the Jewish faith. The case is also important because it shows that as early as 1970, courts were experiencing a flood of inmate litigation that some had predicted to be a consequence of civil rights extended to people in places of confinement. *Gittlemacker* signals the circuit court's unwillingness to address unfounded and baseless claims alleged by inmates. The case represents an early attempt to eliminate the number of meritless cases that inmates file under Section 1983. Another point of note in this case is that the court of appeals suggested that in cases where inmates allege improper medical treatment, those matters can be addressed in state court under tort actions, especially when they fail to rise to the level of cruel and unusual punishment invoking the Eighth Amendment.

Goff v. Nix

803 F. 2d 258 (1986)

Facts

Inmates George Goff, David Hecton, and Terry Schertz of the Iowa State Penitentiary (ISP) in Fort Madison filed a Section 1983 claim in the U.S. District
Court for the Southern District of Iowa alleging that mandatory visual body cavity (VBC) searches by ISP officials conducted on (1) segregation unit prisoners
who enter and leave the institution or cell house; (2) segregation unit prisoners
who have contact with a member of the general prison population; (3) all prisoners after contact visits; and (4) prisoners whom prison staff view with reasonable suspicion in concealing contraband in a body cavity violated their Fourth,
Eighth, and Fourteenth Amendment rights to be free from unreasonable searches
and seizures, cruel and unusual punishment, and denied them equal protection
of the law. The District Court concluded that the VBC searches violated the prisoners' Fourth Amendment rights and issued permanent injunctive relief prohibiting state officials from enforcing the VBC portion of their strip search policy
before or after visits with attorneys, clergy, or the prison ombudsman, and before going to or coming from medical facilities, court appearances, or exercise areas.
The District Court stated the strip search policy can be used under limited circumstances. Iowa state officials appealed the case to the Eighth Circuit Court.

Issue

Did the mandatory visual body cavity search policy used at the ISP violate
the inmates' Fourth, Eighth, and Fourteenth Amendment rights?

Holding

The Eighth Circuit Court of Appeals reversed the judgment of the District
Court finding that the VBC searches were not unreasonable within the meaning of the Fourth Amendment, nor did they violate the Eighth Amendment's
prohibition against cruel and unusual punishment.

Reason

In *Goff*, the appeals court held that the district court used the medium-level
"substantial interest" test in weighing the prison regulations against the Fourth
Amendment right to be free from unreasonable searches. In finding that the
VBC searches were unreasonable, the District Court determined that the

searches were inhibiting prisoners from exercising other rights, such as access
to the courts by visiting law libraries, exercise, and their right to receive medical care. It also stated that the ISP security concerns in conducting the searches
did not outweigh constitutional concerns about the prisoners' rights. The district court even suggested that ISP's strip search policy was exaggerated in light
of the lack of contraband that the policy was made to prevent. Moreover, the
district court found that ISP officials could exercise a less restrictive alternative
to the VBC searches by hiring more correctional officers to meet their security goals. The Court of Appeals rejected use of the medium-level "substantial
interest" test in favor of the lower level "reasonable rotation" test in reversing
the District Court's ruling. The Appeals Court relied on the *Bell v. Wolfish* (441
U.S. 15, 1971) court decision, which held that VBCs conducted after visits and
without probable cause are legal and that courts should rely on the prison administration for determining a rational reason for a given prison rule. More specifically, *Wolfish* held that judicial deference should be given to prison administrators
to make "ranging" policies that are needed to preserve internal order and discipline and to monitor institutional security. In this case, in balancing the interests articulated in *Wolfish*, the appeals court weighed the need for the VBC
searches against the intrusion on the inmates' personal rights that accompany
those searches. The prison officials asserted the searches were a necessary component of the overall security policy and essential for safety of prison visitors,
ISP personnel, and inmates themselves. Under the "reasonable relations" test,
the appeals court noted that ISP officials need only demonstrate that prison
regulations were "rationally related" to legitimate security goals. The Court of
Appeals strongly emphasized that using the lower level test gave maximum
deference to the judgment of prison officials on matters regarding running
prisons, in finding that the VBC searches were reasonably related to ISP officials' concerns to prevent prisoners from smuggling contraband into the prison.
Being reasonably related to legitimate security goals, the court determined that
the searches outweighed any Fourth Amendment privacy rights the prisoners
might have.

As to the allegations of a violation of the Eighth and Fourteenth Amendments,
the appeals court held that the issues were not explicitly addressed at trial and
the State had not raised these contentions on appeal. Because of this, the appeal court was brief in handling these claims. In citing the U.S. Supreme Court,
the Appeals Court stated that Eighth Amendment violations are construed as
punishment that inflicts "unnecessary and wanton" pain or that "are grossly
disproportionate to the severity of the crime." The Court indicated that conduct that does not purport to be punishment must involve more than ordinary lack of due care for prisoners' interests or safety. Moreover, the Court

stated that obduracy and wanton, not inadvertence or error in good faith, characterize the conduct prohibited by the cruel and unusual punishment clause. The Court of Appeals stated that it did not find anything in the record that supported Eighth or Fourteenth Amendment violations.

Case Significance

This case clearly puts the needs of prison administrators to control contraband and promote safety and security above the needs and rights of prisoners. The case is an interesting ruling because it upholds a blanket policy that allows strip searches on every inmate. Despite the fact that inmates have refused to visit medical facilities, access the court by consulting with lawyers, make court appearances, exercise to enhance their physical well-being, the policy is allowed to stand largely because the Appeals Court relied on the language in *Wolfish*, which states that prison administrators should be given deference to create policies as needed to maintain internal control and safety.

Goring v. Aaron

350 F. Supp. 1 (1972)

Facts

Goring, an Oglala Indian prisoner at the Federal Correctional Institution at Sandstone, Minnesota, presented a petition for a writ of habeas corpus on which the court held a trial and evidentiary hearing at Minneapolis on September 22, 1972. He was sentenced by the U.S. District Court in South Dakota in 1969 to a five-year prison term for breaking and entering. On January 4 and 5, 1972, he was granted a furlough to leave the correctional institution to attend his father's funeral. Before departing, he promised that in return for such a privilege, he would obtain a haircut prior to or on his return so as to comply with prison regulations. Goring testified that on his father's grave, he made a "ceremonial Indian vow" that he would return to the old Indian tradition and religion, part of which includes not cutting his hair. On returning to the institution, he kept his prior promise and received a haircut that met the prison regulations. Later, he refused to have his hair cut and was confined to the isolation area of the Sandstone Institution, where he was told he was in violation of the haircut regulation. Goring has no mustache, sideburns, or beard, but his hair at the time of his confinement extended below the collar line and at the time of trial was an inch or more below the collar line. He had fifty-five days remaining on his original prison sentence.

Issue

Do prison haircut regulations deprive prisoners of their First and Fourteenth Amendment rights to religious freedom or expression and the equal protection of the law?

Holding

The U.S. District Court for the District of Minnesota ruled that prison haircut regulations do not deprive prisoners of their First Amendment right to religious expression, nor do such policies deny them the equal protection of the law guaranteed by the Fourteenth Amendment.

Reason

In this case, the petitioner argued that the hair regulations were not reasonable or necessary and did not accomplish any objective. In its rejection of this contention, the District Court cited *Blake v. Pryse* (444 F.2d 218, 8th Cir. 1971). In *Blake,* the court held that prison hair regulations were valid and reasonably supported by the requirements of identification, hygiene, and security. Moreover, the district court acknowledged that the regulation may apply to different persons in different ways depending on the amount and position of hair grown. Nevertheless, it posed the question, "Should the regulations not apply to one who has a limp or a big identifying scar and who washes his hair every night because as to him the purposes of identification and hygiene are needless?"

In addressing the First Amendment claim in this case, the court stated that the question became whether the valid regulations should apply to inmates except those who object based on religious grounds. While considering this question, the court indicated that it is important to consider whether the petitioner is sincere in his religious beliefs regarding long hair, and the court finds substantial doubt here. The court indicated that in the petitioner's testimony, he stated that he has gone thirty-six and a half years of his life without following Indian customs (the last ten of which he has spent in prison). No other Indians at the prison are motivated by religious customs the way the petitioner claims to be, and he has only fifty-five days remaining on his sentence. At that time he will be free and can pursue religion and may grow his hair the way he sees fit. The court sees no reason the petitioner cannot make a similar vow as he made on his father's grave on release. A rabbi testified that the vow would then begin anew. The court also does not believe that the petitioner has become so devout that he cannot go for a brief period without receiving a haircut. Even if the petitioner is devout and sincere, he still does not have an entitlement to the relief he seeks. The hair regulation does not deprive him of any federal civil or constitutional right. The District Court also held that freedom of religion can never mean freedom to flagrantly disregard reasonable rules of conduct in or out of prison.

Where the Fourteenth Amendment is concerned, the petitioner alleges that the regulation permits afro hairstyles for black prisoners and mustaches for other inmates, which constitutes separate classifications, but makes no specific provisions for Indians. Thus, the petitioner alleges the regulation violates the equal protection clause guaranteed by the U.S. Constitution. The District Court held that through testimony, it learned that Indians do not and apparently cannot grow facial hair, and the hair of blacks is genetically different from that of other races because it grows tightly curled. The hair regulation recognizes this difference and so permits a modification of the afro hairstyle, but prohibits basket-shaped styles. Because of these inherited differences, the court does not believe the regulation violates the Fourteenth Amendment.

Case Significance

The case is important because it reveals that a legitimate prison policy will be given deference over an inmate's constitutional right, even if the right is a preferred amendment. If the case had been decided in favor of the petitioner, other inmates would have sought a religious exemption from having to comply with the hair regulation. The consequence could have compromised safety concerns, because weapons and contraband can be secreted or hidden in long hair. Moreover, the District Court, before rendering its decision, listened to testimony from a rabbi and a lawyer who was himself a Sioux Indian. The latter discussed serving in the military, cutting his hair, and being able to practice the same religious tradition as the petitioner. The former discussed how the vow could be resumed upon the petitioner's release without any religious repercussion. Essentially, the District Court took the issue seriously before deciding the case in favor of the Federal Correctional Institution at Sandstone.

Gregg v. Georgia
428 U.S. 153 (1976)

Facts

Petitioner was charged with committing armed robbery and murder on the basis of evidence that he had killed and robbed two men. At the trial stage of Georgia's bifurcated procedure, the jury found Gregg guilty of two counts of armed robbery and two counts of murder. At the penalty stage, the judge instructed the jury that it could recommend either a death sentence or a life prison sentence on each count, that it could consider mitigating or aggravating circumstances, and that it would not be authorized to consider imposing the death sentence, unless it first found beyond a reasonable doubt that (1) the murder was committed while the offender was engaged in the commission of other capital felonies, that is, the armed robberies of the victims; (2) he committed the murder for the purpose of receiving the victim's money and automobile; and (3) the murder was "outrageously and wantonly vile, horrible, and inhumane" in that it "involved the depravity of the mind of the defendant." The jury found the first and second of these aggregating circumstances and returned a sentence of death. The Georgia Supreme Court affirmed the convictions.

Issue

Whether the imposition of the death penalty prohibited under the Eighth and Fourteenth Amendments is "cruel and unusual punishment" and violates the equal protection clause.

U.S. Supreme Court Holding

The U.S. Supreme Court affirmed the judgment of the Georgia Supreme Court by holding that the death penalty does not violate the U.S. Constitution within the statutory scheme under which Gregg was sentenced to death.

Reason

In this case, the U.S. Supreme Court argued that the imposition of the death penalty does not violate the U.S. Constitution in all circumstances. It was accepted by the framers of the Constitution, and for nearly two centuries the Court has not viewed it as an invalid punishment for the crime of murder. Although the Court expressed concern in *Furman v. Georgia* over the death penalty being imposed in an arbitrary or capricious manner, it was not over the constitutionality of the death penalty per se. Since *Furman*, and at the time of the case, thirty-five states had passed new death penalty statutes to ensure that those with sentencing authority are given adequate information and guidance, such as a method that provides for a bifurcated proceeding at which the sentencing authority is apprised of the information relevant to the imposition of sentence and provided with standards to guide its use of information. Therefore, the Georgia statutory system under which the petitioner was sentenced to death is constitutional. The new statutory scheme on its face satisfies the deficiencies expressed in *Furman*. The Court rejected the petitioner's claim that Georgia's new sentencing statutes have not removed the elements of arbitrariness and capriciousness addressed in *Furman* and found that the new statute guides the jury in its exercise of discretion as to whether it will impose the death penalty for first-degree murder. But the holding gives the Georgia Supreme Court the power and imposes the obligation to decide whether the death penalty was being administered for any class of crime in discriminating, standardless, or rare fashion.

Case Significance

This case is important because prior to *Gregg*, there were no national standards or procedures governing the implementation of capital punishment. In fact, it was well known that the death penalty was mostly given to minorities and the poor, even if the crime they committed was disproportionate to the sentence. Because of this, the Court ruled in *Furman* that the death penalty was meted out in an arbitrary and capricious manner that violated the Eighth and Fourteenth Amendments' cruel and unusual punishment and equal protection clauses. In *Gregg*, Georgia created a scheme requiring a jury to consider at least one aggravating factor found beyond a reasonable doubt before capital punishment could be imposed. The statute indicated that juries could also consider other aggravating and mitigating factors. It even required that Georgia provide an automatic appeal of all death sentences to the state Supreme Court. This case is also important because it addressed how the death penalty would be imposed in every state in the United States. For that reason, it is arguably the most important death penalty case. *Gregg* looked at the Eighth Amendment and evolving standards of decency. The Court interpreted this to mean excessive. In fact, the Court stated that punishment must not involve the unnecessary and wanton infliction of pain. It must not be grossly out of proportion to the severity of the crime the defendant was charged with committing. After *Gregg*, no state could legally impose the death sentence without considering the conditions decided on in *Gregg*, nor could states impose capital punishment on an offender who committed any crime less than a murder offense. Even when murder is committed, the death penalty is not automatic.

Harris v. Thigpen
941 F. 2d. 1495 (1991)

Facts

In 1987, Carmen Harris, an inmate at the Tutwiler Prison for Women, filed a complaint challenging the Alabama Department of Corrections (DOC) actions in testing her for HIV antibodies and in segregating her in a separate unit when her results were reported as positive. Moreover, in 1988, Harris and other prisoners filed a motion for class certification. Thereafter, inmates Stewart Hughey and Adam Robinson, two non-HIV general population inmates incarcerated at Limestone Correctional Facility, filed a motion to intervene as defendants under Fed. R.C.V.P. 24. The trial court subsequently consolidated the case with a number of similar actions pending in various federal courts in Alabama requesting similar injunctive relief and certified two classes: the plaintiff class, consisting of all current or future inmates of the DOC, except those inmates who had indicated an intention to intervene on behalf of the defendants, and another class consisting of intervening inmates opposing the relief sought by the plaintiffs. At trial, the plaintiffs challenged the mandatory testing of present and future Alabama state prisoners for HIV antibodies, as well as the policy of forced segregation and other practices associated with the system's care for and treatment of seropositive inmates. The plaintiffs claimed that such practices violated their Fourth, Eighth, and Fourteenth Amendment rights to the U.S. Constitution as well as Section 504 of the Rehabilitation Act of 1973. More specifically, the plaintiffs argued that the DOC had (1) required all prisoners to submit involuntarily to blood tests on entrance into and exit from Alabama penal institutions; (2) failed to advise prisoners as to the inconclusive and sometimes misleading significance of the results; (3) failed to provide emotional support and mental health counseling to those prisoners who tested positive; (4) compelled seropositive prisoners to live in segregated units with other prisoners who have tested positive for HIV; (5) publicly branded the inmates, through the fact of their segregation, as carriers of a dreaded socially unacceptable and fatal disease; (6) caused the infected inmates to lose the opportunity to participate in vocational and educational programs, earn good time credits, and participate in work release and similar programs, thus limiting the prisoners' opportunities for early release and parole; and (7) provided the inmates with grossly deficient medical, mental health, and dental care.

Issue

Whether the Alabama DOC policies regarding the treatment of HIV-positive inmates are in violation of the First Amendment right to access the courts, the Fourth Amendment's protection against unreasonable search and seizure, the Eighth Amendment's protection against cruel and unusual punishment, and the Fourteenth Amendment violation of equal protection.

Holding by the Eleventh Circuit Court

The Eleventh Circuit Court of Appeals affirmed the District Court's ruling and dismissed the plaintiffs' lawsuit regarding the Eighth Amendment claim of deliberate indifference to medical care by the Alabama DOC. The court also found no merit in the claims against mandatory testing and involuntary segregation. The circuit court also vacated and remanded the plaintiffs' claims regarding violations of the Rehabilitation Act of 1973 and the right to access the court back to the District Court for future hearings.

Reason

In this case, when addressing the appellants' claim of an Eighth Amendment violation, they contend that the Alabama DOC was deliberately indifferent to the medical needs of seropositive inmates at Limestone and Tutwiler. The Appeals Court agreed with the District Court's finding that the preponderance of the evidence revealed no violation of any prisoner's rights to medical, psychological, or psychiatric care and no deliberate indifference to any medical or psychological need. Moreover, the Appeals Court held that "we simply cannot agree with plaintiffs' contention that the treatment received by the inmates was so inadequate as to manifest the kind of 'conscious or callous indifference' necessary to raise the Alabama DOC perhaps negligent care to certain AIDS-infected prisoners to violations of a constitutional magnitude." Appellants contend the DOC is "deliberately indifferent" to inmates' serious medical needs because physician staffing is numerically inadequate for the HIV unit, and the physicians assigned to Limestone and Tutwiler are not competent to treat AIDS and serious HIV-related conditions. For this contention, the Appeals Court stated, "We find that there is enough evidence to support district court's conclusion of no deliberate indifference." In fact, the court held, "We agree with the district court in that the units were not so understaffed as to manifest systemic deliberate indifference to the seropositive inmates' needs."

In regard to the appellants' Fourth Amendment claim of an invasion of their privacy rights, they charged that the DOC's policies of mandatory testing and segregation, as well as certain disclosure practices, violated the seropositive prisoners' constitutional rights of privacy. The Court of Appeals argued that appellants' privacy attack is focused on the DOC's blanket policy of isolating inmates from the general population who have tested positive for HIV. Appellants argue that the involuntary disclosure of inmates' seropositive status resulting from such segregation is unnecessary, gravely stigmatizing, and ultimately violates constitutionally guaranteed rights. The Appeals Court disagreed with this assertion citing *Turner v. Safley*. In denying the HIV-positive prisoners' claim that involuntary segregation violates their privacy rights because other prisoners and staff can readily identify prisoners who tested positive, the court found that Alabama's segregation policies were consistent with *Turner* and reasonably related to the danger presented by HIV-positive prisoners, noting that when weighing an inmate's privacy right against prison policies, a showing of rationality by prison officials allows them to regulate in areas normally protected by constitutional rights. With respect to the plaintiffs' claim that DOC policies violated the Rehabilitation Act of 1973, the court remanded the issue back to the District Court for further hearings because it found that the Act required each prison program to be evaluated separately regarding the suitability for participation by HIV-positive inmates. Current DOC policies uniformly excluded HIV-positive inmates from all prison programs, including recreation, employment, educational, housing, chapel use, and community programs. Finally, the Court of Appeals found inconsistencies in the District Court's access to the court's ruling and remanded the issue back to the District Court for clarification.

Case Significance

The case is important because it notes that only a minority of states involuntarily segregate HIV-positive inmates. In those states that have segregation programs, prisoners often complain that the exclusion of HIV/AIDS-infected inmates from prison programs makes life very difficult and bring lawsuits challenging the constitutionality of such programs and policies. They often allege that such policies violate the equal protection clause of the Fourteenth Amendment. Nevertheless, because of the threat to health that HIV/AIDS presents, state prison systems have been able to successfully practice and defend constitutionally protected segregation programs and policies when officials demonstrate that these programs are rationally related to furthering legitimate penological interests on the safety and health of offenders not infected with HIV/AIDS. Segregation is a strategy in prison to contain and isolate the spread of sexually transmitted disease. Without being able to end state segregation programs, the Rehabilitation Act may be the best way for segregated AIDS inmates to gain access to prison programs to relieve the long-term effects of idleness associated with prison segregation.

Heflin v. Stewart County
958 F. 2d (1992)

Facts

A Section 1983 claim was brought by the family of a twenty-year-old pretrial detainee (Heflin) who committed suicide in the Stewart County, Tennessee, jail. Those sued in the claim included the county, the sheriff (Hicks), one deputy (Crutcher), and the jailer (Hoffman). A jury awarded damages to the plaintiff, and the defendants appealed. The defendants' appeal was based on the fact that the District Court denied their motion for a directed verdict of acquittal at the conclusion of the plaintiff's case. A second attempt was made by the defendant to renew the motion for a directed verdict of acquittal after both sides presented closing arguments. On appeal, the defendants contend that the evidence was insufficient for the submission of two issues: (1) Whether any act or failure to act of the defendants was the proximate cause of the inmate's death; and (2) Whether any defendant acted with "deliberate indifference" to the inmate's medical needs after he was discovered hanging in his cell. The defendants also argued that they were entitled to judgment based on qualified immunity. Stewart County sought reversal, as well on the ground that no county policy or action led to the inmate's death.

Issue

Did the District Court err in denying Sheriff Hicks and Duty Sheriff Crutcher a directed verdict because the evidence did not show that Hicks and Crutcher's response to Heflin's hanging amounted to deliberate indifference to his serious medical needs?

Holding

The Sixth Circuit Court of Appeals affirmed the District Court's ruling, and the jury awarded Heflin's family after finding sufficient evidence to support the action.

Reason

In *Heflin*, the Court of Appeals cited the U.S. Supreme Court holdings in *Bell v. Wolfish* and *Estelle v. Gamble* in that pretrial detainees have a constitutional right to the same protection afforded convicted prisoners who have serious medical needs that cannot be ignored. To ignore the serious medical needs of prisoners would invoke an Eighth Amendment claim of deliberate indifference to the plight of inmates. In this case, the Court of Appeals held that a motion for a directed verdict is granted when it is determined "that reasonable minds could not differ as to the governing facts." When applying this standard, the court stated that "We cannot find that the District Court erred in denying the defendants, Sheriff Hicks and Deputy Crutcher's motion, because no one attempted to resuscitate Heflin." This seemed odd because both Hicks and Crutcher were trained in CPR. The Court of Appeals also discovered that Hicks was the policy-maker for the sheriff's department and the county jail. He was also present at the time the emergency medical technician arrived at the jail. Even when Dr. Lee informed everyone that he heard a heartbeat and Heflin's body should be cut down and laid on a cot, no resuscitation efforts were made. Resuscitation efforts, if immediately undertaken, could have carried a 95 percent chance of survival. The Court of Appeals found that this was clear evidence that signaled to the jury that Heflin died as a proximate result of Hicks and Crutcher's failure to take any steps to save his life, since they left him hanging twenty minutes or more after he was discovered, even though his body was still warm and his feet were touching the floor. The court believed that Hicks and Crutcher's inaction amounted to showing deliberate indifference to Heflin's serious medical needs in violation of the Eighth Amendment based on the testimony of a plaintiffs' expert witness (Totten) in the field of corrections. Totten testified that the Tennessee Corrections Institute and every other jailer training program required a jailer to call for assistance and immediately cut the hanging victim down to apply first aid and CPR until told by a physician to stop. The Court of Appeals reasoned that a jury could find that when Hicks and Crutcher found Heflin's body, there was a "pervasive risk of harm to Heflin," which supports a finding of deliberate indifference and that the sheriff and deputy sheriff took no reasonable steps to attempt to save Heflin's life. In this case, the defendants also argued that the District Court should have submitted their qualified immunity defense to the jury. The Appeals Court disagreed, citing *Poe v. Haydon* (853 F.2d 418, 6th Cir. 1988) where it ruled that resolution of qualified immunity was a question of law. In fact, the Appeals Court held that the trial judge bears the responsibility of resolving the question raised by a qualified immunity defense. The official must first plea qualified immunity, and the court then decides the issue on which immunity turns. It also cited the U.S. Supreme Court ruling that whether an official protected by qualified immunity may be personally liable for an allegedly unlawful official action generally turns on the "objective legal reasonableness" of the action. In the present case, the unlawfulness of doing nothing to attempt to save Heflin's life would have been apparent to a reasonable official in Hicks and Crutcher's position. Therefore, the qualified immunity judgment is not granted.

Case Significance

The case is important for several reasons. First, the Eighth Amendment applies to pretrial detainees in jails, as well as in prisons. A major source of lawsuits comes from the surviving family members of inmates who have committed suicide, thus creating a body of Eighth Amendment pretrial detainee "suicide law." This case is important because the federal courts found that the jailers acted with "deliberate difference" in violation of the Eighth Amendment when they failed to cut down the hanging body of a suicide victim, failed to immediately call for help, and did not administer first aid/CPR. The Court of Appeals was clear in its determination of deliberate indifference. It stated that officials' action must rise to a level that is higher than mere negligence to invoke such a claim. Ultimately, the holding in this case becomes part of the body of suicide law, which helps the future courts decide whether jailers act with deliberate indifference to inmates who commit suicide. Second, it also highlights the need to provide adequate training to jailers (sheriffs and deputy sheriffs) charged with managing or processing pretrial detainees. More specifically, they should be trained to recognize warning signs of suicide, monitor suspicious inmates, and respond with CPR, if needed. These presuicidal prevention strategies could save inmates' lives and minimize prison litigation.

Helling v. McKinney
509 U.S. 25 (1993)

Facts

In 1986, McKinney, a prisoner at Nevada State Prison, filed a Section 1983 claim in the U.S. District Court seeking injunctive relief and damages for being subjected to cruel and unusual punishment. His complaint alleged that his involuntary exposure to environmental tobacco smoke (ETS) from his cellmate, who smoked five packs of cigarettes a day, and other inmates who smoked posed an unreasonable risk to his health, and that in not transferring him from his cell, or curtailing smoking at the prison, prison officials acted with "deliberate indifference" to this serious health problem in violation of his Eighth Amendment right to be free from cruel and unusual punishment. The District Court held that McKinney had no constitutional right to be free from ETS because society could not agree on the right to a "smoke-free" environment, and it directed a verdict for the prison officials because McKinney failed to present evidence linking serious medical problems to secondhand cigarette smoke, or that prison officials were deliberately indifferent to any serious medical problem. On appeal, the Ninth Circuit Court of Appeals held that involuntary exposure to unreasonably dangerous levels of ETS violated current standards of decency and ruled the District Court erred in giving prison officials a directed verdict without giving McKinney the opportunity to prove that involuntary exposure to ETS was sufficient to constitute an unreasonable danger to his health. The Nevada prison officials appealed to the U.S. Supreme Court, and it granted certiorari.

Issue

Whether an inmate can sue to prove that his Eighth Amendment right to be free from cruel and unusual punishment has been violated by prison officials who acted with deliberate indifference to the future health risks associated with secondhand smoke.

U.S. Supreme Court Holding

The U.S. Supreme Court affirmed the decision of the Ninth Circuit Court of Appeals holding that an inmate is entitled to smoke-free environment under the Eighth Amendment claim based on how involuntary exposure to ETS can endanger his future health. However, the inmate must first show that being exposed to unreasonably high levels of ETS is a condition that today's society refuses to tolerate and that prison officials acted with deliberate indifference to alleviating the harmful conditions. The Court remanded the case back to the district court with instructions.

Reason

On appeal, prison officials alleged that McKinney did not state a valid Eighth Amendment claim because his claim was based on future medical effects from ETS and that an Eighth Amendment claim required that a prisoner suffer present ill health effects. The U.S. Supreme Court dismissed the prison officials' contention citing *Estelle v. Gamble,* where it ruled that although accidental or inadvertent, failure to provide adequate medical care to a prisoner would not violate the Eighth Amendment. However, deliberate indifference to serious medical needs of prisoners violates the amendment because it constitutes the unnecessary and wanton infliction of pain contrary to contemporary standards of decency. Moreover, the Court stated, "We have great difficulty agreeing that prison authorities may not be deliberately indifferent to an inmate's current health problems that may ignore a condition of confinement that is sure or may be likely to cause serious illness and needless suffering the next week or month or year. Also, it would be odd to deny an injunction to inmates who plainly proved an unsafe, life-threatening condition in their health."

In remanding the case back to the District Court, the U.S. Supreme Court commented that to be successful, McKinney would have to prove both objective and subjective components of an Eighth Amendment claim. The Court cautioned that with respect to the objective factor, McKinney must show that he is being exposed to unreasonably high levels of ETS, which may prove difficult because he has been moved from Carson City to Ely State Prison and no longer has a cellmate who smokes five packs of cigarettes a day. Although he could be moved back to Carson City, he is currently not exposed to ETS. Furthermore, the director of the Nevada State Prisons adopted a formal policy that restricts smoking in several areas of the prison. The policy allows wardens to designate non-smoking areas and create committees to make reasonable efforts to respect the wishes of non-smokers who are double-bunked. With respect to the objective factor, the U.S. Supreme Court stated that McKinney would have to prove with more than scientific and statistical data the seriousness of the potential harm and the likelihood that such injury to health will actually be caused by exposure to ETS to show that his condition of confinement constitutes a violation of the Eighth Amendment. A court must also assess whether society considers the risk that McKinney complained about as so grave that it violates contemporary standards of decency. The prisoner must show that the risk of which he complains is not one that today's society chooses to tolerate.

Case Significance

This is the leading case regarding the right of prisoners to be free from the effects of ETS or secondhand tobacco smoke. It also speaks to what prison administrators should do to avoid acting in a manner that is deliberately indifferent to the long-term health of its inmate population. As mentioned in

Helling, a statewide policy was passed to designate areas in the prisons as smoke-free. More specifically, the state restricted smoking in programs, food preparation/serving, recreational, and medical areas. However, the policy in some cases depends on space availability, designated non-smoking areas in dormitory settings, and created committees to entertain reasonable efforts to respect the wishes of inmates who are double-bunked. These reasonable accommodations on the part of the Nevada prison director could send a message to a judge or jury presiding over a similar claim addressing the issue of cruel and unusual punishment as it relates to an Eighth Amendment violation, that it does not constitute a show of deliberate indifference. What is particularly interesting about this ruling is that it was affirmed and remanded with instructions that could signal that the U.S. Supreme Court did not want to decide the case and opted to send it back to the District Court to make a decision with the caveat that the inmate be given an opportunity to prove both the subjective and objective elements necessary to establish the Eighth Amendment violation. The case is important because although the U.S. Supreme Court affirmed the decision of the Ninth Circuit Court of Appeals, it did not rule definitively on the case. It can, however, be used by other circuit courts addressing similar issues of secondhand smoke in correctional settings.

Hewitt v. Helms
459 U.S. 460 (1983)

Facts

Helms was a prisoner at the State Correctional Institution at Huntingdon, Pennsylvania. On December 3, 1978, another prisoner assaulted two guards, and before the prisoner was subdued, one guard received a broken nose and the other a broken thumb. Later that evening, a riot erupted; before it was quelled, one guard received cuts and bruises on the face and another received a skull fracture, broken jaw, broken teeth, and an injured collarbone. Helms was removed from the general population and confined to administrative segregation pending an investigation into his role in the riot. The next day, he received notice of the misconduct charge against him. Five days after his transfer to administrative segregation, a hearing committee reviewed evidence against him, and he acknowledged, in writing, that he had an opportunity to have his version of the events reported, but no finding of guilt was made. On December 11, criminal charges based on his involvement in the riot were filed but were later dropped. A prison review committee reviewed Helms's status and recommended he remain in segregation because he posed a threat to the safety of other inmates and prison officials and to the security of the prison. On January 19, 1979, a second misconduct report alleging that Helms assaulted another guard was given to the respondent. On January 22, a hearing committee composed of three prison officials dropped the first misconduct charge, but found Helms guilty of the second charge and sentenced him to six months in administrative segregation. Helms brought a Section 1983 claim in the U.S. District Court for the Middle District of Pennsylvania alleging his confinement to administrative segregation violated the Fourteenth Amendment Due Process Clause. The District Court granted the prison officials motion for summary judgment. The U.S. Court of Appeals for the Third Circuit reversed, holding that Helms had a protected liberty interest in continuing to reside in the general prison population created by the Pennsylvania regulation governing the administration of state prison. The appeals court also cited *Wolff v. McDonnell,* which required that inmates be given a hearing before they are deprived of a liberty interest.

Issue

Whether the Fourteenth Amendment's Due Process Clause is violated when a prisoner is placed in administrative segregation without being given a formal hearing.

U.S. Supreme Court Holding

The U.S. Supreme Court reversed the decision of the Third Circuit Court of Appeals, holding that Pennsylvania law gave Helms a liberty interest in remaining in the general prison population and that the prison officials' hearing procedure regarding placing a prisoner in administrative segregation satisfied the due process requirement of the Fourteenth Amendment.

Reason

In *Helms,* the U.S. Supreme Court disagreed with the respondents' contention that because Pennsylvania created a law regarding a procedure to regulate the use of administrative segregation, it naturally created a liberty interest. However, the Court focused on the language used in the procedure, such as *shall, will,* or *must* and that administrative segregation will not occur unless substantive predicates occur. Because of the wording, the Court was persuaded that the repeated use of explicitly mandatory language in connection with requiring specific substantive predicates draw a conclusion that the state created a protected liberty interest. With this, the Court was forced to decide whether the process afforded to Helms satisfied the minimum requirement of the Due Process Clause. The Court held that the requirements imposed by the clause are flexible and variable depending on the particular situation being examined. Within the prison setting, the Court ruled in *Wolff v. McDonnell* that one cannot automatically apply procedural rules designed for free citizens.

The Court also considered the competing interests involved and argued that petitioners had two closely related reasons for confining Helms to administrative segregation prior to conducting a hearing on the charges against him. First, they stated he was removed from the general prison population because he was perceived as a threat to the safety of inmates, prison officials, and the security of the institution. Second, prison officials believed it wiser to separate the respondent from the general population until the institutional investigation was completed. The respondent's interest is of no great consequence. The U.S. Supreme Court held the safety of the institution's guards and inmates is the most fundamental responsibility of the prison administration. The Court held that neither of the grounds for confining Helms in administrative segregation would have required a detailed adversary proceeding. Moreover, in *Wolff*, the Court held that prison administrators should be accorded wideranging deference in the adoption and execution of policies and practices that in their judgment, are needed to preserve internal order and discipline to maintain institutional security. Finally, the Court held that it was satisfied that Helms received all the process that was due after being confined to administrative segregation, especially since he acknowledged on the misconduct form that he had the opportunity to have his version reported as part of the record. The Court also stated, "We think an informal, non-adversary evidentiary review is sufficient both for the decision that an inmate represents a security threat and the decision to confine an inmate to administrative segregation pending completion of an investigation into misconduct charges against him." The informal procedure permits a reasonably accurate assessment of probable cause to believe that misbehavior occurred.

Case Significance

This case is important because the U.S. Supreme Court essentially ruled that within the context of correctional settings, every due process claim does not mean that inmates are entitled to a formal adversarial process. In *Helms*, the Court, in its interpretation of *Wolff*, concluded that as long as inmates are given an opportunity to give their statement to a hearing committee when faced with administrative segregation, this satisfies the due process requirement of the Fourteenth Amendment. In fact, in the matter of transferring an inmate from the general prison population to administrative segregation (usually to ensure prison safety or protection), an informal, nonadversary, evidentiary review is sufficient pending a complete investigation of the alleged misconduct. However, the *Wolff* decision should be interpreted to mean if punitive segregation is being considered, *Wolff* requires a formal process. Therefore, the case means that inmates can be removed from the general prison population without a formal hearing if prison officials can justify such an action on protecting the inmate involved in an altercation, other inmates and prison guards, or security reasons in general. Interestingly enough, the Court did not specify a time limit on administrative segregation. Prison officials should be careful not to use administrative segregation as a pretext for punitive segregation. This could be a point of litigation in the future.

Holt v. Sarver

300 F. Supp. 825 (1969)

Facts

Several petitioners housed at the Cummins Farm Unit of the Arkansas Penitentiary located near Pine Bluff filed a Section 1983 claim to the U.S. District Court for the Eastern District of Arkansas alleging that prison officials denied them adequate medical and dental care, failed to protect them from assaults from other inmates, and subjected them to substandard conditions when confined in isolation cells amounting to cruel and unusual punishment in violation of the Eighth and Fourteenth Amendments' equal protection clauses. The District Court ruled that the plaintiffs failed to sustain their burden of proof with respect to the medical and dental facilities. The court did not consider the deficiencies rising to the level of a constitutional problem. The court also ruled that the plaintiffs failed to sustain their complaint about food served to prisoners while in isolation. It argued that although the food was not appetizing, the U.S. Constitution does not require that prisoners in isolation be served tasty or attractive dishes. The court ruled that the evidence presented by the plaintiffs alleging assaults of certain prisoners was not sufficient to justify relief. However, the District Court found that from a preponderance of the evidence, the state failed to discharge its constitutional duty with respect to the safety of certain convicts and that the conditions existing in the isolation cell, including overcrowding, rendered confinement in those cells under those conditions as unconstitutional.

Issue

Whether Arkansas prison officials at the Cummins Farm Unit were in violation of the Eighth Amendment's cruel and unusual punishment clause because they failed to respect the safety of inmates housed in barracks to sleep and conditions of confinement in isolation cells.

Holding by the District Court

The District Court held from a preponderance of evidence, the state of Arkansas failed to discharge its Eighth Amendment constitutional duties with respect to the safety of certain inmates, and that conditions existing in the isolation cells, including overcrowding, rendered confinement in those cells unconstitutional.

Reason

With respect to the prisoners' personal safety issue, the District Court found that within the previous eighteen months, there were seventeen stabbings at Cummins and all but one was in the barracks where prisoners slept. Four of the stabbings were fatal. Sleeping arrangements in the barracks allowed one inmate to attack a sleeping inmate. Most inmates possessed small weapons, such as scissors and knives, and the court found that efforts by officials to keep the weapons away from the inmates were impractical. Many stabbings arose from deadly feuds among inmates and involved "crawlers," or an inmate who would catch his enemy asleep before crawling over and stabbing him. The barracks were patrolled at night by "floorwalkers." It was these inmate guards that the court found ineffective in preventing the assaults. In sum, the District Court found that the inmates sleeping in the barracks were being subjected to "cruel and unusual" punishment because they could not sleep at night without fear of having their throats cut before morning and that the state of Arkansas failed to do anything about changing these conditions. To comply with the constitution, the District Court ordered Arkansas prison officials to enter into a decree to do away with the floorwalkers and hire free-world guards to ensure inmate safety in the barracks when the inmates slept. It recommended transferring problem inmates to the Tucker Farm. It suggested that a minimum number of inmates be confined in isolation cells. The court recommended that inmates not be confined for extended periods in isolation before a hearing, and that prison cells be sanitary, especially mattresses. The unsanitary conditions were aggravated when infectious inmates were placed in the small cells with others. In all, the District Court found conditions in the solitary units to be mentally and emotionally traumatic, physically uncomfortable, hazardous to health, degrading, debasing, offensive to modern sensibilities, and amounting to cruel and unusual punishment.

Case Significance

This is one of the first Eighth Amendment conditions of confinement cases. It came seven years before the U.S. Supreme Court's first ruling in this area in its decision in *Estelle v. Gamble* (1976). In 1969, the district court judges had broad discretionary powers to interpret the Eighth Amendment and intervene in the operations of prisons by issuing compliance orders to prison officials. Some commentators refer to this period as the Judicial Activism Era of prison law. It was not until the 1990s that the District Courts were bound to decide conditions of confinement cases under strict "deliberate indifference" guidelines provided by the U.S. Supreme Court, which also discouraged judicial activism and discouraged courts from intervening in how prisons should be operated. In *Holt*, the District Court interpreted the Eighth Amendment concept of cruel and unusual punishment as "flexible and expanding, and that a punishment is unconstitutional if it offends concepts of decency and human rights and precepts of civilization which Americans profess to possess or if it is disproportionate to the offense, or if it violates fundamental standards of good conscience and fairness." The District Court found the Arkansas conditions unconstitutional after judging evidence presented by the prisoners in light of this standard. Orders were issued to prison officials to ensure compliance. This is a far cry from the way federal courts decide Eighth Amendment cases today, being bound by evidentiary standards to base decisions on and prevented from issuing compliance orders to prison officials.

Houchins v. KQED, Inc.

438 U.S. 1 (1978)

Facts

The Sheriff of Alameda County, California (as the person controlling all areas to the Alameda County jail), refused the request of an operator of radio and television broadcasting stations (KQED) to inspect and take pictures within an area of the jail that was the site of an inmate suicide and was the scene of alleged rapes, beatings, and adverse physical conditions. The operator filed a Section 1983 suit in the U.S. District Court for the Northern District of California alleging that the sheriff (Houchins) had violated the First Amendment by refusing to permit media access and by failing to provide any effective means by which the public could be informed of conditions prevailing at the suicide site (Greystone portion of the jail) or could learn of prisoners' grievances. Several weeks after the complaint was filed requesting injunctive relief to prevent the sheriff from excluding the station's news personnel from the suicide site and jail facilities, and from preventing full and accurate news coverage of prevailing conditions, the sheriff announced a program of regular monthly tours of the jail, which were open to the public (including news media personnel). However, these tours did not include access to the area of the jail where the suicide and alleged violent activities took place. Moreover, during the tours no cameras, tape recorders, or interviews with inmates were allowed. The District Court ruled in favor of KQED, enjoining Houchins from denying news personnel access to jail facilities, including the area where the suicide and alleged violent activity had occurred, at reasonable hours and times and for full news coverage. On interlocutory appeal, the U.S. Court of Appeals for the Ninth Circuit affirmed. The case was appealed to the U.S. Supreme Court, and it granted certiorari.

Issue

Whether the news media have a constitutional right under the First and Fourteenth Amendments to access a county jail above that of the public to interview inmates and make sound recordings, films, and photographs for publication by newspaper, radio, and television.

U.S. Supreme Court Holding

The U.S. Supreme Court reversed and remanded the decision of the Ninth Circuit Court of Appeals holding that under the U.S. Constitution, the press does not have a right of access to the jail superior to that of the public.

Reason

In this case, the U.S. Supreme Court rejected the Court of Appeals' assertion that the public and the media have a First Amendment right to government information regarding the conditions of jails and their right is superior to that of the public. Citing *Pell v. Procunier* and *Saxbe v. Washington Post*, the Court held that neither the First nor the Fourteenth Amendment provides a right of access to government information or sources of information within the government's control. The news media have no constitutional right of access to the county jail over and above that of other persons to interview inmates and make sound recordings, films, and photography for publication and broadcasting by newspaper, radio, and television. Moreover, the Court held that the argument put forth by the respondent is flawed for several reasons. First, it goes against previous decisions made by the U.S. Supreme Court. Second, it invites the Court to perform a legislative task (make policy), which the Constitution has reserved for the political process—open penal institutions in the manner sought by respondents. Respondents contend that the public has a right to know about conditions in jails and prisons, and the media personnel are the best qualified persons for discovering malfeasance in public institutions. The Court disagreed, stating that there are a number of alternatives available to prevent problems in penal facilities from escaping public attention. In fact, petitioners cannot prevent respondents from learning about jail conditions in a variety of ways. Respondents have a First Amendment right to receive letters from inmates criticizing officials and reporting conditions. Second, respondents are free to interview those who provide legal assistance to inmates. Third, they are free to seek out former inmates, visitors to the prison, public officials, and institutional personnel. Moreover, under California law, health inspectors are required to inspect prisons and provide reports. Another avenue to learn about what is occurring in prison is to contact fire officials because they are legally responsible for inspecting prisons. The U.S. Supreme Court further stated that in the current case, after the suicide, the County Board of Supervisors called for a report from the County Administrator and held a public hearing on the report, which was open to the media, and called for continued reports when the initial report failed to describe the conditions in the cell in the Greystone portion of the jail.

Case Significance

This case is important because the U.S. Supreme Court reiterated its decisions in *Pell v. Procunier* and *Saxbe v. Washington Post* regarding media access to penal institutions and the First and Fourteenth Amendments. In *Pell* and *Saxbe*, the Court allowed prison regulations that forbade the press from accessing specific prisoners for interviews based on the prisons' perception that such alternatives contributed to problems associated with the "Big Wheel" Theory whereby certain inmates (those interviewed by the press) would rise in popularity, which would lead to problems with security and order. What is interesting about *Pell* and *Saxbe* (other than both cases being decided on the same day) is that the press had full access to penal institutions for reporting purposes, leaving it unclear as to how far prison authorities can go in restricting access to prison officials. However, in *Houchins*, the U.S. Supreme Court makes it clear that prison officials have unlimited discretion to limit public and press access to penal facilities by ruling that the press has no First Amendment right that exceeds the amount of right or protection given to other U.S. citizens. Furthermore, although penal systems are closed institutions, there are alternative ways to collect information on what is occurring in them.

Howe v. Smith

452 U.S. 473 (1981)

Facts

Robert Howe was convicted in Vermont of first-degree murder arising out of the rape and strangulation of an elderly female neighbor and sentenced to life imprisonment. The Classification Committee of the Vermont Department of Corrections determined that Howe should be in a maximum security facility. Vermont, however, previously closed its only maximum security prison pursuant to 18 U.S.C. Section 5003(a), which authorized the Attorney General to contract with a state for the custody, care, subsistence, education, treatment, and training of persons convicted of criminal offenses in the state's courts when the Director of the U.S. Bureau of Prisons certifies that proper and adequate treatment facilities are available. Before Howe's hearing was held to determine whether to transfer him to a federal facility, he was afforded advance notice of the hearing and reasons for the proposed transfer, and was represented by a legal advisor from the facility's staff who presented evidence on his behalf. After the hearing, officers found Howe to be dangerous and determined that he could not be integrated into a community-based program due to the threat he posed to women. Vermont transferred Howe to a maximum security federal prison in Terre Haute, Indiana, for proper custody and care. Howe brought a civil action in the U.S. District Court for the District of Vermont challenging his transfer, claiming that to transfer him to a federal prison under Section 5003(a), federal authorities are required to make an individual determination that the prisoner needs a particular specialized treatment program available in the federal prison system. The District Court denied the prisoner's request for relief, holding that Section 5003(a) requires no showing of specialized treatment needs and requires nothing more than a certification that facilities exist within the federal prison system to accommodate the state prisoners. The U.S. Court of Appeals for the Second Circuit affirmed the District Court's holding; Howe appealed to the U.S. Supreme Court, and it granted certiorari.

Issue

Whether a state may transfer a prisoner to federal custody pursuant to 18 U.S.C. Section 5003(a) in the absence of a prior determination that the prisoner who is being transferred has a need for specialized treatment.

U.S. Supreme Court Holding

The U.S. Supreme Court affirmed the decision of the Second Circuit Court of Appeals holding that Section 5003(a) authorizes a state that has contracted within the United States to transfer its prisoner to federal custody despite the absence of a prior determination that the prisoner has a need for specialized treatment available in the federal prison system.

Reason

In this case, the U.S. Supreme Court agreed with the Second Circuit Court of Appeals in its interpretation of Section 5003(a) in that nothing in the plain language restricts or limits the states' use of federal prison facilities to those state prisoners in need of some particular treatment. Moreover, the U.S. Supreme Court argued that the legislative history of 5003(a) reveals that Congress perceived a need to respond to state requests for the federal prison system to undertake custody, treatment, and training of state prisoners where the state lacked an institutional capacity to do so, and nothing in the legislative history makes this case one of the rare exceptions requiring a departure from the plain language of the statute. Furthermore, the Court ruled that the contemporaneous and uniform construction of 5003(a) by the Bureau of Prisons has been that the text authorizes contracts based on a broad range of purposes, including the transfer shown by the record of this case, and absent any evidence of congressional objection, the Bureau's interpretation must be given great weight.

Case Significance

The case is significant because it is one of the only cases that addresses the transfer of state prisoners to federal custody. Its ruling is clear. The U.S. Supreme Court gives weight to the plain language used in Section 5003(a) and holds that it makes no sense to interpret the section as requiring federal authorities to transfer only inmates in need of treatment to federal prisons. In this case, the Court found that the petitioner had an erroneous understanding of the concept of "treatment" because he argued that it should be limited to medical treatment, psychiatric treatment, and alcohol or drug rehabilitation programs, and not secure incarceration. The U.S. Supreme Court approves of such transfers.

Hudson v. McMillian
502 U.S. 1 (1992)

Facts

Keith Hudson, an inmate in a Louisiana state penitentiary (Angola) brought a Section 1983 claim against three corrections security officers (McMillian, Woods, and Mezo) in the U.S. District Court for the Middle District of Louisiana claiming that the officers had violated the Cruel and Unusual Punishment Clause of the Eighth Amendment. More specifically, Hudson alleged that (1) one officer, after arguing with him, punched him in the mouth, eyes, chest, and stomach while another officer held him in place and kicked and punched him from behind; (2) the third officer (Mezo), who was the supervisor on duty, watched the beating but merely told the other officers "not to have too much fun"; and (3) as a result of the beating, the inmate suffered minor bruises and swelling of his face, mouth, and lips, loosened teeth, and a cracked partial dental plate. The parties consented to disposition of the case by a U.S. Magistrate, who found that the first two officers had used force when there was no need to do so and that the supervising officer had expressly condoned their actions. The inmate was awarded damage in the amount of $800. On appeal, the U.S. Court of Appeals for the Fifth Circuit reversed on the grounds that (1) prisoners who allege use of excessive force in violation of the Eighth Amendment must prove significant injury, and (2) although the officers' use of force was objectively unreasonable, clearly excessive, and occasioned unnecessary and wanton infliction of pain, the inmate could not prevail on his claim because his injuries were minor and required no medical attention. The case was appealed to the U.S. Supreme Court, and it granted certiorari.

Issue

Whether the use of excessive physical force against a prisoner may constitute cruel and unusual punishment when the inmate does not suffer serious injury.

U.S. Supreme Court Holding

The U.S. Supreme Court reversed the decision of the Fifth Circuit Court of Appeals holding that the use of excessive physical force against a prisoner may constitute cruel and unusual punishment when the prisoner does not suffer serious injury.

Reason

In this case, the U.S. Supreme Court reversed the decision of the Fifth Circuit Court of Appeals citing its previous ruling in *Whitley v. Albers*. In *Whitley*, the Court held that the legal standard to use in Eighth Amendment claims is that "the unnecessary and wanton infliction of pain constitutes cruel and unusual punishment forbidden by the Eighth Amendment." However, what is necessary to establish an "unnecessary and wanton" infliction of pain varies according to the nature of the alleged constitutional violation. More specifically, the Court held that whenever prison officials are accused of using excessive physical force in violation of the Cruel and Unusual Punishment Clause, the core judicial inquiry is what was established in *Whitley*: whether force was applied in a good-faith effort to maintain or restore discipline or maliciously and sadistically to cause harm. Under *Whitley*, the extent of injury suffered by an inmate is one factor that may suggest "whether the use of force could plausibly have been thought necessary" or the unjustified infliction of harm. When determining if the use of force was wanton and unnecessary, it may be proper to evaluate the need, the relationship between the need and the amount of force used, the threat "reasonably perceived" by the responsible officials, and any effort made to temper the severity of a forceful response. The absence of serious injury is relevant to the Eighth Amendment inquiry but does not end it. In the present case, the U.S. Supreme Court stated that it disagreed with the respondent's assertion that a significant injury requirement must exist as part of the objective component of the Eighth Amendment analysis decided in *Wilson v. Seiter*. In *Wilson*, the Court suggested that the objective aspect of an Eighth Amendment claim can be distinguished from the subjective aspect of the same claim. Thus, courts considering Eighth Amendment claims must ask both if "the officials acted with a sufficiently culpable state of mind" and if the alleged wrongdoing was objectively "harmful enough" to establish as constitutional violation.

In *Wilson*, the U.S. Supreme Court held that what is necessary to show sufficient harm for the purpose of cruel and unusual punishment claim is a showing of deliberate indifference on the part of correctional personnel, and a level of care below the minimal needs of the inmates [depends on two parts]. First, the Eighth

Amendment claimant must show the unnecessary and wanton infliction of pain was applied. Second, since the Eighth Amendment's prohibition of cruel and unusual punishment draws its meaning from the evolving standards of decency that mark the progress of a maturing society, when prison officials maliciously and sadistically use force to cause harm, they violate the Eighth Amendment by engaging in behavior that runs counter to contemporary standards of decency. This is true whether or not significant injury is evident. Moreover, the Eighth Amendment's prohibition of cruel and unusual punishment excludes from constitutional recognition *de minimus* uses of physical force, provided that the use of force is not of a sort "repugnant to the conscience of mankind." In this current case, the Fifth Circuit Court of Appeals found Hudson's claim of an Eighth Amendment violation untenable because his injuries were minor despite the blows he received about the face that caused bruises, swelling, loosened teeth, and a cracked dental plate. These are not *de minimus* for Eighth Amendment purposes. Thus, the extent of Hudson's injuries provides no basis for dismissal of his Section 1983 claim.

Case Significance

This case is important because it sends a clear message that the U.S. Supreme Court has ruled that extreme use of force, when not required, is unconstitutional and should not be tolerated or used as a common practice in places of confinement to discipline or punish prisoners. The case should also be taken very seriously because it demonstrates that out-of-control, malicious, or sadistic guards could mean that correctional institutions may face economic hardship resulting from expensive lawsuits that could be decided in favor of inmates. Perhaps it also signals the need to properly screen and train current and future employees carefully and provide the training that is needed for them to perform their correctional duties in a constitutionally-correct manner. At the same time, this decision reaffirmed *Whitley* in that the standard to be used in Eighth Amendment cases regarding excessive force alleging cruel and unusual punishment is whether the force caused the wanton and unnecessary infliction of harm on the inmate.

Hudson v. Palmer

468 U.S. 517 (1984)

Facts

Respondent Palmer, an inmate at a Virginia penal institution was serving a sentence for forgery, grand larceny, and bank robbery convictions. Palmer was accused of damaging state property, given a disciplinary hearing, and found guilty of the charges. He was ordered to reimburse the state for the cost of the materials destroyed. He was also reprimanded, and with the incident being placed on his prison record. He subsequently filed a Section 1983 claim in federal District Court against petitioner Hudson, an officer at the Bland Correctional Center alleging that the petitioner had conducted an unreasonable "shakedown" search of his prison locker and cell and had brought a false charge against him under prison disciplinary procedures for destroying state property (a ripped pillow case) solely to harass and humiliate him. More specifically, the respondent contended that the petitioner had intentionally destroyed certain noncontraband personal property during the search, which constitutes a violation of his Fourteenth Amendment right not to be deprived of property without due process. The District Court granted summary judgment for the petitioner, and the Court of Appeals for the Fifth Circuit affirmed in part, reversed in part, and remanded holding, that Palmer was not deprived of his property without due process, but that he had a limited privacy right in his cell that entitled him to protection against searches conducted solely to harass or humiliate. The case was appealed, and the U.S. Supreme Court granted certiorari.

Issue

Whether a prison inmate has a reasonable expectation of privacy in his prison cell entitling him to the protection of the Fourth Amendment against unreasonable searches and seizures. Whether unauthorized intentional deprivation of property by state officials violate the Fourteenth Amendment due process rights.

U.S. Supreme Court Holding

The U.S. Supreme Court affirmed, in part, and reversed, in part, the ruling of the Fifth Circuit Court of Appeals holding that a prisoner does not have a reasonable expectation of privacy in his prison cell entitling him to the protection of the Fourth Amendment against unreasonable searches and seizures. The Court also held that unauthorized intentional deprivation of property by a state employee does not constitute a violation of the procedural requirement of the Due Process Clause of the Fourteenth Amendment if a meaningful post-deprivation remedy for the loss is available.

Reason

In this case, the U.S. Supreme Court disagreed with the Fifth Circuit Court of Appeals position that Palmer had a limited privacy right that entitled him to protection from searches. The Court held that when considering the issue of privacy, the applicability of the Fourth Amendment turns on whether "the person invoking its protection can claim a reasonable or legitimate expectation of privacy, and whether society is prepared to recognize it as reasonable." The Court argued that society is not prepared to recognize as legitimate any subjective expectation of privacy that a prisoner might have in a prison cell, and the Fourth Amendment protection against unreasonable searches does not apply within the confines of prison cells. Thus, the recognition of privacy rights for prisoners in their cells cannot be reconciled with incarceration and the objectives of penal institutions. More specifically, the Court ruled that prison officials are required to take the necessary steps to ensure safety and prevent the introduction of drugs, weapons, and other contraband.

When determining whether an expectation of privacy is reasonable, the Court does a balancing of interests. In this case, it considered the interest of society and its penal institutions and the interest of prisoners, and decided the balance in favor of the institution. The Court also mentioned that the loss of privacy is a condition that is inherent in confinement. The Court also disagreed with the Fifth Circuit Court's position on how to resolve the privacy issue in *Palmer*. It suggested that officials at Bland could resolve the matter by informing inmates of planned searches. The Court admonished the Fifth Circuit Court and asserted that "the uncertainty that attends random searches of cells renders these searches perhaps the most effective weapon of the prison administrator in the constant fight against the proliferation of knives, guns, illicit drugs, and other contraband." However, a requirement that even random searches be conducted pursuant to an established plan would undermine the effectiveness of this weapon.

Where the second issue is concerned, the respondent argued that the destruction of his property constituted an unreasonable seizure within the meaning of the Fourth Amendment. The Supreme Court disregarded holding that the protection against unreasonable searches is inapplicable in a prison cell because prison officials must be free to seize from cells any contraband that can counter legitimate institutional interests. However, the Court also held that because the Fourth Amendment does not extend to seizures in prison cells does not mean that an inmate's property can be destroyed with impunity. In the present case, the respondent was afforded a grievance procedure and had adequate remedies for the alleged destruction of his property. In addressing this issue, the Court cited its ruling in *Parratt v. Taylor*. In *Parratt*, the Court ruled that when deprivations of property are effected through random and unauthorized conduct of a state employee, predeprivation procedures are simply "impracticable" because the state cannot know when such deprivations will occur. The Court, in *Palmer*, ruled it could not discern a logical distinction between negligent and intentional deprivations of property insofar as the "practicability" of affording predeprivation process is concerned. Therefore, the Court extended *Parratt* to intentional deprivations of property. For the Court, the next step was to determine if the Commonwealth of Virginia provided the respondent an adequate postdeprivation remedy for the alleged destruction of Palmer's property. Because both the District Court and the Fifth Circuit Court of Appeals held that several common law remedies were available to the respondent, the Court held that this satisfied the Due Process Clause of the Fourteenth Amendment because adequate compensation for Palmer's property could have been made. The Court even suggested that the respondent could have invoked the Eighth Amendment claim of cruel and unusual punishment.

Case Significance

This is an important case because it indicates that prisoners do not have reasonable expectations to privacy in their cells. Thus, the Fourth Amendment does not lend its protection to searches and seizures that prisoners view as unreasonable. Moreover, it is also important because the issue of due process was addressed. The Court found no due process violation after Palmer had been deprived of his personal property by a state employee. The Court ruled in favor of the prison system for several reasons, one of which was that the state law provided for several meaningful postdeprivation remedies for the loss. The case indicates that the Court believes that some issues that are brought by inmates can be resolved through other remedies before rising to the level of being addressed in federal court. It also signals the need for states to develop postdeprivation remedies for inmate claims.

Hutto v. Finney

437 U.S. 678 (1978)

Facts

This litigation began in 1969. It is a sequel to two earlier cases holding that conditions in the Arkansas prison system violated the Eighth and Fourteenth Amendments of the U.S. Constitution. The case began as *Holt v. Sarver*. The two earlier cases were *Talley v. Stephens* and *Jackson v. Bishop*. In *Holt*, the U.S. District Court for the Eastern District of Arkansas found that conditions of confinement for prisoners in punitive isolation were unconstitutional with an average of four and sometimes ten or eleven prisoners confined to a single isolation cell that contained no furniture and a toilet that could be flushed only from outside the cell. Often prisoners with infectious diseases were placed in the same cells as healthy prisoners, and the mattresses the infectious prisoners slept on were jumbled up at the beginning of the day and redistributed randomly at night to all prisoners. However, the District Court did not impose a detailed remedy and ordered Arkansas prison officials to improve conditions using their own remedy. In *Holt* II, the District Court was not satisfied with the improvements made by Arkansas prison officials to alleviate unconstitutional conditions and issued guidelines for authorities to meet in regard to four areas, one of which was the isolation units. In a third set of hearings held in 1972 and 1973, the District Court found that Arkansas prison officials made substantial improvements to the system and that supervision by the courts was no longer needed. At that time, the District Court also held that prior decrees were still in effect and court costs and attorneys fees would be imposed on prison officials if the violations reoccurred. In 1976, a fourth set of hearings occurred, and the District Court found that conditions in the isolation units had seriously deteriorated since 1973. There were twice as many prisoners as beds in some cells, and the overcrowding led to violent antisocial prisoners victimizing weaker prisoners. Also, the "gruel" diet being fed isolation prisoners was resulting in prisoners losing weight and an inadequate number of guards led to the use of nightsticks, mace, and physical beatings of prisoners to maintain control of the unit. Consequently, the District Court declared conditions in the isolation unit unconstitutional and ordered officials to place limits on the number of men that could be placed in each isolation unit cell, requiring that each man have a bunk, discontinuation of the grue diet, and thirty days as the maximum isolation sentence. The District Court concluded that prison officials acted in bad faith and awarded opposing counsel a fee of $20,000 to be paid from Department of Corrections funds. On appeal to the Eighth Circuit Court of Appeals, prison officials were unsuccessful in having the District Court's decision overturned. In fact, the Court of Appeals assessed them an additional $2,500 to cover fees and expenses. Arkansas did not appeal the District Court's finding that conditions of confinement in the isolation units were unconstitutional in violation of the Eighth and Fourteenth Amendments. The case was appealed to the U.S. Supreme Court, and it granted certiorari.

Issue

Could the District Court order Arkansas prison officials to limit isolation unit sentences to thirty days and could the District Court and the Eighth Circuit

Court of Appeals assign attorney's fees and court costs to the Arkansas Department of Corrections for failing to comply with previous court orders?

U.S. Supreme Court Holding

The Supreme Court affirmed the decision of the Eighth Circuit Court of Appeals holding that (1) the federal District Court did not err in placing a maximum limit of thirty days on confinement in punitive isolation because (a) the court had given prison officials repeated opportunities to remedy the cruel and unusual conditions in the isolation cells, (b) because of the interdependence of the conditions producing the violation, the thirty-day limit would help correct overcrowding and enmities growing out of confinement in the cells, (c) the limit presented danger of interference with prison administration, and (d) the trial judge had years of experience with the problem and recognized the limits on a federal court's authority in such a case; (2) the award of attorney's fees to be paid out of the department's funds was adequately supported by the court's finding of bad faith and did not violate the substantive provisions of the Eleventh Amendment, even though the court did not assess the award against the officers in their official capacities; and (3) the award of attorney's fees by the Court of Appeals was supported by the Civil Rights Attorney's Fees Award Act of 1976 and was not barred by a state's immunity under the Eleventh Amendment from retroactive relief.

Reason

In this case, the Court reviewed whether past orders from the District Court to the Arkansas Department of Corrections to address Eighth and Fourteenth Amendment violations had been remedied. According to the Supreme Court, the District Court was entitled to consider the severity of these violations in assessing the constitutionality of conditions in the isolation cells. More specifically, the District Court took note of the inmates' diet, the continued overcrowding, the rampant violence, the vandalized cells, and the lack of professionalism and good judgment on the part of maximum security personnel. The Court concluded the conditions in the isolations cells continued to violate the prohibition against cruel and unusual punishment. The Court also ruled that the District Court had the authority to go beyond its earlier orders and address each element that contributed to the violation. The District Court had given the Department of Corrections opportunities to remedy the "cruel and unusual conditions" in the isolation cells. If petitioners had fully complied with the court's earlier orders, the time limitation would not have been necessary. In citing *Milliken v. Bradley* (418 U.S. 717, 1974), the Court held that when state and local authorities fail in their affirmative obligations, judicial authorities may be invoked. However, when invoked, the scope of a District Court's equitable powers to remedy past wrongs is broad—for breadth and flexibility are inherent in equitable remedies.

In this case, the Court ruled that the petitioner does not disagree with the District Court's finding that the Arkansas Department of Corrections' punitive isolation cells are operating in violation of the Eighth Amendment, but rather disagrees with the District Court's most recent order that forbids the Department to sentence inmates to more than thirty days in punitive isolation. The petitioner assumed that the District Court held that an indeterminate sentence to punitive isolation always constitutes cruel and unusual punishment. The Supreme Court disagreed with the Arkansas Department of Corrections' reasoning and argued that the District Court's opinion is clear in that the length of isolation sentences was not considered in a vacuum. In fact, the District Court states, "punitive isolation" is not necessarily unconstitutional, but it may be depending on the duration of the confinement and the conditions. The Court held, "We think it quite clear that the court was describing the specific conditions found in the Arkansas penal system."

Where the attorney's fees and additional court costs are concerned, the Court of Appeals relied on the Civil Rights Attorney's Fees Act of 1976 and supported the findings of the District Court that the conduct of state officials justified the award under the bad faith exception established in *Alyeska Pipeline Service Co. v. Wilderness Society* (421 U.S. 240, 1975). In *Alyeska Pipeline*, the Court ruled that an equity court has the unquestioned power to award attorney's fees against a party who shows bad faith by delaying or disrupting the litigation or by hampering enforcement of a court order.

Case Significance

This case is significant because it reveals the seriousness the federal courts give to Eighth Amendment conditions of confinement cases, especially when an entire prison system has been ruled as operating in violation of the U.S. Constitution. This case is particularly important to prison litigation because prior to the 1960s, judicial officials had taken a hands-off approach to addressing complaints from inmates. Needless to say, in 1978, the present case challenged the conditions of confinement in the entire Arkansas Prison System. In *Hutto*, it is clear that the Supreme Court reinforces the decision ordered by the District Court and later the Court of Appeals that reforms needed to be made to make the Arkansas system constitutionally correct. The case reveals that despite prior orders to make corrective measures in the system, prison officials refused to comply. As a result, the system was revisited, and it was found that conditions were still operating in violation of the Eighth and Fourteenth Amendments. Subsequently, the federal District Court issued additional orders. In this case, the Supreme Court also upheld the District Court's ruling to the dismay of the state that a thirty-day limitation on solitary confinement should be a matter of policy, and it affirmed the Appeals Court's award of attorney's fees and additional court fees. From this case, the message is clear: Prison officials must abide by federal court orders to make sure their penal systems function in a constitutionally correct manner.

Jackson v. Bishop
404 F.2d 571 (1968)

Facts

Three inmates of the Arkansas Penitentiary appealed a 1967 decision by the U.S. District Court for the Eastern District of Arkansas that enjoined the use of a leather strap three-and-a-half to five-feet long, four inches wide, and half an inch thick attached to an eight- to twelve-inch wooden handle to whip the bare skin of prisoners until appropriate safeguards were developed by prison authorities. The inmates sought permanent injunctive relief in their action on the basis that corporal punishment violated the proscription against cruel and unusual punishment. Administrators contend that corporal punishment is meted out when inmates commit such major offenses as homosexuality, agitation, insubordination, making or concealing weapons, refusal to work when medically certified able to work, and participating in or inciting a riot. The Arkansas inmates claimed that the District Court erred in not holding that the whipping of prisoners with the leather strap is in itself cruel and unusual and should be banned as a punishment. While citing *Talley v. Stephens*, the District Court ruled that the leather strap whippings were constitutional as long as they were accompanied by rules announced to the prisoners, and necessary safeguards existed in the Arkansas prison system. In January 1966, Arkansas reinstated the practice of whipping prisoners with the strap by publishing a set of rules and safeguards to control the whippings, which were in effect until June

1967 when the District Court found that Arkansas prison officials repeatedly whipped prisoners outside those rules and safeguards.

Issue

Whether whipping prisoners with a leather strap constituted a violation of the Eighth Amendment's prohibition against cruel and unusual punishment.

Holding

The Eighth Circuit Court vacated and remanded the District Court's decision holding that the use of a leather strap to discipline inmates runs counter to the Eighth Amendment prohibition of cruel and unusual punishment.

Reason

In reviewing the case, the Eighth Circuit Court relied on the U.S. Supreme Court's ruling in *Trop v. Dulles* (356 U.S. 86, 1958) where the Court invalidated a statute that denationalized a native-born citizen who deserted his military service during World War II. In *Trop*, the Court declared that such drastic action was cruel and unusual punishment prohibited by the Eighth Amendment. In reaching its decision, the Court ruled that punishment is cruel and unusual when it runs counter to "evolving standards of decency that mark the progress of a maturing society." In the present case, the Eighth Circuit Court judged the practice of whipping prisoners as contrary to evolving standards of decency in society. It also held that such punishment was outside the standards of contemporary society and comparative law. The Eighth Circuit Court vacated and remanded the case because: (1) It was not convinced that any rule or regulation of the strap would prevent abuse; (2) Rules governing corporal punishment often went unobserved; (3) Regulations were often circumvented; (4) Corporal punishment is easily subject to abuse in the hands of the sadistic and unscrupulous; (5) Excessive whipping or an inappropriate manner of whipping constitutes cruel and unusual punishment; (6) Corporal punishment creates hate toward the keepers and undermines correctional and rehabilitative goals; and (7) Whipping creates other penological problems and makes readjusting to society more problematic. The Court of Appeals also observed that Arkansas and two other states still used whipping as a form of discipline that other states had uniformly abolished.

Case Significance

This case is significant for a number of reasons, chief among them that the Arkansas penitentiary system joined all but two states in prohibiting the use of corporal punishment as a disciplinary measure on the prison population. In fact, the Court of Appeals states that it was not convinced Arkansas needed corporal punishment as a tool to discipline inmates. It also stated that Arkansas cannot claim that it is too poor to offer other acceptable means to enforce prison regulations. The court stated that the failure to treat prisoners humanely cannot be attributed to the lack of financial resources. Second, the ruling is important because it prevents not only physical abuse inflicted by correctional guards on inmates but also inmate-on-inmate violence because inmate trustees were allowed to whip other inmates. Third, today there are two types of prisoner Eighth Amendment cruel and unusual punishment cases: those involving prison conditions that deprive the prisoner of adequate medical care, nutrition, and/or protection; and those that involve excessive punishment. This is the first prison case where punishment practiced by prison authorities was declared excessive and, therefore, cruel and unusual punishment.

Johnson v. Avery
393 U.S. 483 (1969)

Facts

A state prisoner in Tennessee assisted other inmates to prepare and file petitions for postconviction relief, such as petitions for writ of habeas corpus. Petitioner Johnson was punished for the infraction by being placed in disciplinary confinement and deprived of certain privileges for violating the regulation prohibiting inmates from helping other inmates prepare writs or other legal papers. In response to Johnson's challenge, the District Court for the Middle District of Tennessee trial court held that the prison regulation banning the assistance of a jailhouse lawyer impeded prisoners' rights, especially those of illiterate prisoners to seek postconviction relief, thus violating inmates' federal right to habeas corpus. The court ordered that the petitioner be restored to his status as an ordinary prisoner. The decision was appealed to the Sixth Circuit Court, where it was reversed, holding that the state's interest in preserving prison discipline and limiting the practice of law to licensed attorneys justified the burden the regulation placed on access to federal habeas corpus. The case was appealed to the U.S. Supreme Court, and it granted certiorari.

Issue

Can state prison authorities enforce a penal regulation that prohibits prisoners from assisting other prisoners in preparing federal habeas corpus petitions for postconviction relief?

U.S. Supreme Court Holding

The U.S. Supreme Court reversed and remanded the judgment of the Sixth Circuit Court of Appeals, holding that unless and until the state provided some reasonable alternative to assist inmates in the preparation of petitions for postconviction relief, it could not validly enforce the prison regulation banning inmates from providing such assistance to other prisoners.

Reason

The U.S. Supreme Court ruled that the writ of habeas corpus is fundamental to the U.S. system of jurisprudence. Its basic purpose is to enable those unlawfully incarcerated to obtain their freedom. In fact, the Court stated that it and Congress have always worked so that prisoners can have access to the courts for the purpose of presenting their complaints without obstruction. Moreover, the Court has held that a state may not make the writ available only to prisoners who can pay a filing fee. The Court has insisted that the writ be provided to poor, as well as affluent, prisoners during postconviction proceedings and not be viewed as a mere formality. Therefore, the state is obligated to provide prisoners with a transcript or equivalent recordation applicable to inmates housed at all prison facilities. Any prison regulation that conflicts with this position is invalid. To highlight this point, the Court cited a state regulation it invalidated because it required that habeas corpus petitions first be submitted to prison authorities and then approved by the "legal investigator" to the parole board as "properly drawn" before being transmitted to the court. In that case, like the current one, the state argued the requirement was necessary to maintain prison discipline. However, the Court ruled the state and its officers may not abridge or impair a petitioner's right to apply to a federal court for a writ of habeas corpus. The Court, in the current case, stated the states do not have the power to control the practice of law to the extent where they can abrogate federally protected rights. The Court suggested that if writ writers were to be abolished, indigent offenders should be provided regular assistance programs that may include (1) providing prisoners access to lawyers in the state public offender system, (2) the employment of senior law students for writ writing assistance, and (3) voluntary programs within the state bar association that provide prisoners with access to private attorneys. However, the Court did not specifically express what a state must do to satisfy its regular assistance requirement.

Case Significance

This case is important because the U.S. Supreme Court ruled that state prison officials cannot obstruct state inmates from seeking a federal writ of habeas corpus for postconviction relief. The case demonstrates the state's attempt to ban the use of jailhouse lawyers from assisting convicted inmates seeking release. The U.S. Supreme Court states that the federal writ of habeas corpus is a right guaranteed to those who claim their confinement is illegal and therefore the "Great Writ," as it is referred to, has enjoyed protection from the Court as well as Congress. Moreover, the Court is aware that jails and penitentiaries include a high percentage of offenders who are either totally or functionally illiterate; therefore, they need assistance in bringing or filing such claims. Essentially, the case represents a victory for granting inmates access to court.

Jolly v. Coughlin
894 F. Supp. 734 (1995)

Facts

Paul Jolly, a Rastafarian inmate, refused to submit to a mandatory tuberculosis (TB) screening program instituted by the New York State Department of Corrections. He claimed the tests violated his religious beliefs because they involved injecting an artificial substance into his body. As a result of his refusal, he was placed in medical keeplock at New York's Attica Correctional Facility, where he remained for three and a half years. In all, the tuberculosis program involved taking a PPD test, being x-rayed, and being checked for physical signs of tuberculosis. An inmate must show positive results for TB on all three measures before being placed in respiratory isolation. Jolly displayed no physical signs of TB and had submitted to three chest x-rays in the past three years that did not indicate TB, but he remained in medical keeplock at the time of the trial because of his refusal to submit to the PPD test, which was not considered a reliable indicator of TB. At the time of the trial, Jolly sought a prelim-

inary injunction to be released back to the general population. He also claimed
that his confinement had rendered him unable to stand. As a result of his confinement, Jolly could not stand up to go to the shower and developed physical problems such as rashes, severe headaches, shortness of breath, and hair loss.
He claimed that his treatment violated his right to the free exercise of religion
under the Religious Freedom Restoration Act of 1993 (RFRA) and the Eighth
Amendment right to be free from cruel and unusual punishment.

Issue

Whether Jolly was entitled to relief of preliminary injunction that ordered
his release from medical keeplock.

Holding

The District Court for the Southern District of New York granted Jolly a
preliminary injunction prohibiting New York correctional officials from keeping him in medical keeplock while his case was being litigated.

Reason

In this case, the Southern District Court only ruled on whether to grant
Jolly a preliminary injunction that would release him from medical keeplock
while he pursued his First and Eighth Amendment claims in the federal courts.
In granting the injunction, pursuant to court policy, the district court ruled that
Jolly (1) demonstrated a substantial and clear showing of possible success on
his First and Eighth Amendment claims, and (2) that irreparable injury could
result because of the possible violation of his constitutional rights. First, the
District Court found that Jolly's inability to stand during showers and his other
medical ailments constituted irreparable injury, or injuries for which he could
not be adequately compensated for monetarily. In regard to his First Amendment free exercise of religion claim, the District Court interpreted the RFRA
to require that New York correctional officials demonstrate a compelling reason that involved the least restrictive means of advancing their interests in preventing TB among the inmate population to justify keeping Jolly in medical
keeplock because the PPD test violates his religious beliefs. The District Court
thought that although New York correctional officials had a compelling reason
to prevent the spread of TB among inmates, they had not provided Jolly with
a less restrictive way of demonstrating that he did not have TB, and for that reason, he could prevail on his First Amendment claim. The District Court also
thought that Jolly could prevail on his Eighth Amendment claim. Applying

the U.S. Supreme Court's two-part test for a medical cruel and unusual punishment claim, the District Court thought confining Jolly for three and a half years without any daily exercise could constitute cruel and unusual punishment in the objective sense, and that New York correctional officials ignoring his complaints about the resulting physical ailments could amount to their acting with deliberate indifference to his medical condition in the subjective sense.

Case Significance

The case is important because the District Court found the correctional policy to be unreasonable and injurious because Jolly had no signs of TB. It also highlights the fact that he had incurred injury as a consequence of his prolonged stay in medical keeplock for three and a half years because of his refusal to be tested on the grounds that to do so would constitute an infringement on his First Amendment to the free exercise of religion. The fact that New York correctional officials ignored his complaints about the ailments that resulted from his detention constituted deliberate indifference on the part of prison officials. The court also reasoned that because Jolly was not contagious, letting him out with a preliminary injunction caused no harm.

Jones v. Bradley
590 F.2d 294 (1979)

Facts

Richard Jones, a Washington State inmate, brought a suit seeking injunctive relief and damages in the U.S. District Court of Eastern Washington contending that prison officials denied him the right to freely exercise his religion guaranteed by the First Amendment to the U.S. Constitution. More specifically, Jones, a self-proclaimed pastor of the Universal Life Church (ULC), was denied the use of the prison chapel to perform study sessions and the right to perform marriages for inmates. He argued that because others practicing religions were allowed these privileges, they must be extended to him and his followers. Prison officials argued that the ULC was not recognized as a church and denied Jones's request. The District Court dismissed Jones's complaint, holding the ULC was not a religion and therefore not entitled to the First Amendment protection. The case was appealed to the Ninth Circuit Court of Appeals.

Issue

Whether Jones was entitled to the First Amendment protection to the free exercise of his religion by state prison officials to have access to a chapel for study sessions and the right to perform marriages for inmates.

Holding

The Ninth Circuit Court affirmed the decision of the District Court, holding that it was not necessary to address the question as to whether the ULC was a religion because its free exercise was not denied by the defendant's refusal to allow Jones access to perform study sessions in the chapel and to perform marriages.

Reason

The Ninth Circuit Court reasoned that the District Court did not exceed its authority or act improperly when it concluded that ULC was not a religion. Moreover, the Circuit Court contended that it understood the basis of the District Court's conclusion that the ULC was not a religion because it had no traditional doctrine and the church sold a variety of doctoral degrees to anyone wishing to start a branch of the ULC. The Circuit Court of Appeals did not review the District Court's finding that the ULC was not a religion because it ruled that even if the ULC was an established religion, prison authorities did not violate its free exercise of religious rights. In regard to chapel use, Jones was denied for several reasons, such as his wish to have study groups and not worship services, and prison chaplains refused to sponsor meetings by ULC because they did not recognize the church as a religion. In this case, the circuit court cited *Cruz v. Beto* where the Supreme Court ruled a prisoner must be given a reasonable opportunity to pursue his faith comparable to the opportunities afforded fellow prisoners who practice conventional religious precepts. In citing *Beto,* the Circuit Court reasoned that the free exercise of religion did not mean that every religious group have identical facilities or personnel, and they found because Jones did not intend to use the chapel as it was intended to be used (worship services), and not find an outside sponsor to supervise chapel activities in accordance with prison regulations, or request use of another room presenting less security risk for the study group, prison officials did not deny him free exercise of religious rights. Moreover, the Circuit Court reasoned that efforts to provide prisoners a reasonable opportunity to exercise religion must be evaluated in light of the state's legitimate interest in prison security (see *Pell v. Procunier*). The Ninth Circuit Court also ruled that the claim of a First Amendment right to perform marriages is also without merit. The Appeals Court ruled that such matters are of state law.

Case Significance

The case signals the federal court's unwillingness to extend the First Amendment rights to the free exercise of religion to groups that have no history connected with a traditional religion. The case also suggests that not every religious group must have identical facilities or personnel. However, the case makes it clear that the courts are concerned that prisoners be given the opportunity to reasonably engage in the free exercise of their religion in light of the prison's need to maintain security.

Jones v. North Carolina Prisoners' Labor Union

433 U.S. 119 (1977)

Facts

The North Carolina Prisoners' Labor "Union" brought a Section 1983 action in the U.S. District Court for the Eastern District of North Carolina seeking injunctive relief, attorney fees, and damages. The prisoners claimed their rights under the First and Fourteenth Amendments were violated by North Carolina prison administrators because (1) they were prohibited from soliciting other prisoners to join the Union, (2) Union meetings were barred, and (3) they were prevented from making bulk mailings on behalf of the Union from outside sources to individual prisoner's for redistribution among other prisoners. The District Court ruled in favor of the prisoner's union on all three claims, holding that if the prison permitted the Union to exist in the past, it permitted it to meet and invite others to join. Because this practice was extended to some, it must be extended to others. However, the prison could impose reasonable restrictions. The District Court further held that the state of North Carolina presented no evidence that prisoner-to-prisoner solicitation or Union meetings actually disrupted prison operations, and because North Carolina allowed organizations such as the Jaycees and Alcoholics Anonymous do bulk mailings, the equal protection clause required that all organizations could participate in bulk mailings. North Carolina prison officials appealed the District Court's ruling, arguing that prison regulations used to control the Union were necessary because of the potential loss of control and violence that could occur because of a powerful prison union.

Issue

Whether North Carolina prison regulations prohibiting Union prisoners from soliciting other prisoners from joining the Union, banning Union meetings, and preventing them from communicating in bulk mailings violated the First and Fourteenth Amendments to the U.S. Constitution.

U.S. Supreme Court Holding

The U.S. Supreme Court reversed the decision of the District Court holding that the North Carolina prison regulations did not infringe on the First and Fourteenth Amendment rights of the Union because the prison policies represented reasonable security interests consistent with the Union members' status as prisoners.

Reason

The U.S. Supreme Court ruled in favor of the North Carolina prison system, basing its decision on the general principles that the needs of the penal institution impose limitations of the constitutional rights of prisoners and that incarceration brings about a necessary withdrawal and limitation of constitutional rights and privileges. In regard to the prisoner-to-prisoner solicitation and Union meeting claims, the Court disagreed with the District Court's reasoning that prison officials must support prison regulations with actual evidence of disruption and violence. The Court accepted the North Carolina prison officials' contention that the regulations were reasonably justified by the potential for disruption and violence that could exist in a union of prisoners, and although officials presented no actual evidence of disruption or violence by the Union, it did not have to wait for a volatile situation to develop to justify its regulations. In regard to the District Court ruling that the equal protection clause required prison officials to allow bulk mailings on behalf of the Union from outside sources because other organizations were allowed to do so, the Court ruled that the prison was not a public forum. The equal protection clause prohibited officials from discriminating between groups for communication purposes only if the place of communication is a public forum, and because the prison was a public forum, the Union was protected. The Court accepted the North Carolina prison officials explanation that security required prisoner mail to be monitored and that it was impossible to monitor the content of the bulk mailings to individual prisoners for redistribution among them, and that prison officials could discriminate among organizations it allowed to bulk mail based on security interests. North Carolina prison officials saw security interests in the Union's bulk mailings, whereas it did not in the bulk mailings by the Jaycees and Alcoholics Anonymous.

Case Significance

This case is important for several reasons. First, it is the only case heard by the federal courts regarding a prisoners' union. Second, the case signals that while each group or organization is supposed to be allowed or provided equal protection under the Fourteenth Amendment, the Court is inclined to depart from this reasoning. In the present case, the North Carolina Prisoners' Union had become large. In fact, its membership had increased to 2,000 prisoners. The Union had all along maintained that its main purpose was to work for prison reform. Penal administrators were concerned that the Union would create a power bloc to cause work slowdowns or stoppages or other undesirable activity. This speaks to collective bargaining power that the U.S. Constitution does not afford prisoners. Though Union inmates speak to disparate treatment they received compared to other groups/organizations in the prison, such as the Jaycees, Alcoholics Anonymous, and the Boy Scouts of America, the latter groups have a history of advocating rehabilitation, not better working conditions or prison reform. Moreover, in its decision, the U.S. Supreme Court emphasized the security problems of prison officials in restricting the rights of prisoners. Thus, the Court rejected the District Court ruling that prison regulations must be justified by a showing of actual evidence of disruption and violence. The Court accepted North Carolina's justification for its prison regulations based on a reasonable concern for potential disruption and violence, especially losing control of inmates.

Jordan v. Gardner

986 F. 2d 1521 (9th Cir. 1993)

Facts

State prison officials at the Washington Corrections Center for Women (WCCW) appealed an order from the U.S. District Court for the Western District of Washington enjoining them from implementing a policy allowing male guards to conduct random pat-down nonemergency, suspicionless clothed body searches of female prisoners. These cross-gendered clothed body searches are routine and rare, usually conducted at prison checkpoints. The District Court found that such policies violated the prisoners' First, Fourth, and Eighth Amendment rights. The WCCW held about 270 minimum-, medium-, and maximum security prisoners and employed both male and female guards. Before the lawsuit, male guards were not allowed to conduct suspicionless searches and could only search female prisoners in emergency situations. Female guards conducted almost all searches, including the routine suspicionless searches and those done under suspicion that the prisoner possessed contraband. In February 1989, to make routine suspicionless searches more effective, Eldon Vail, the new WCCW Superintendent, instituted a policy that increased the number of suspicionless searches at the prison and allowed male guards to conduct them. The searches required the male to run his hands over the clothed body of the female prisoner and included the "squeezing and kneading" of the upper thighs and crotch area and "flattening of the breasts." After one day of males conducting searches, one female inmate who had been severely abused by men in her past suffered severe mental distress. She had to have her fingers pried from bars she had grabbed during the search, and she vomited after returning to her cell block. That same day, female prisoners filed suit with the District Court and obtained a preliminary injunction barring the male searches.

Issue

Whether the male guards' nonemergency, suspicionless clothed body searches of female prisoners at WCCW violated the female prisoners' First, Fourth, and Eighth Amendment rights.

Holding for the Ninth Circuit Court of Appeals

The Ninth Circuit Court affirmed the decision of the U.S. District Court for the Western District of Washington. The male guards' nonemergency suspicionless clothed body searches of female prisoners violated the Eighth Amendment's prohibition against inflicting unnecessary and wanton pain. The court dismissed the claims of First and Fourth Amendment rights violations.

Reason

The Appeals Court did not address the issue of whether the searches violated the female prisoners' First and Fourth Amendment right to religion and privacy because they found the searches violated the female prisoners' Eighth Amendment right to be free of cruel and unusual punishment. In determining whether the searches violated the Eighth Amendment, the court used a "traditional" Eighth Amendment analysis grounded in Supreme Court case law. The two-part traditional analysis first involved an inquiry into whether the searches "inflicted pain upon the female prisoners." After reviewing several dispositions, live testimony from the female prisoners, and testimony from prison psychologists and counselors, the Ninth Circuit Court found that there was a high probability that even properly conducted searches would cause severe psychological injury and emotional pain to previously physically and sexually abused women. The second part of the court's traditional analysis involved determining whether the inflicted pain was "unnecessary and wanton." In deciding that the pain was unnecessary, the court found that the prison security interests were adequately fulfilled before officials instituted the policy allowing males to perform the routine suspicionless pat-down searches. The court found that such searches were wanton because prison officials who were mandating the male search policy acted with deliberate indifference to warnings from prison psychologists that the searches would cause psychological trauma in some of the prisoners. In this case, Superintendent Vail commented on how he could be sued by the employees' union if he did not allow the men to search the female prisoners. The court decided that violating a constitutional right did not justify a labor grievance suit.

Case Significance

This case is significant for several reasons. In it, women prisoners filed a class action suit alleging a violation of their First, Fourth, and Eighth Amendment rights, due to a policy that allows cross-gendered body searches of clothed prisoners. Despite the first two Amendments being considered preferred amendments, the Appeals Court, in this case, found no merit in the appellees' assertion that to be searched by a male guard violated their religious beliefs because the male guard was not their spouse and also found no merit in their Fourth Amendment objection to having a reasonable expectation of privacy from unreasonable searches. In a surprising ruling, the Ninth Circuit discovered that most of the women in prison had been abused in the past. Because of this, being touched by male guards caused them emotional distress, which the court interpreted as an infliction of pain on the inmate. Moreover, the court interpreted the new policy allowing male guards to search female inmates as unnecessary and wanton as required because there was no security justification and prison officials acted with deliberate indifference to the plight of inmates even after staff psychologists had warned them of this probability. During the case, the Appeals Court discovered that what the prison had described as a mere pat-down typically involved rubbing, squeezing, and kneading. Furthermore, the court found the injunction issued by the trial court to be proper. The case signals a victory for women inmates who find it offensive and degrading to be touched by male guards. It also places limitations and restrictions on the physical touching of cross-gendered clothed body searches.

Kahane v. Carlson
527 F. 2d. 492 (1975)

Facts

In 1971, Kahane, an Orthodox Jewish rabbi, was sentenced to one year in the Eastern District of New York for conspiracy to violate the federal Firearms Act. His sentence was suspended, and he was placed on probation. Kahane and his family relocated to Israel with permission of the court. While there, he became a candidate for election to the Knesset, the Israeli Parliament. Kahane subsequently admitted to violating the conditions of his probation. Therefore, his probation was revoked. During his incarceration, he filed an order in the form of mandamus in the Eastern District of New York requiring federal prison administrators to accommodate the Jewish religious diet and prayer. More specifically, Kahane requested that prison officials provide him with a special Kosher diet so that he could maintain a state of good health without violating Jewish dietary laws. The District Court ruled in favor of Kahane. Prison officials appealed the decision, arguing that the lower court was not the proper venue for Kahane's order.

Issue

Whether the First Amendment to the U.S. Constitution requires prison authorities to provide special diets to prisoners whose religions prevent them from eating regular diets.

Holding

The Second Circuit Court of Appeals modified the order and affirmed the decision of the District Court, citing the venue was proper due to the inmate's long residence and probation obligation in the location.

Reason

In this case, the Second Circuit Court of Appeals held that it has long been established that as a consequence of incarceration, restrictions are placed on many of the freedoms enjoyed by free citizens. Where fundamental rights are concerned, such as the right to freely practice one's religion, the U.S. Supreme Court has recognized that the degree of restriction placed on a prisoner must be only that amount justified by an "important or substantial government interest." The court cited the Supreme Court decisions in *Price v. Johnston* (334

U.S. 266, 1948), *Cruz v. Beto,* and *Pell v. Procunier* with respect to restrictions and limitations of inmate rights because of penal system needs. The court also stated that the First Amendment allows inmates to retain those rights that are not inconsistent with their status as a prisoner or with the legitimate penological objective of penal systems. In the present case, the court held that to deny an inmate kosher food is not justified by any substantial governmental interest or compelling government interest. The court also stated that courts have long recognized that prison authorities must accommodate the rights of prisoners to receive diets in a manner consistent with their religious beliefs. Moreover, the Jewish faith has a long-established history found in the laws of kashruth, which addresses its dietary laws and how its observance is an integral part of the covenant between the Jewish people and God. Furthermore, the court ruled that accommodating the Jewish inmates would not represent an insurmountable task because only a small number (twelve) of practicing Orthodox Jews were in federal prisons at the time. Thus, this would not cause a financial hardship on the prisons. Since state and city prisoners were already providing Kosher food to inmates, the idea of the federal system following the same course of action is not novel.

Case Significance

This case is important because it provides that inmates are to be accommodated if they have special dietary needs that are required of their religion. Thus, prison authorities must extend more protection to the First Amendment right to freedom of religion of inmates. However, the court suggests that when it can be shown from an established history that such diets are legitimate and not false, such requests should be met. The court's reasoning also presupposes that such dietary accommodation should not create an economic hardship on correctional budgets. The case is also important because it appears that this is the first time a federal correctional institution was asked to address this issue.

Kentucky Department of Corrections v. Thompson
490 U.S. 454 (1989)

Facts

In September 1976, Kentucky prisoners filed a class action suit in the U.S. District Court for the Western District of Kentucky challenging the general conditions of confinement in the state prisons. The District Court settled the action in 1980 by issuing a consent decree containing provisions governing general prison conditions, which included a provision requiring the Bureau of Corrections to maintain an open visiting policy with minimal restrictions. Prior to this decision, the Commonwealth had issued regulations containing a nonexhaustive list of categories of state prison visitors who, being either a threat to the security or order of the institution or nonconducive to the successful reentry of the inmate to the community, "may be excluded." In 1985, the Kentucky State Reformatory issued changes in their visitation policy allowing prison officials to deny visits to those constituting "a clear and probable danger to the safety and security of the institution or who would interfere with the orderly operation of the institution." A nonexhaustive list of nine specific reasons for excluding visitors accompanied the new visitation policy, which also gave power to the duty officer to exclude visitors. In the present suit, the Kentucky prisoners claimed that the new policy violated the 1980 consent decree mandating an open visitation policy and the Fourteenth Amendment's Due Process Clause because the visitation suspensions are decided without a hearing. The District Court found that the new policy did not violate the 1980 consent decree but ordered prison officials to develop due process procedures for excluding state prison visitors. The U.S. Court of Appeals for the Sixth District largely affirmed and remanded the case, finding that the prisoners had a Fourteenth Amendment liberty interest in visitation based on the consent decree and the regulations and stated policies. The Appeals Court found that the relevant language was sufficiently mandatory to create a liberty interest. The corrections department and officials petitioned the Court for a writ of certiorari, and the Court granted the petition.

Issue

Whether the Kentucky prison officials' decision regarding the exclusion of any particular visitor implicates a prison inmate's Fourteenth Amendment rights.

U.S. Supreme Court Holding

The U.S. Supreme Court reversed the decision of the Sixth Circuit Court of Appeals, holding that the petitioner, the Kentucky Department of Corrections, did not have to provide state inmates with a minimum due process standard because a prison regulation did not establish a liberty interest protected by the Due Process Clause because its regulation did not use "explicitly mandatory language" in connection with the establishment of specific substantive predicates to limit official discretion.

Reason

The Supreme Court stated that two things could create a Fourteenth Amendment liberty interest: A direct guarantee by the Fourteenth Amendment itself and the wording of state law. While quickly dismissing the idea that prisoners have liberty interests in visitation protected by the Fourteenth Amendment itself, the Court addressed the issue of whether the prison regulations created a liberty interest for prisoners. In deciding that the regulations did not create such a liberty interest in receiving visitors for the state prisoners, the Court stated that in a prison context, state regulations must use "explicitly mandatory" language in connection with the establishment of "specifically substantive predicates" to limit official discretion, which would require that a particular outcome be reached after a finding that relevant criteria have been met. The Court found that the Kentucky regulations lacked mandatory language in creating a liberty interest in visitation for prisoners because visitors "may" be, but not necessarily excluded if they fell within one of the listed categories of excludable visitors, and visitors could still be excluded if they did not fall within one of the categories. The regulation was not worded in a way that gave an inmate an "objective expectation" that a visit would be allowed if the visitor did not fall into one of the exclusion categories, nor did it entitle prisoners to force prison officials to allow visits absent one of the exclusion conditions.

Case Significance

This case is important because the U.S. Supreme Court ruled that prison officials can create criteria to determine who can be excluded from prison visitation. The decision is significant because it affects inmates and others in the free community. After setting aside the edits of the consent decree, the Court held that the denial of prison access to a particular visitor is well within the terms of confinement ordinarily contemplated by a prison sentence, and therefore is not protected by the Due Process Clause. The Court held that the procedure governing who is unfit to visit was fair because exclusion was based on maintaining security and order in the institution. For example, the policy excluded visitation from visitors (1) whose presence in the institution constituted a clear and probable danger to the institution's security or interfered with the orderly operations; (2) with a past record of disruptive conduct; (3) under the influence of alcohol and drugs; (4) who refuse to submit to a search or show proper identification; (5) who are directly related to the inmate's criminal behavior; and (6) who are currently on probation or parole who do not have special written permission from the probation/parole officer and the institutional superintendent. The Court was also aware of the two incidents that ultimately led to the creation of the ban on visitation. Both cases involved contraband that was smuggled into the prison by visitors. So, in an attempt to stop the flow of drugs and weapons, the policy was instituted. One has to wonder if the case would have been decided differently if family members and friends in the free community had filed a class action suit alleging the policy violated their constitutional right to visit inmates. Perhaps the question would have been "Must a law-abiding citizen be granted a due process hearing before being denied access to a family member or friend?" Or would the Court in its infinite wisdom conclude that as a condition of confinement inmates have no legal entitlement to visitation and such a right cannot be extended to those in the free community because no liberty interest is at issue? Nevertheless, the ruling is clear in that while visitation may contribute to rehabilitation and healthy postrelease adjustment when visitors have a positive influence on inmates, the opposite is also true. Visitors may have a negative impact on the inmate and prison if they engage in criminal behavior and smuggle contraband into the institution.

Lanza v. New York
370 U.S. 139 (1962)

Facts

In 1957, while Lanza, the petitioner, visited his brother, who was confined at the Westchester County Jail in New York, authorities electronically eavesdropped and recorded their conversation, which took place in the jail visiting room. Six days later, Lanza's brother was paroled under unusual circumstances by order of one member of the State Parole Commission, prompting a committee of the state legislature to hold an investigation for possible corruption of the state parole system. During the investigation, parole experts determined that Lanza's brother should not have been paroled, and Lanza was called on to testify before the legislative committee. The prosecution granted him immunity in exchange for answering questions at the committee hearing. At the hearing, Lanza was arrested for refusing to answer the questions directed to him by the committee because the questions were based on the conversation he had with his brother that had been electronically intercepted and recorded by jail authorities. He argued that the conviction violated the Fourth Amendment and the Due Process Clause of the Fourteenth Amendment because the conversation was intercepted by state officials through an electronic device. He was subsequently convicted under New York Penal Law. His conviction was affirmed by the New York Court of Appeals. He appealed his case to the U.S. Supreme Court, and it granted certiorari.

Issue

Is the visiting room of a jail a constitutionally protected area where electronic eavesdropping of a jail inmate's conversation could amount to a Fourth Amendment violation?

U.S. Supreme Court Holding

The U.S. upreme Court affirmed the decision of the New York Court of Appeals, holding that the Fourth Amendment protections against unreasonable searches and seizures do not extend to jails because they do not share any of the attributes of privacy of a home, an automobile, an office, or a hotel room. Moreover, in prison, official surveillance has traditionally been used to maintain safety and order and to stop the flow of contraband from being smuggled into prisons.

Reason

At the time of *Lanza*, the U.S. Supreme Court analyzed Fourth Amendment cases based on whether a person had a reasonable expectation of privacy in the place to be searched. With its decision in *Katz v. United States* (389 U.S. 347, 1967), the Court declared that the Fourth Amendment protects people and not places and switched its Fourth Amendment analysis to whether the person had a reasonable expectation of privacy when searched regardless of the place. Over time, the *Lanza* holding has withstood a *Katz* person analysis, but the *Lanza* holding is limited because the Court used its place analysis to conclude that people do not have reasonable expectations of privacy in jails or jail visiting rooms. The Court determined that because people do not have this reasonable expectations of privacy in jail visiting rooms, this place is not protected by the Fourth Amendment, making electronic eavesdropping a permissible activity. The Court concluded that Lanza's arrest for refusing to answer the legislative committee's questions was valid.

Case Significance

In this case, the Supreme Court ruled that private conversations conducted at a public jail that have been electronically intercepted and recorded do not enjoy any constitutional protection and are not viewed as a Fourth Amendment violation against the prohibition of unreasonable searches and seizures because jails, unlike homes, do not afford prisoners or visitors a reasonable expectation of privacy. The case empowers prisons, jails, and other correctional institutions to better monitor and safeguard security and order within places of confinement. It also highlights that inmates have a diminished degree of privacy as a consequence of confinement. Likewise, people who visit places of confinement must, for the time being, expect to have no protection when they visit correctional institutions. They should be aware that any communication can be admitted in criminal court to gain a criminal conviction.

Lee v. Downs

641 F. 2d 1117 (1981)

Facts

Debra Lee, a Virginia state prisoner housed at the Women's Correctional Center in Goochland, was transferred to a kitchen job, prompting a group of prisoners to demand that she steal sugar from the kitchen so they could make whiskey. When the inmates threatened to set Lee's cell on fire if she did not steal the sugar, Lee requested a cell transfer several times. Frustrated at the guard's refusal to transfer her, Lee threatened one of the guards and immediately was placed in a maximum security section as a result of the threat. Within a half hour after the transfer, Lee was seen in her new cell with an electrical cord wrapped around her neck, clad in only a bra and underpants. Guards of both genders were summoned. The guards removed her to a medical unit because she was seen as a suicide threat, where two male guards forcibly held her while a female nurse removed her undergarments so she could not make a noose out of them. Lee was given a paper dress to cover herself. She contended that at this time her menstrual cycle started, and she asked the nurse for sanitary napkins, but her requests were denied. A few days later she set the paper dress on fire and was seen dancing naked among the flames and clapping her hands before being restrained by two male guards, who asked her if she had more matches. She replied, "In some place where they would never be found." A female nurse wearing a surgical glove searched her vagina for matches while male guards restrained her arms and legs. Lee filed a Section 1983 claim seeking injunction and damages against correctional officials for (1) failure to provide her with protection against the threat of fire in her first cell; (2) invasion of privacy when the two male guards forcibly removed her undergarments; (3) deprivation of essential medical care; and (4) invasion of privacy because her vagina was searched in front of two male guards. The U.S. District Court for the Eastern District of Virginia entered judgment for Lee on the invasion of privacy count. Each side appealed.

Issue

Did the forceful removal of Lee's undergarments and involuntarily exposing her genitals to two male guards constitute a violation of her right to privacy?

Holding by the Fourth Circuit Court of Appeals

The Fourth Circuit Court of Appeals affirmed the decision of the District Court, holding that it was wholly unnecessary for the male guards to remain in the room and restrain the plaintiff while her undergarments were forcibly removed.

Reason

The Fourth Circuit Court affirmed the District Court's finding. Regarding the failure to protect Lee from her allegation, the Court of Appeals did not find her complaint actionable because she did not show actual harm. While satisfied with her transfer to the medical unit and subsequent treatment, the Court of Appeals also dismissed her deprivation of medical care allegation. Regarding the complaint about the two male guards viewing her vaginal search, the Appeals Court thought that Lee setting her dress on fire presented the male guards with a situation where she needed to be restrained immediately, and because they did not have time to call for female guards, their actions were reasonable. However, on the one count that Lee prevailed, the Court found the forcible removal of her undergarments by male guards amounting to an unwarranted invasion of privacy. The Appeals Court cited cases that the Supreme Court decided that protected the privacy rights of inmates subjected to unnecessary and unreasonable searches in prison. For example, in *Forts v. Ward*, the Court issued an injunction holding that a woman's right to privacy in the most private portions of their person must prevail despite male guards having the right to work with female inmates and equal employment opportunities. Moreover, the case found that male guards cannot be stationed in rooms where females are required to dress or undress. Also see *Sterling v. Cupp* (290 Or.611 P.2d 123, 1981), where a court ruled that male inmates are not to be subjected to partial touching by female guards. In the current case, the Court of Appeals found that the male guards acted improperly because Lee offered to voluntarily remove her undergarments if the officers would withdraw from her cell. When she made this offer, the Fourth Circuit Court thought that the male guards should have complied and allowed female guards to supervise the removal of her undergarments. The court noted that prisoners have privacy rights that protect them from involuntarily exposing their genital areas to members of the opposite sex who work as prison staff, and the male guards viewing Lee's genital area after she agreed to voluntarily remove her undergarments in the presence of female guards was an unwarranted invasion of privacy.

Case Significance

This case is important for several reasons. First, it indicates that although prisons are places where people have diminished expectation of privacy as a condition of confinement, most people, inmates included, have a special sense of privacy and involuntary exposure of them in the presence of people of the opposite gender. The Fourth Circuit Court in this case found the experience of a female inmate having her genitals exposed to male guards as being degrading and humiliating, which are not intended consequences of confinement. Second, the case is important because it reveals the need to have more women employed in female correctional facilities so that when issues such as the current case occurs, female guards may respond and assist the same-gendered prisoner to prevent a humiliating and demeaning result. The case is also important in that it reveals that more training needs to occur among correctional guards with respect to emergency situations, response time, and being able to physically restrain inmates who are strong or who are experiencing psychotic mood swings. The latter reason should be of particular concern to penal administrators and correctional guards because, in the current case, substantial damages were awarded to the defendant. Despite the efforts of those named in the suit, the Superintendent of the Correctional Center for Women and several officers, the court refused to accept the "good faith" defense. Thus, the Circuit Court may have been more impressed with a record indicating that all officers, both male and female, had been trained to respond to such incidents in an appropriate manner. This would have signaled that those at the Women's Correctional Center in Goochland were sensitive to the needs of its prison population.

Lee v. Washington
390 U.S. 333 (1968)

Facts

The U.S. Court for the Middle District of Alabama declared that Alabama statutes that required racial segregation in prisons and jails violated the Fourteenth Amendment's prohibition of racial discrimination and established a schedule for the desegregation of institutions. The state of Alabama appealed the district court's ruling directly to the U.S. Supreme Court, claiming the statutes of its Rule 23 of the federal Rules of Civil Procedure were constitutional and necessary to maintain prison security and discipline.

Issue

Whether the Alabama statutes are constitutional and whether the District Court's orders to desegregate the state prisons allow for the necessities of prison security and discipline.

U.S. Supreme Court Holding

The Court affirmed the decision of the Alabama District Court holding that the state's contention that the challenged prison statutes were constitutional was without merit, and the District Court orders were affirmed after finding that they allowed for the necessities of prison security and discipline.

Reason

The Court did not consider the logic behind any of Alabama's argument contending that the challenged statutes were constitutional, simply dismissing the arguments without discussion by stating they were without merit. Similarly, the Court provided no discussion on prison order and security. The concurring opinion of the case given by Justices Hugo Black, John Marshall Harlan II, and Potter Stewart noted that Alabama prison officials could take racial tensions into account when considering prison security, order, and discipline but warned that Alabama should not unwillingly assume that this meant they could dilute the Court's firm commitment to the Fourteenth Amendment's prohibition of racial discrimination.

Case Significance

This case is significant because it signals that the Supreme Court is committed to ending social segregation in all aspects of the American experience and not just in education, employment, and living accommodations, but also in prisons and other places of confinement throughout the United States. Because the case was decided by the U.S. Supreme Court, all state and federal prison systems cannot legally segregate inmates based on race. In the Court's concurring opinion, several justices stated that prison officials have a right, when acting in good faith and when circumstances require, to factor racial tension in how they go about maintaining security and discipline in prisons and jails. The concurring opinion suggests that racial segregation should be the exception and not the rule. Moreover, it should be used situationally or temporarily rather than for the long term to address specific institutional needs regarding safety and order. Perhaps in cases of racial and ethnic gangs, segregation must be required to prevent gang wars that are often violent and could end in death.

Lewis v. Casey

518 U.S. 343 (1996)

Facts

Inmates at various Arizona prisons brought a class action suit against the Arizona Department of Corrections and prison officials to the U.S. District Court for the District of Arizona alleging that prison officials were denying their fundamental right to access the courts by failing to provide them with adequate law libraries or assistance from people trained in law in violation of the U.S. Supreme Court's ruling in *Bounds v. Smith*. Inmates alleged that their First, Sixth, and Fourteenth Amendment rights were being violated. In *Bounds*, the Court ruled that a prisoner's fundamental right to access the courts required that prison officials assist inmates in the preparation and filing of meaningful legal papers by providing them with adequate law libraries or adequate assistance from persons trained in law. A special master was appointed to investigate and report about appropriate relief. After eight months of investigation, a report was given to the District Court. The District Court ruled in favor of the Arizona prisoners, ordering changes in state law libraries and legal assistance programs after finding that prison officials failed to comply with constitutional standards set out in *Bounds*, and that two groups of inmates, were particularly affected by inadequacies in the system. The state of Arizona appealed the decision to the Ninth Circuit Court of Appeals. The Appeals Court affirmed both the finding of a *Bounds* violation and the injunction's major terms. The case was appealed to the U.S. Supreme Court, and it granted certiorari.

Issue

To what extent under *Bounds v. Smith* must prison authorities provide prisoners with adequate law libraries or adequate legal counsel to ensure prisoners have meaningful access to the courts?

U.S. Supreme Court Holding

The Supreme Court reversed the judgment of the Ninth Circuit Court of Appeals and remanded the case, holding that the District Court's injunction was improper because (1) prisoners alleging *Bounds v. Smith* violations must show that the inadequacies of state legal assistance programs resulted in actual injury, (2) only one Arizona prisoner who was illiterate could show that inadequacies in the system caused him injury, and (3) the District Court failed to accord adequate deference to the judgment of prison authorities on this matter.

Reason

Justice Clarence Thomas, in his concurrence, summed up the case the best, commenting that *Bounds v. Smith* imposed no affirmative obligations on the part of the state to finance and support prisoner litigation by providing them a lawyer or law library. The majority clarified what constituted a *Bounds* violation, ruling that the Supreme Court's doctrine of standing required that the prisoner show an actual injury before a constitutional right is violated. Prisoners must demonstrate (1) deficiencies in the prison legal facilities prevented an inmate from learning of technical requirements resulting in dismissal of a legal complaint, or (2) prison law libraries are so inadequate that they stymie prisoners from filing legal complaints to redress actionable claims. Although the majority did find that one illiterate prisoner suffered a *Bounds* injury because he failed to file an appeal as a result of Arizona not providing assistance in reading legal papers, the U.S. Supreme Court determined that the injury was not enough to justify systemwide changes.

Case Significance

This case is significant because it clarifies the Court's decision in *Bounds v. Smith*. For example, after the *Bounds* decision was handed down by the Supreme Court, it was widely interpreted to mean that correctional facilities across the country had an affirmative duty to provide each inmate access to a law library and assistance in the preparation of filing meaningful legal papers. In this case, the Court clarifies by saying this was not the intended meaning of *Bounds*. To interpret *Bounds* in such a manner would open the door to frivolous lawsuits because inmates would file suits about any and every issue. However, inmates citing a *Bounds* violation must be able to demonstrate receiving actual injury after alleging a violation of right of access to courts. For example, a prisoner cannot establish actual injury by alleging that his prison law library or legal assistance program was subpar. The Supreme Court is firm in the current case that *Bounds* established a right of access to the courts and not a right to a law library or to legal assistance. The decision should lead to a reduction in the number of cases from inmates and perhaps a small financial benefit to correctional budgets because the law does not require prisons to keep and maintain expensive law libraries.

Logue v. United States
412 U.S. 521 (1973)

Facts

Reagan Logue was arrested by U.S. Deputy Marshal Del Bowers in May 1968 for smuggling 229 pounds of marijuana into the United States. After his first hearing, he was taken to a local jail, the Nueces County Jail in Corpus Christi, Texas, to await trial. The Nueces County Jail was one of 800 state and local institutions that contracted with the Federal Bureau of Prisons for the safekeeping of prisoners. One day after his incarceration at the Nueces County Jail, Logue attempted suicide by slashing the veins in his left arm. The wound turned out to be minor, but he was admitted to the hospital's psychiatric unit because the attending doctor found him to be hallucinating and out of touch with reality. A psychiatrist recommended that Logue be admitted to a medical facility for rehabilitation. He was transferred back to the Nueces County Jail to await a transfer to a federal medical facility. On the transfer, Deputy Marshal Del Bowers informed the chief local jailer of Logue's suicidal tendencies and gave instructions to prepare a special cell removed of all dangerous objects for him. Jail authorities prepared the special cell for Logue, but because Bowers gave no instructions to provide constant surveillance, jail officials did not place Logue under constant surveillance, only periodically checking on him. One day after returning to the jail, Logue removed a gauze bandage that had been applied to his laceration and hanged himself. His parents sued the U.S. government for damages under the Federal Tort Claims Act for negligence and being the proximate cause of their son's death. The U.S. District Court for the Southern District of Texas found that (1) the local jail authorities were negligent in providing inadequate surveillance of the prisoner; (2) Bowers was negligent for failing to make specific arrangements for the constant surveillance of Logue; and (3) the U.S. government was liable for the negligent acts of both the deputy marshal and the Nueces County Jail employees. The Court of Appeals for the Fifth Circuit reversed the District Court's decision, holding that under the "contractor clause" the county jail fell within exclusion from the Federal Tort Claims Act. Hence, the local jail authorities were not acting as agents of the U.S. government, and because the Deputy Marshal had no power over any jail employee or control of the inner functions at the jail, he violated no duty of safekeeping in regard to the prisoner. The case was appealed to the U.S. Supreme Court, and it granted certiorari.

Issue

Could the United States be sued because of negligent actions of Nueces County Jail officials and Deputy Marshal Bowers in regard to the suicide of prisoner Logue?

U.S. Supreme Court Holding

The Court vacated the judgment of the Fifth Circuit Court of Appeals and remanded the case for reconsideration of the liability of government because its liability was based on the negligence of the federal Deputy Marshal. More specifically, because the county jail employees were employees of a "federal agency" or acting on behalf of a federal agency in official capacity, and the government could therefore not be held liable for the employees' negligence, but because the Court of Appeals did not consider the distinct question regarding the Deputy Marshal's negligence, the case was remanded for consideration of government's liability concerning the Deputy Marshal's negligence.

Reason

In reviewing the Federal Tort Claims Act and its contractor clause exclusion, the Court decided that Congress authorized the U.S. government to make contracts similar to the one between the Federal Bureau of Prisons and the Nueces County Jail. In authorizing such contracts, the Court determined that Congress intended that the day-to-day operations of the contractor's facilities be in the hands of the contractor, giving no authority to federal officials regarding the conduct of the employees of agencies with which it contracts. Re-

garding the liability of the federal government for the negligent actions of the
county jail employees, the Court thought that the federal tort law was clear, the
jail officials or any other contracting agents were not acting on behalf of the
U.S. government, and the U.S. government could not be held liable for the actions of county employees. Addressing the question of Bowers's liability, the
Court remanded the case back to the Fifth Circuit Court of Appeals to rehear
the issue of the deputy marshal's liability because Bowers' liability in this case
was not limited to his alleged failure to make specific arrangements for the
constant surveillance of the prisoner.

Case Significance

This case is important because the U.S. Supreme Court ruled that if county
employees are contracted by the federal government to perform a duty and
through negligence someone in their custody or charge is harmed, there can
be no recourse through the Federal Tort Claims Act. In the current case, a federal inmate in the custody of a county jail that was contracted by the federal
government committed suicide, and his family was seeking damages under a
federal law that makes federal agencies and employees liable when someone in
their care is injured as a result of their negligence. The Court stated that such
protection does not extend to nonfederal agencies or employees. However, as
the Court's ruling regarding Bowers indicates, this does not mean that federal
jail officials are immune from liability in cases involving private agencies. The
United States could still be held liable for contributing to the negligence of the
private agency. Moreover, the outcome of the case may have been decided differently if the surviving family members had sought legal recourse under Section 1983 or a state tort action against the county jail.

Lyons v. Gilligan
382 F. Supp. 198 (1974)

Facts

Michael Lyons and another prisoner at the Marion Correctional Institution
in Ohio, and their wives, filed a Section 1983 lawsuit with the U.S. Court for
the Northern District of Ohio, Eastern Division, alleging that various state officials, because of the absence of opportunity for conjugal visits with their
spouses, denied them their constitutional rights to marital privacy, and this
constitutes cruel and unusual punishment prohibited by the Eighth Amendment.

Both prisoners were married before their incarceration and regularly engaged in intimate sexual intercourse with their wives. The prisoners also contended that sex and private displays of sexual intimacy between inmates and their visitors are prohibited. They also argued that the correctional facility did not have facilities where couples could engage in sexual intimacy. The prisoners claimed that the correctional institution's rules prohibiting sexual intimacy between married inmates denies them their privacy. Moreover, the fact that inmates are married places an affirmative duty on prison officials to provide private places for conjugal visits.

Issue

Do married prisoners have a constitutional right to have marital relations?

Holding by the U.S. District Court

The court granted the state officials motion to dismiss the inmates' complaint. The court held that prisoners have no fundamental right to privacy that requires officials to provide private facilities for married couples and no privcy right to prevent rules prohibiting sexual intimacy between prisoners and their spouses. Also, the absence of conjugal visits does not amount to cruel and unusual punishment within the meaning of the U.S. Constitution.

Reason

In deciding this case, the court cited several cases where other federal courts held that inmates and prisoners did not have a constitutional entitlement to conjugal visits or sexual intimacies with their spouse. The cases included *Stuart v. Heard* (359 F.Supp. 921, S.D. Tex. 1973), *Tarlton v. Clark* (441 F.2d 384, 1971), and *Payne v. District of Columbia* (253 F.2d 867, D.C. Cir. 1958). In these cases, the courts ruled that the denial of marital relations to prisoners did not constitute a violation of the Eighth or Fourteenth Amendments. Where the Eighth Amendment is concerned, inmates contend that policies against conjugal visits have subjected them and their spouses to cruel and unusual punishment. The court disagreed with this contention, reasoning that under the Eighth Amendment, punishment must be meted out only for crimes committed, must comport with human dignity, and not be excessively severe in proportion to the crime committed. Moreover, acceptable punishment "must draw its meaning from the evolving standards of decency that mark the progress of a maturing society." In the present case, the court held that the absence of conjugal visits in prison is not the equivalent of excessive punishment that is disproportional to the plaintiff's crime; it is merely an aspect or a consequence of being incarcerated.

Whereas plaintiffs allege that they are suffering physical and psychological stress, loneliness, boredom, wasted time, and less than ideal physical conditions, these do not, in fact or law, constitute cruel and unusual punishment. The court also reasoned that constitutional rights to privacy are meant to protect rights of private citizens and do not apply to prisoners. Also, a lack of conjugal visits for married couples does not result in a loss of dignity required for a cruel and unusual punishment claim.

Case Significance

The case is important because the ruling makes it clear that conjugal visits between spouses is not a fundamental right and denying such a privilege does not constitute a deprivation of privacy, nor is it cruel and unusual punishment within the meaning of the Eighth Amendment. The ruling rejects the claim that the denial of marital privacy creates physical and psychological injuries to inmates. If such claims had been ruled valid by the court, it would have essentially opened the door to claims seeking monetary damages and redress concerning these types of deprivations. Furthermore, the decision enables prison officials to reward good inmate behavior if they see fit by perhaps making conjugal visits a privilege, rather than an affirmative duty that they must perform. The case indicates that one condition of confinement is that inmates must be deprived of personal privileges that free citizens enjoy. The ruling means that places of confinement are not meant to be treated as hotels or motels. Despite this, one has to ponder the outcome of this case, if the parties concerned had filed an equal protection claim. Perhaps the ruling would be more complicated if plaintiffs had claimed that all inmates in a prison must be treated the same, and one cannot deprive a few inmates the privilege to have access to conjugal programs without there being legitimate reasons in place.

Marquez-Ramos v. Reno

69 F. 3d. 477 (1995)

Facts

Marquez-Ramos was a Mexican national incarcerated at the federal prison in Florence, Colorado. In 1991, he pleaded guilty to conspiracy to possess with the intent to distribute marijuana and was sentenced to 144 months in prison. While serving his sentence, he was convicted of conspiracy to escape and was sentenced to an additional eighteen months. In July 1992, he filed a petition with the Attorney General of the United States requesting transfer to a Mexican prison pursuant to the Treaty on the Execution of Penal Sentences—a Mexican treaty that allowed offenders from foreign countries to transfer to prisons within their own country to serve out their sentences. On February 15, 1994, the U.S. Attorney General denied the transfer on the basis of "the seriousness of the offense and the prisoner's significant ties to the United States." Marquez-Ramos then filed an action seeking a writ of mandamus directing the Attorney General to transfer him to a Mexican prison pursuant to the treaty. The Attorney General responded with a motion to dismiss. The action was referred to a magistrate judge, who recommended that the motion be granted on the basis that the Attorney General had discretion in deciding whether to transfer Marquez-Ramos under the treaty and mandamus relief was not available to challenge the Attorney General's discretion. After considering Marquez-Ramos's objections, the District Court adopted the magistrate judge's recommendation, granted the Attorney General's motion, and dismissed the case with prejudice. On appeal, Marquez-Ramos argued that based on the legislative history behind the treaty Act, the Attorney General owes him a "nondiscretionary ministerial duty to grant his transfer request."

Issue

Whether Marquez-Ramos is entitled to mandamus relief because the U.S.-Mexican Prisoner Exchange Treaty places a nondiscretionary duty on the Attorney General to transfer a foreign prisoner in the United States to a prison in the country where he or she has citizenship on request by the prisoner.

Holding by the Tenth Circuit Court

The Tenth Circuit Court of Appeals affirmed the District Court's ruling that Marquez-Ramos is not entitled to mandamus relief because the U.S.-Mexican Prisoner Exchange Treaty allowed the Attorney General to exercise discretion in determining whether Marquez-Ramos should be transferred from a U.S. to a Mexican prison.

Reason

The Tenth Circuit Court noted that a writ of mandamus is intended to provide a remedy for petitioners only if the defendant owes him or her a clear nondiscretionary, ministerial duty. It examined the language of the treaty to see if it called for the nondiscretionary transfer of Mexican national prisoners housed in the United States to Mexican prisons on request of the prisoner. The court found that the treaty allowed the Attorney General a considerable amount of discretion in making the decision on whether to transfer Mexican nationals convicted in the United States to Mexican prisons to serve out their sentences. Therefore, the Tenth Circuit Court of Appeals reviewed Article IV, Section (2) of the treaty: It stated that if the authority of the transferring state finds the transfer of the offender appropriate, and if the offender gives express consent for the transfer, said authority shall transmit a request for transfer, through diplomatic channels, to the authority of the receiving state. As such, this section creates a necessary precondition to a prisoner's transfer under the treaty. In this case, the Attorney General did not find the transfer appropriate.

Case Significance

The case is important because it has profound implication on the criminal justice system, especially in the area of corrections and the treatment that foreign national prisoners are to receive. The case deals with a treaty that could allow a foreign national to return to his or her native land to serve a prison sentence if it is agreeable to the U.S. Attorney General and the prisoner in question. Because of the drug war, it is likely that many foreign nationals will be arrested for drug smuggling, human trafficking, and other criminal activities. Perhaps it is better to have them spend their prison sentence in the United States than to trust that other countries will administer punishment in an equitable and humane manner. In the current case, the Treaty states that factors to be considered include whether rehabilitation and the social life of the offender are acceptable conditions of transfer. While some U.S. prisons have programs that allow for rehabilitation, this is certainly not the case in many other countries, including Mexico. Moreover, while prisons are tough and physically and psychologically challenging in the United States, prisoners are afforded many constitutional liberties and safeguards that are not practiced or allowed in many foreign countries. As such, a prisoner's social life or even his or her physical safety could be forfeited if returned to his or her respective country.

Mary of Oakknoll v. Coughlin
475 N.Y.S. 2d 644 (1984)

Facts

Petitioners Calvin of Oakknoll, a prisoner at New York's Auburn facility, and Mary of Oakknoll appealed a ruling from the New York Supreme Court at Special Term, that refused to allow the petitioners' acceptance into a prison family reunion program, to the Supreme Court of New York, Appellate Division. The lower court upheld prison regulations requiring participants in the family reunion program, to possess valid marriage licenses to participate in the conjugal visitation program. Calvin and Mary of Oakknoll were members of the Religious Society of Families and participated in a church marriage ceremony in Cleveland, Ohio, on June 20, 1963. While they claimed to have passed a blood test and obtained a marriage license, no official performed the state-required ceremony. As such, they did not have a marriage license. They claimed that the New York prison authorities' refusal to admit them to the family reunion program because they did not have a marriage license violated their First Amendment right to freedom of religion. The trial court dismissed the petitioners' application to annul the department's decision. The case was appealed to the Supreme Court of New York's Appellate Division.

Issue

Whether the New York prison regulations requiring participants in the family reunion program to have marriage licenses is justified by reasonable security interests and whether it violates the petitioners' First Amendment freedom of religion rights.

Holding

The New York Appellate Court affirmed the trial court ruling that there is no constitutional right to conjugal visitation within the state penal system.

Reason

The New York court found that prison officials' marriage license requirement was intended to serve as a screening mechanism to prevent the reunion program from being overwhelmed with inmates claiming spouses without supporting documentation. Moreover, the requirement had a rational basis in that it permitted administrative convenience and efficiency. The requirement was applied in a neutral manner, without respect to one's religion. As such, there was no infringement of the First Amendment.

Case Significance

The case is important because it demonstrates that married inmates do not have a constitutional entitlement to conjugal visits. In fact, while marriage is deemed a fundamental practice, one must surrender marital intimacy as a condition of confinement or such intimacies are "precluded by the exigencies and operational considerations of the penal system." In this case, the New York Appellate Court ruled that there is no constitutional violation when an inmate is denied a conjugal visit because there is no such right. However, correctional institutions can allow conjugal visits as a privilege to inmates. When it occurs, prison officials can stipulate requirements to participate in such programs. In the current case, the petitioners were denied participation in the family reunion program because they failed to produce a valid marriage license. The court in this case ruled that the state may allow conjugal visits as a privilege as long as these programs are implemented in a reasonable manner and are consistent with the inmates' status as prisoners and the legitimate operational considerations of the institution. This ruling is only applicable in the circuit where the case was decided because it was not heard by the U.S. Supreme Court.

McCorkle v. Johnson
881 F. 2d 993 (1989)

Facts

Plaintiff Charles McCorkle, a state inmate at Alabama's Holman Facility, filed a Section 1983 claim in the U.S. District Court for the Southern District of Alabama alleging a deprivation of his constitutional right to freely exercise his chosen religion of Satanism. He argued that the defendants, prison officials, refused his request for access to satanic books and articles, including the Satanic Bible, the *Satanic Book of Rituals*, and a Satanic medallion. The District Court dismissed McCorkle's complaint. In District Court, Alabama prison officials argued (1) that Satanism is not a religion entitled to First Amendment protection; (2) that McCorkle was not a true believer in Satanism; and (3) access to the requested books would pose a threat to prison security. McCorkle appealed the judgment to the Eleventh Circuit Court of Appeals.

Issue

Whether Alabama prison regulations prohibiting McCorkle from exercising his First Amendment right to worship in the religion of his choice, Satanism, are reasonably related to legitimate security interests.

Holding

The Eleventh Circuit Court of Appeals held that the Alabama prison policy that prohibited the practice of Satanism does not violate the First Amendment's free exercise of religion clause or the Fourteenth Amendment equal protection clause because the policy is reasonably related to penological interests.

Reason

The Eleventh Circuit Court of Appeals did not consider whether Satanism was a religion within the meaning of the First Amendment or if McCorkle was a true believer of Satanism or finding that the prison regulations preventing access to Satanic literature were reasonably related to legitimate security concerns. The Appeals Court examined three factors when considering the reasonableness of the policy that placed restrictions on McCorkle's free exercise of his religion. First, the court argued that there must be a valid rational connection between the policy and the legitimate governmental interest used to justify the policy. The court saw that the Satanic Bible encouraged violence, required human sacrifice, and advocated that its members engage in behavior without regard to consequences. Second, the court examined if the prison restriction allowed for an alternative means of exercising the asserted right and found that other worshippers of Satanic sects were able to practice Satanism without use of the Satanic Bible. Third, the court considered the impact that making accommodations would have on guards, other inmates, and prison resources and concluded that the plaintiff's form of worship could only occur at the expensive costs to guards, other prisoners, and society in general. The Eleventh Circuit Court of Appeals used the minimum level test from *Turner v. Safley* to judge the prison regulations against McCorkle's First Amendment freedom of religion rights. Under the *Turner* decision, prison officials had to show (1) there was a valid, rational connection between the regulation and the legitimate government interest justifying it; (2) that alternative means of exercising the right remain open; (3) accommodating the right will negatively impact guards and other prisoners; and (4) workable alternatives were available as evidence that the restrictions were unreasonable. The Appeals Court found that because the requested Satanic materials encouraged violence, the regulations prohibiting them were related to a legitimate prison security interest. Also, the court found that the alternative means of practicing Satanism were open to McCorkle because other inmates at Holman, despite being denied the religious materials, were still able to practice Satanism. Moreover, the court found that allowing prisoners to read books that legitimate violence and teach hatred would negatively affect both guards and other inmates, and noted that the defendant did not offer the court any reasonable alternatives.

Case Significance

This case is important because it demonstrates that even the right to freely exercise one's religion, a fundamental right protected by the U.S. Constitution, can be restricted within the context of a prison if the practice poses a threat to others, including inmates, other prisoners, and guards, or presents an undue expense on the correctional facility. The Eleventh Circuit Court of Appeals reaffirmed *Turner v. Safley* by drawing from its tenets, holding that as soon as a prison regulation is shown to be reasonably related to legitimate penological interests, the policy will stand. Essentially, the court stated in this case that after weighing opposing interests—the plaintiff's alleged constitutional right to practice Satanism and the defendants' policy designed to ensure prison safety it sided in favor of prison officials. After discovering what the practice of Satanism entailed, the court determined that allowing rituals, such as sacrificing a female virgin, wrist slashing, blood drinking, and consumption of human flesh, were not unreasonable restrictions to place on an inmate's religion. The policy did not prove arbitrary but promoted the governmental interest asserted by prison officials. That is, there is the need to maintain safety and security for everyone in a correctional setting.

Meachum v. Fano
427 U.S. 215 (1976)

Facts

Based on reports from prison informants that the six inmate respondents were involved in a series of nine serious fires at the Massachusetts Correctional Institution at Norfolk, a medium security institution, the six men were placed in an administrative detention area. Proceedings were then conducted before the Norfolk Classification Board to determine whether the inmates should be transferred to a more secure institution. The Board recommended that one inmate be placed in administrative segregation for thirty days, three be transferred to a maximum security prison where conditions were substantially less favorable than those at Norfolk, and two be placed in a maximum-medium security facility. While the inmates were made aware of the allegations against them, they were not made aware of the details of the information used against them or reasons for the transfers. Respondent inmates filed a Section 1983 claim against the petitioner, Massachusetts prison officials, alleging their due process rights under the Fourteenth Amendment had been violated by their transfer to another prison without adequate fact-finding hearings. The inmates sought injunctive and declaratory relief and damages. The District Court held that the notices and hearings given to the inmates were constitutionally inadequate and ordered the inmates returned to the general population at the Norfolk facility until proper notices were served and hearings conducted. The prison officials appealed the decision to the U.S. Court of Appeals for the First Circuit. The Circuit Court affirmed the District Court's decision, the case was appealed to the U.S. Supreme Court, and it granted certiorari.

Issue

Whether the Due Process Clause of the Fourteenth Amendment entitles a state prisoner to a hearing when he is transferred to a prison where the conditions are substantially less favorable to the inmate, absent a state law or practice conditioning the transfers on proof of serious misconduct or the occurrence of other specified events.

U.S. Supreme Court Holding

The Supreme Court reversed the decision holding that the Due Process Clause of the Fourteenth Amendment does not entitle a state prisoner to a hearing when he is transferred to a prison where the conditions are substantially less favorable to the inmate, absent a state law or practice conditioning the transfers on proof of serious misconduct or the occurrence of other specified events. Such a transfer does not infringe or implicate a liberty interest of the prisoner within the meaning of the Due Process Clause.

Reason

The Due Process Clause prohibits the state from depriving a person of life, liberty, or property without due process of the law. However, a valid conviction constitutionally deprives a criminal defendant of his liberty to the extent that the state may confine him and subject him to its prison system. The main issue for the Supreme Court to determine in this case was whether the inmates had a liberty interest in the conditions of confinement they were subject to within the Massachusetts state prison system. If the Court found that the inmates had a liberty interest in their conditions of confinement, then the state would be required to follow constitutionally mandated procedures before they could transfer the prisoners against their will. If not, then the state could transfer the prisoners at will. The Court held that the inmates had no liberty interest in conditions of confinement in a state facility, and the state was free to transfer its prisoners between institutions for any reason. In making their determination that the inmates had no liberty interest in their conditions of confinement, the Court reasoned that the U.S. Constitution does not mandate that a state have more than one prison, nor does it guarantee that a prisoner would be put in one type of prison for a certain type of crime if a state has more than one type of prison. In addition, the initial classification decision on where to place the prisoner is not subject to the Due Process Clause even though it could result in substantially different prison conditions for the inmate, and a state does not have to have a disciplinary reason to transfer a prisoner. The Court further reasoned that state officials frequently transfer prisoners to other facilities to serve a number of different penological goals, and state prison transfers are better decided by prison officials who are in charge of the day-to-day running of the prisons than federal judges.

Case Significance

The case is important because it empowers prison officials with the ability to transfer inmates for any reason. The case means that due process is not an issue that needs to be considered when a decision is being made to transfer prisoners from one facility to the next even if it means that the next prison is substantially worse. The Court held that after inmates received a valid conviction, there can be no due process claim because there is no liberty interest where a transfer is concerned. The case signifies that the Court believes that when it comes to the issues of safety and security, prison officials are in a better position to address them. In fact, the Court held that the day-to-day functioning of state prisons should not be the business of federal judges.

Montanye v. Haymes

427 U.S. 237 (1976)

Facts

On June 7, 1972, Haymes, a New York prisoner who was an inmate clerk in the law library, claimed the state of New York violated his constitutional rights by transferring him without a hearing from Attica, a maximum security New York state prison, to Clinton Correctional Facility, another maximum security state prison. Haymes was transferred to Clinton without punishment after prison officials observed him circulating a petition he prepared for a federal judge that was signed by eighty-two other prisoners at Attica, each claiming they had been deprived of legal assistance as the result of the removal of Haymes and another inmate from the law library. Haymes was dismissed from his job at the law library after he repeatedly violated a prison rule of furnishing legal assistance to other inmates without official permission. He filed a Section 1983 claim seeking relief against Montanye, Superintendent of Attica at the time. The petition complained that the seizure and retention of the document violated Administrative Bulletin No. 20, and also infringed Haymes's federally guaranteed right to petition the court for redress of grievances. The claim also asserted that the transfer to Clinton was to prevent him from pursuing his remedies and as reprisal for giving other inmates legal assistance to petition the courts for redress. The U.S. District Court for the Western District of New York dismissed the action, finding that removing Haymes from the law library, the seizure of his petition, and the prison transfer did not violate his constitutional rights and was within the scope of prison officials exercising proper custody of inmates. The Second Circuit Court of Appeals reversed the District Court decision, stating its judgment was erroneous because there were two unresolved issues of material fact: (1) whether Haymes's removal to Clinton was punishment for a disobedience of prison rules, and if so, (2) whether the effects of the transfer was sufficiently burdensome to require a hearing under the Due Process Clause of the Fourteenth Amendment. The case was appealed to the U.S. Supreme Court, and it granted certiorari.

Issue

Whether the Due Process Clause of the Fourteenth Amendment requires a hearing when a state prisoner is transferred to another institution in the state for disciplinary or punitive reasons.

U.S. Supreme Court Holding

The Court reversed the Fourth Circuit Court of Appeals and remanded the case to that court for further proceedings consistent with this opinion.

Reason

The Supreme Court reaffirmed its holding in *Meachum*, where it ruled that there is no Due Process Clause liberty interest of an inmate who has been duly convicted. There is a right to a hearing when prisoners are transferred from one prison to another within the state. Absent some right or justifiable expectation rooted in state law, he or she will not be transferred except for misbehavior or on the occurrence of other special events. As long as the conditions of confinement that a prisoner receives is within the sentence imposed on him by the state, there is no constitutional violation. The Court also ruled that it agreed with the state of New York in that under its law, Haymes had no right to remain at any one particular facility in the state and no justifiable expectation that he would not be transferred. New York law states, "Adult persons sentenced to imprisonment are not sentenced to particular institutions, but are committed to the custody of the Commissioner of Corrections." Therefore, the Commissioner has the authority, by statute, to transfer inmates from one correctional facility to another.

Case Significance

The case is important because the U.S. Supreme Court reaffirms its ruling in *Meachum v. Fano*. In this case, the Court is essentially telling the Second Circuit Court of Appeals that its interpretation of *Meachum* is erroneous. The Circuit Court of Appeals was suspicious of the circumstances of the Haymes transfer, believing it to be due in part to administrative retaliation for assisting prisoners with the petitions to seek redress from the courts. In fact, the Circuit Court felt that Haymes could even argue that being transferred from Attica to Clinton (though both are maximum security prisons) could come with burdensome consequences. The U.S. Supreme Court ruled that the inmate's claim is without merit for the same reasons cited in *Meachum v. Fano*.

Moskowitz v. Wilkinson

432 F. Supp. 947 (1977)

Facts

Petitioner Moskowitz, an Orthodox Jewish prisoner at the Federal Correctional Institution in Danbury, Connecticut, brought a habeas corpus petition and filed a motion for a temporary restraining order, which the court granted by the U.S. District Court for the District of Connecticut, claiming a federal prison regulation that prohibited beards violated his First Amendment free exercise of religion. Moskowitz refused to cut his beard pursuant to a prison policy that prohibited inmates from wearing them. He argued that his religious beliefs forbade any cutting or shaving of his beard. He was the subject of four disciplinary proceedings for violating the policy. The disciplinary committee ordered that he be placed in disciplinary segregation and that he forfeit the good time he had accumulated. Federal authorities placed Moskowitz in disciplinary segregation for refusing to shave his beard in violation of prison regulations. He maintained that his religious beliefs forbid the shaving of his beard while federal authorities argued that recognition problems associated with beard removal made a No-Beard Rule necessary to identify prisoners within the prison system to prevent escapes.

Issue

Does Moskowitz's First Amendment free exercise of religion protect him from prison regulations requiring him to shave his beard?

Holding by the U.S. District Court

The U.S. District Court for the District of Connecticut held that the federal prison regulation that requires inmates to shave their beards is unconstitutional when applied to prisoners who refuse to shave their beards for sincerely held religious reasons.

Reason

In this case, the actual issue for the District Court was whether the government's interest reasonably justified the regulation that prevented the petitioner's ability to observe his religious belief. The government held the No-Beard Rule was needed to effectively identify inmates to ensure prison security and to facilitate apprehension of inmates who escaped. The court cited *Cruz v. Beto*, where the Supreme Court held that prisoners do not lose their right to practice religion as a consequence of incarceration. The District Court also cited the Court's decision in *Procunier v. Martinez* where it required as a test that the prison must show that a restriction on religious freedom is justified by an important or substantial government interest and that such a restriction is reasonable to achieving that objective. The District Court used the middle-level "substantial interest" test to weigh Moskowitz's First Amendment religious rights against the prison regulation. The court selected the substantial interest test reasoning that regulations limiting First Amendment freedoms should be no greater than necessary to protect a government interests. Under the substantial interest test, prison authorities must demonstrate that (1) an important or substantial government interest justifies its restriction on religious freedom, and (2) the regulation is the least restrictive way to reasonably achieve their objectives. Ruling in favor of Moskowitz's religious right to wear a beard, the District

Court reasoned (1) since about half of the states allowed beards in their prison systems, the federal government's beard-shaving rule was not necessary to advance their security interests in the identification of prisoners, and (2) the government could achieve its security interests in identifying prisoners in less restrictive ways, such as rephotographing a prisoner who changes his appearance through beard shaving.

Case Significance

This case is significant because it demonstrates that in some cases, the right of inmates will prevail over penal policies. For example, in this case, the District Court ruled that if it can be determined that an inmate engages in a longstanding practice that is deeply rooted in his or her religion, it is sufficient to trigger that the government justifies its restriction of an inmate to continue to engage in such a practice and do so in a manner that is reasonably necessary for it to achieve its interest. Moreover, the court held that the state cannot simply resort to any measure to assure that inmates are identifiable, recognizable, or easy to discover after escape, the consequence would violate many liberties that inmates enjoy. In relying on the U.S. Supreme Court's decision in *Procunier*, the district court held the "No-Beard" Policy could not be raised to justify the First Amendment restriction because half of the states allow inmates to wear beards. In *Procunier*, the Court held that "the policies followed at other, well-run institutions are relevant to a determination of the necessity for the restriction and the fact that half of the states operate their prisons with a No Beard Rule certainly casts doubt on the government's claim."

Muhammad v. Carlson

845 F. 2d 175 (1988)

Facts

Defendant Muhammad, a prisoner at Leavenworth Federal Prison, was transferred to the U.S. Medical Center for Federal Prisoners in Springfield, Missouri (MCFP) because he lost coordination in his legs and right hand. Blood tests revealed he developed antibodies against the AIDS virus, and pursuant to Bureau of Prisons regulations, was classified as pre-ARC, which meant that he tested positive for AIDS and had developed one or more AIDS symptoms but had no damage to his immune system. He was placed in the restricted AIDS unit without a hearing and isolated from other prisoners. Seven months later, the Bureau of Prisons changed its AIDS regulations and released Muhammad and other restricted inmates back into the general population at MCFP. Muhammad brought a pro se complaint to the U.S. District Court for the Western District of Missouri, contending that his transfer to and seven-month confinement in the restricted AIDS unit violated his Fourteenth Amendment due process rights because the transfer was conducted without a hearing and stigmatized him. The District Court dismissed the complaint because it failed to allege conduct arising to the level of a constitutional violation. The defendant challenged the District Court's decision and the case was appealed to the Eighth Circuit Court of Appeals.

Issue

Whether federal prison medical regulations establishing procedures for the diagnosis, treatment, and isolation of AIDS carriers created a liberty interest under the Due Process Clause of the U.S. Constitution for prisoners to remain within the general prison population.

Holding by the Eighth Circuit Court of Appeals

The Eighth Circuit Court of Appeals affirmed the District Court decision to dismiss the pro se claim, holding that federal prison medical regulations did not create any liberty interest for prisoners to remain within the general prison population because the interest was too insubstantial to trigger due process protection.

Reason

In this case, the Eighth Circuit Court of Appeals first noted that a Fifth Amendment liberty interest may arise from two sources: the Due Process Clause itself, and the laws of the United States. Since the Due Process Clause itself does not create a liberty interest for prisoners in being confined to the general prison population, the Court of Appeals reasoned that if Muhammad had a liberty interest in remaining in the general prison population, it must have been created by the federal medical regulations that governed the diagnosis, treatment, and isolation of AIDS carriers. The Court of Appeals then cited *Hewitt v. Helms*, the leading U.S. Supreme Court case in this area at the time, to determine whether the prison medical regulations created a liberty interest for prisoners that is protected by the Due Process Clause. *Hewitt* directs courts to look to the language of the regulation to determine if the regulation creates a liberty interest. If the language of the regulation is "mandatory" and limits the discretion of decision-makers, then, according to *Hewitt*, the regulation creates a liberty interest for prisoners, which is protected by the

Due Process Clause. Otherwise, regulations that do not limit decision-making create no protected due process liberty interest. Applying *Hewitt* to the prison medical regulations, the Eighth Circuit Court of Appeals found no language in the regulation from which a prisoner could deduce he would not be transferred to the AIDS unit without an opportunity to challenge his medical classification or which limited the prison official's discretion in making AIDS transfers, and concluded that the regulations did not create a protected liberty interest.

Case Significance

The case is important because the Eighth Circuit Court of Appeals did not expand any due process rights or protection to the inmate in the current case. The inmate did not contend that the conditions of his confinement violated due process protection. However, he claimed that before being transferred to an AIDS unit pursuant to a prison policy, he should have been afforded a hearing before such a determination could be made. In this case, both the District and Appeals Courts agree that the pro se claim should have been dismissed because there is no liberty interest at issue in this case. In fact, both courts held that the matter at issue does not rise to the level of a constitutional violation. In fact, the prisoner was unable to show that he sustained any injury from being transferred in and out of an AIDS-restricted unit at the prison. This case empowers correctional administrators by allowing them to make quick decisions that are in the best interest of perceived threats to the safety and security of their facilities without having to expand or increase due process protections in areas that are not guaranteed such rights.

Murray v. Giarratano

492 U.S. 1 (1989)

Facts

Respondent Joseph M. Giarratano, a Virginia prisoner sentenced to death, filed a civil rights action against state prison officials seeking declaratory and injunctive relief in the U.S. District Court for the Eastern District of Virginia. He claimed that the U.S. Constitution required that prison officials provide him with an attorney at the state's expense to represent him in postconviction proceedings. The District Court included all current and future Virginia death row inmates awaiting execution in a class action suit holding that they should also be afforded counseling in postconviction proceedings. In compliance with constitutional requirements and the Supreme Court's decision in *Bounds v. Smith*, Virginia had provided death row inmates access to adequate law libraries, allowed the inmates to borrow library materials for use in their cells, and allowed the death row inmates to consult with state-appointed "unit attorneys," who were assigned to each of the state's penal institutions to assist inmates in filing lawsuits. The District Court ruled in favor of the death row inmates, finding that Virginia's law library policies and assignment of unit attorneys did not provide the death row inmates with meaningful access to the courts under the Constitution. Such inmates had a limited amount of time to prepare postconviction petitions, their cases were unusually complex, and the shadow of impending death would interfere with their ability to do legal work. The District Court then ordered Virginia to appoint individual counsel to assist the death row inmates in their postconviction proceedings. The case was appealed to the Fourth Circuit Court, where it affirmed the District Court's decision. The case was later appealed to the U.S. Supreme Court, and it granted certiorari.

Issue

Do constitutional requirements mandating that prison officials provide all state prisoners meaningful access to the courts require prison officials to provide death row inmates with individual legal counsel at the state's expense?

U.S. Supreme Court Holding

The U.S. Supreme Court reversed and remanded the case to the District Court to see if it could remedy the situation without expanding the Court's decision in *Bounds*.

Reason

The U.S. Supreme Court reasoned that the Fourth Circuit Court of Appeals did not properly understand its decision in *Bounds v. Smith*. The Court also cited *Pennsylvania v. Finley* (481 U.S. 551, 1987), where it ruled that the U.S. Constitution did not require states to provide counsel in postconviction proceedings. The Court held the Sixth and Fourteenth Amendments to the Constitution assure the right of an indigent defendant to counsel at various stages of criminal proceedings (*Gideon v. Wainwright*, 372 U.S. 335, 1963), and an indigent defendant is entitled to a counsel for the initial appeal (*Griffin v. Illinois*, 351 U.S. 12, 1956). In reversing the appeals court, the U.S. Supreme Court first ruled that *Finley* was to be applied no differently in capital or noncapital cases and that Virginia was not required to provide attorneys to death row inmates for the purpose of helping them with postconviction appeals. The Court next ruled that its decision in *Bounds* that required states to provide inmates access to adequate law libraries so the prisoners could prepare petitions for judicial relief, was controlling for this case. The Court found no Eighth Amendment cruel and unusual punishment violation and remanded the case to the District Court to remedy the situation without expanding its decision in *Bounds*. Essentially, the U.S. Supreme Court disagreed with the respondent's contentions that the Eighth and Fourteenth Amendments' Due Process Clauses provide an entitlement to a state-appointed counsel for indigent death row inmates seeking postconviction relief because a state collateral proceeding is not required under the Constitution as part of a state's criminal proceeding. Additional safeguards imposed by the Eighth Amendment at the trial stage of a capital case are sufficient to ensure the reliability of the process in which the death penalty is imposed. The Court also held that many considerations the District Court entertained should not have been held as factual because to do so would permit different constitutional rules to apply in different states. Finally, the Court indicated that on remand, the District Court would be able to remedy allegations of denying death row inmates adequate and timely access to a law library.

Case Significance

This case is significant because the U.S. Supreme Court uses it as an opportunity to clear up its meaning in both the *Finley* and *Bounds* decisions. The Court does not disagree with the idea or belief that prisoners are entitled to have access to court, and it should in fact be accomplished with the assistance of law libraries, jailhouse lawyers, and even volunteers from the legal community who may choose to assist prisoners in filing meaningful documents. However, the Court does not agree that the Constitution ensures prisoners any legal representation that goes beyond their initial conviction. In fact, the Court is clear on its ruling in the current case: Death row inmates or anyone else who has been found guilty and convicted are not entitled to the continued assistance of legal representation at the state's expense. To allow such a right or guarantee would place too much of an economic strain on the prison system and also encourage the filing of frivolous lawsuits. Essentially, the right to a lawyer extends in all stages prior to the actual conviction of an offender. When the accused is sentenced to prison, he or she is no longer guaranteed the right to an attorney.

Myers v. County of Lake

30 F. 3d 847 (1994)

Facts

At age sixteen, Steven Myers was a juvenile in the custody of the Lake County Juvenile Detention Center (LCJC) in Indiana, where he stole a car. It was suggested that he be transferred to a more secure custody facility in Maine specializing in intelligent children who treated ordinary detention centers as challenges to overcome. Reluctant to go to Maine, eight days later Myers hanged himself with a sheet at the LCJC. He survived the attempt but suffered from severe and permanent brain damage. As the result of a trial in the U.S. District Court for the Northern District of Indiana, a jury concluded that the LCJC negligently failed to take precautions to prevent the suicide attempt and awarded Myers and his father $600,000 in damages. The LCJC appealed to the U.S. Court of Appeals for the Seventh Circuit seeking review of the judgment, claiming that Myers and his father should be precluded from recovering damages on a negligent action because Myers intentionally committed the act that was the contributing cause of his brain damage.

Issue

Whether Myers and his father should be precluded from filing a negligent action against the LCJC officials because Myers contributed to his own injuries by intentionally attempting suicide.

Holding by the Seventh Circuit Court of Appeals

The Court of Appeals for the Seventh Circuit affirmed the District Court's judgment holding that Myers's intentional act does not protect the county from liability based on the county's failure to provide sufficient psychological personnel to detect suicidal symptoms of inmates at risk of such behavior.

Reason

This case began with both federal and state law issues to be litigated in the Federal District Court. However, the District Court granted LCJC officials summary judgment on the plaintiff's constitutional claim, leaving the Myers family with only a state law negligence claim. The District Court exercised supplemental jurisdiction to hear the state law negligence claim in which a jury awarded the Myers family $600,000. On appeal, the Seventh Circuit Court had to interpret Indiana state law to determine if the case was correctly decided. After finding that the jury was entitled to find that LCJC acted negligently in regard to the attempted suicide of Steven Myers, the remaining issue became whether Indiana state law allowed the LCJC a defense to the negligence claim on the basis that Myers contributed to his own injuries by intentionally trying to commit suicide. Finding that Indiana state law was silent on the contributory negligence defense issue, the Court of Appeals determined that Indiana would most likely follow the majority of states that had laws preventing contributory defenses to negligent actions involving suicides. The Court of Appeals reasoned that "the duty to protect the others against unreasonable risk of harm extends to risks arising out of the actor's own conduct."

Case Significance

This case is important for several reasons. First, it reveals that correctional facilities can be civilly liable when inmates commit suicide. Second, it reveals that the lawsuits from these actions can be very large. In this case, the Appeals Court states that the appellant could not use the defense of not being legally responsible because the victim intentionally attempted suicide. Moreover, it held that the county owed the inmate a duty to provide protection even against himself. The court found that the victim had a history of suicide risk factors that were recorded at LCJC and at other youth detention facilities where he had been incarcerated. However, LCJC was facing a financial hardship and was short-staffed and unable to provide the facility with a full-time psychologist to monitor juveniles who exhibited suicidal behavior. LCJC also failed to place Myers under suicide watch. Such a lack of reasonable care makes the facility civilly liable for the suicide attempt.

Although no monetary figure can replace the value of human life, LCJC was ordered to pay $300,000 (reduced from $600,000 on appeal). This amount is devastating to a correctional facility already facing a financial strain. Nevertheless, the award could have been more. The lesson in this case is that unless correctional facilities take precautionary measures to identify suicidal symptoms in inmates, they will be held responsible for their death or damages they sustain from suicide attempts. The court is unwilling to accept a lack of money as an excuse not to find fault in a facility charged with having custody of inmates. Perhaps a central message is that the defense of using the victim as a contributing cause of an attempted suicide is not acceptable. Therefore, correctional officials would do well to ensure that guards are properly trained to detect symptoms of depression and suicidal behavior. They should also monitor those inmates who are at risk of harming themselves.

Olim v. Wakinekona

461 U.S. 238 (1983)

Facts

Respondent Wakinekona, a Hawaii state prisoner, was serving a life sentence without the possibility of parole for murder, as well as other sentences for rape, robbery, and escape. Wakinekona was housed in the maximum security unit at the Hawaii State Prison outside of Honolulu. Olim was an administrator with the Hawaii prison system and a member of the Program Committee, which was holding hearings to determine the reasons for a breakdown in discipline and failure of certain programs within the maximum security unit. Wakinekona and another prisoner were singled out as troublemakers at the prison and received notice they were to appear before the Program Committee to determine whether they should be reclassified or transferred to a prison on the mainland. Five days later, the hearing was held and the committee recommended that Wakinekona remain classified as a maximum security prisoner and be transferred to Folsom State Prison in California. Wakinekona filed a Section 1983 suit with the U.S. District Court for the District of Hawaii alleging that he had been denied procedural due process by the Program Committee because the people who recommended his transfer were the same people who initiated the hearing. He alleged that they were biased against him in violation of a Hawaii Corrections Rule that requires transfer hearings to be conducted by an impartial committee. The District Court dismissed the suit, holding that the prison regulations did not create a substantive liberty interest protected by the Due Process Clause of the Fourteenth Amendment. The Court of Appeals for the Ninth Circuit reversed, holding that the Hawaii prison regulations created a liberty interest for inmates in remaining imprisoned in Hawaii and that the rule gave prisoners a constitutionally protected liberty interest that they would not be transferred to the mainland without an impartial hearing. The case was appealed to the U.S. Supreme Court, and it granted certiorari.

Issue

Whether the interstate transfer of a prisoner from a state prison in Hawaii to one in California implicates a liberty interest protected by the Due Process Clause of the Fourteenth Amendment.

U.S. Supreme Court Holding

The Supreme Court reversed the decision of the Ninth Circuit Court of Appeals, holding that an interstate transfer of an inmate does not deprive an inmate of any liberty interest protected by the Due Process Clause of the Fourteenth Amendment and that Hawaii's prison regulations did not create a protected liberty interest that placed limitations on the prison officials' discretion regarding the transfer of an inmate.

Reason

The Supreme Court's reasoning in the case was twofold. First, the Court reasoned that an interstate prison transfer itself did not implicate the Due Process Clause. The Court found that the statutes and compacts regarding the interstate transfer of prisoners were so common that it is "neither unreasonable nor unusual" for an inmate to serve his entire sentence in another state or part of his sentence in another state because of a transfer. Citing *Meachum v. Fano* and *Montanye v. Haymes*, where the Court held that intrastate transfers did not implicate the Due Process Clause because they were within the normal range of custody, the Court did not find much difference between interstate prison transfers and intrastate prison transfers. It concluded that interstate transfers were common and that prisoners had no liberty interest in being imprisoned in the state where they committed their crime. Second, the Court determined that even Hawaii prison regulations did not create a constitutionally protected liberty interest for prisoners to remain within Hawaii's prisons that would implicate due process protections. The Supreme Court noted that regulations that create liberty interests in prison involve objective and defined criteria that limit official discretion and reasoned that Hawaii's regulations regarding interstate prison transfers did not limit the use of official discretion in making those transfers.

Case Significance

This case is important because it informs inmates that simply because they committed a crime and were tried in a certain state, there is no guarantee or reason to believe that they will be sentenced to a prison in that state or serve the remainder of their sentence there. At the same time, if they are sentenced to serve time in a particular state, there is no liberty interest of due process attached if they are later transferred from that facility. The Court stated that inmates cannot expect for there to be a formal remedy in place that observes a due process interest, such as a formal hearing, where guilt needs to be determined before the transfer can be made. The case allows prison administrators flexibility to expedite solving internal matters that may involve transferring problem or trouble inmates for various reasons, such as disciplinary action, to prevent riots or gang wars, or for the safety of everyone in the prison setting. If the ruling had been decided the other way, the decision would probably have empowered inmates by requiring institutions to tolerate their behaviors up to the amount of time it would take before inmates could be transferred. This type of inaction would put guards, administrative officials, and inmates at the mercy of prisoners who need to be transferred for the safety of others.

O'Lone v. Estate of Shabazz
482 U.S. 342 (1987)

Facts

The Islamic prisoners at New Jersey's Leesburg State Prison filed a Section 1983 suit in the U.S. District Court for the District of New Jersey alleging the Department of Corrections regulations preventing them from attending Jumu'ah, a weekly congregational service, violated their First Amendment rights to the free exercise of religion. Leesburg Prison classified prisoners into three categories: (1) maximum security, (2) intermediate minimum security, and (3) full minimum security, with minimum security prisoners having substantially more freedom than maximum security prisoners. Because of overcrowding, Leesburg implemented policies that required all minimum security prisoners to work outside the main building. Due to increased security risks and delays at the main prison gate, officials maintained regulations that would not allow prisoners to return to the main building after they reported to work outside the main building. As such, this security regulation prevented the minimum security Muslim prisoners from attending Jumu'ah, an Islamic congregational service held every Friday after the sun reaches its zenith but before afternoon prayer. The District Court ruled in favor of prison officials, holding that the regulations advanced security goals and that no less restrictive way could be adopted without compromising the objectives of prison security. The decision was appealed, and the Third Circuit Court of Appeals vacated the District Court's ruling and remanded the case to find whether the prison regulations served the penological goal of security and that no reasonable alternative could be found without creating security problems. The case was appealed to the U.S. Supreme Court, and it granted certiorari.

Issue

Does the First Amendment right to the free exercise of religion require New Jersey prison officials to make special security accommodations to allow Muslim prisoners access to Jumu'ah services?

U.S. Supreme Court Holding

The Supreme Court reversed and remanded the decision of the Third Circuit Court of Appeals, holding that the prison regulations challenged did not violate the free exercise of religion clause under the First Amendment of the U.S. Constitution.

Reason

In this case, the Court reiterated the need to evaluate penological objectives by relying on prison administrators who are actually charged with and trained in the area of running prisons. Therefore, the Court has always deferred to prison officials. Also, the Court stated that when prison regulations are alleged to infringe on the constitutional rights of prisoners, the Court uses a reasonableness test to determine whether the policy is reasonably related to a legitimate penological interest. The main issue in the case concerned what level of test should be used to weigh the Muslim prisoners' First Amendment religious rights against the prison regulations. The Third Circuit Court of Appeals ruled that a medium-level test should be applied. Under the medium-level test, for a regulation to survive, prison officials would have to show that (1) the regulation advanced an important security goal, and (2) no reasonable alternatives existed to accommodate the prisoners' religious rights. The Court disagreed with the Third Circuit Court's decision when it established a separate burden on prison officials to prove that no reasonable method exists that prisoners' religious rights can be accommodated without creating bona fide security problems. Instead, the Court cited *Turner v. Safley,* ruling that the lowest level reasonableness test was to be used when weighing a prisoner's constitutional rights against prison regulations. Under the reasonableness test, prison officials would only have to show regulations are rationally related to legitimate security interests. It was not necessary to show that regulations were the least restrictive way of achieving security objectives or that no reasonable security alternative existed, making it easier for prison officials to justify their actions before the federal courts.

Case Significance

This case is important because it demonstrates the respect and deference that the U.S. Constitution allows for the judgment of prison administrators. In rejecting the decision made by the Court of Appeals, the U.S. Supreme Court stated that the Appeals Court made an erroneous decision by concluding that prison officials must shoulder the burden of disproving the availability of alternative methods of accommodating prisoners' religious rights. At the same time, the case is concerned with Muslim prisoners being able to freely exercise their right to worship. In this case, the Court considered the accommodations the prison offered so as not to deprive inmates of their right to worship. The Court observed that the inmates had the right to congregate for prayer or discussion except during work time. The Muslim inmates were provided different meals when pork was served in the cafeteria. Moreover, special arrangements were made during the observance of Ramadan, a month-long period of fasting and prayer. Because of these opportunities provided to the Muslim inmates, the Court concluded that the policy that prevented them from reentering the prison during the afternoon was reasonably related to the legitimate penological interest of safety because contraband could have been smuggled into the facility and used in the commission of crime and posed a threat to safety and security. Moreover, it was widely known that some gang members worked with Muslims. Prison officials were aware of existing problems, such as there being only one guard to supervise the entire work detail, and some of the prisoners who had previously been allowed to return during the day presented security risks.

Parratt v. Taylor

451 U.S. 527 (1981)

Facts

Respondent Taylor, a prisoner at the Nebraska Penal and Correctional Complex, paid $23.50 for hobby materials he ordered with two drafts from his inmate account. When the hobby materials arrived at the prison, they were signed for by two employees who worked at the prison hobby center, one a civilian and the other an inmate. The normal prison procedures regarding processing packages were that upon arrival, the packages are either delivered to the prisoner, who signs a receipt for them, or the prisoner is notified to

pick up the package and sign a receipt for it. According to state prison policy, no inmate other than the one the package is addressed to is allowed to
sign for the package. However, in this case, two hobby center employees
signed for the package because Taylor was in segregation at the time his package arrived and was not permitted to have hobby materials. After his release
from segregation, Taylor contacted several prison officials about his package, but the officials never were able to determine its whereabouts or what
caused its disappearance. Taylor brought a Section 1983 action to the Federal District Court for Nebraska against the prison officials to recover the
value of the lost hobby materials, claiming that because mail procedures were
not followed, the state negligently lost his property and that he had been deprived of property without due process of law in violation of his Fourteenth
Amendment rights. The District Court affirmed Taylor's motion for summary judgment, ruling that negligent actions by state officials can be the
basis for an action under Section 1983, that petitioners were not immune
from liabilities, and that the deprivation of the hobby materials implicated
due process rights. The Court of Appeals for the Eighth Circuit affirmed the
District Court's ruling. The case was appealed to the U.S. Supreme Court, and
it granted certiorari.

Issue

Whether a state prisoner's claim for the negligent loss of property by state
prison officials can be the basis for a Fourteenth Amendment due process of
law violation.

U.S. Supreme Court Holding

The Supreme Court reversed the Eighth Circuit Court of Appeals, holding
that the respondent has not stated a claim for relief under 42 U.S.C. Section
1983 and the claim does not rise to the level of a due process violation within
the meaning of the Fourteenth Amendment when the state provides a tort
remedy.

Reason

The Supreme Court reasoned Taylor's claim of a due process violation is sub-
stantiated. However, because the deprivation of property did not occur because
of an established state procedure but from an unauthorized state agent's inability to follow that procedure, Nebraska's prison policy did not cause Taylor to lose
his property and does not raise due process concerns. In addition, the Court reasoned that since Nebraska had a tort claims remedy to compensate Taylor for the

full value of his property loss, his Fourteenth Amendment due process rights were not violated because the state tort remedy protects his due process interests. The Court noted that while Taylor would not be eligible for as much compensation in state law as he would be in federal law, it is the fact that he can be fully compensated in state law for his losses and not how much he could gain in compensation that determines whether due process implications arise in cases involving the loss of property because of negligence on the part of state officials. Moreover, whereas Section 1983 would have provided the respondent with more relief than the state remedy, the state remedy is adequate to satisfy the due process claim.

Case Significance

This is a landmark prisoner's rights case that stands for the principle that a state prison inmate cannot sue state prison officials in the federal courts for the negligent loss of his or her personal property under the Due Process Clause of the Fourteenth Amendment if adequate remedies exist in state law. In this case, the Court indicates that protecting all inmates' property from theft or destruction may be beyond the control of prison officials. As such, it is very likely that inmates may allege a due process violation if they are deprived of property that is lost, stolen, or damaged. The risks are that such mishaps are likely to occur within the context of correctional settings. In this case, the Court says that there is nothing in the Fourteenth Amendment that protects against all deprivations of life, liberty, and property by the state. Rather the amendment protects only those deprivations without due process of law. However, Nebraska has a tort claims remedy through which inmates can seek redress for their property loss or damage, and this mechanism affords the inmate a due process protection. Moreover, when an adequate state remedy exists to redress property damage by state officials, there is no constitutional deprivation of property without due process within the meaning of the Fourteenth Amendment.

The implications here are clear. First, a state tort remedy allows the federal court system to be free from small suits, especially where the amount of injury or property value is small, such as in the present case. These matters can be diverted from the federal to the state remedy. Second, the ruling in this case extends beyond the prison setting to other places where there are officials operating under color of law, such as police officers and their daily encounters with citizens. This decision or ruling prevents cases that are relatively minor or nonserious from clogging the federal courts if states have other remedies in place to protect the interest of injured parties.

Pell v. Procunier
417 U.S. 817 (1974)

Facts

California state prisoners and journalists brought a Section 1983 claim in the U.S. District Court for the Northern District of California alleging that California state prison regulations prohibiting face-to-face interviews between the press and specific individual prisoners violated their First and Fourteenth Amendment rights. Before the regulation was imposed, to gather news about California prisons, members of the press used specific individual prisoners as sources. They were often interviewed on a regular basis. California prison authorities discovered that those prisoners used as news sources gained status and became public figures. This would invariably lead to notoriety and influence among their fellow inmates. Prison officials believed that the newly found status would encourage those inmates interviewed by the media to challenge prison regulations, which endangered prison staff. To maintain control of the prisons, officials passed regulations limiting press access to prisons and prisoners to specific times and locations, and prohibited the specific prisoner interviewing process. The District Court granted summary judgment for the prisoners ruling that California regulations violated their First and Fourteenth Amendment rights, and dismissed the suit by the journalists ruling that in light of the First Amendment rights granted to the prisoners, they had no claim. The case was appealed to the U.S. Supreme Court, and it granted certiorari.

Issue

Whether the California prison regulations that prohibited interviews between the press and specific individual prisoners violated the First and Fourteenth Amendment rights of either the prisoners or the press.

U.S Supreme Court Holding

The Supreme Court reversed and held that since prisoners had alternative ways to express themselves, the regulation did not violate their freedom of speech. The regulation did not violate freedom of the press because the press was not denied media access to sources available to the general public.

Reason

The U.S. Supreme Court reasoned that prisoners retain First Amendment rights that do not conflict with the legitimate penological objectives of the corrections system. Prisoners' rights must be balanced against the security interests of correctional officials. The Court used a medium-level test to balance the prisoners' First Amendment rights against the security interests of the prison officials. For a regulation to withstand constitutional challenges, medium-level tests require that the regulation advance a substantial state interest in the least restrictive way. The Court uses three levels of tests to weigh government regulations: the highest level strict scrutiny test, the medium-level test, and the least restrictive test requiring only that government regulations be rationally related to advancing a rational government interest. The selection of the test that the Court uses to weigh the government regulation depends on the nature of the right that is at issue.

In the current case, the Supreme Court used a medium-level substantial interest test to weigh the prison regulation against the First Amendment rights of prisoners, indicating that the Court considers First Amendment rights of prisoners important. Here, the Court reasoned that the California prison officials were stating legitimate security interests in attempting to prevent the press from building the egos of specific prisoners. The Court also reasoned that alternatively, prisoners could correspond by mail with members of the press, had visitation rights with certain visitors, and could communicate with the press through these visitors. With respect to the media, the Court reasoned that their freedom of the press rights were not violated when they had the same access to information as the general public. Because the general public could not interview specific prisoners at will, the freedom of the press did not grant the journalists a right to do so. The Supreme Court was impressed that California regulations still allowed the press and the general public the right to view prison facilities by scheduling tours and the right to interview any prisoner they encountered on these tours. This signaled to the Court that officials were not trying to hide or conceal conditions inside prisons. The security interests of prison officials allowed them to regulate the time and place of contacts between the press, the general public, and prisoners. The time and place regulations of the California prison system still allowed members of the press access to the prison system to allow for news reporting.

Case Significance

This case is significant for a number of reasons. First, the Supreme Court sent a clear message that it supports the efforts of prison officials in upholding policies that are created to help maintain safety and control in places of confinement, which is a legitimate penological objective. In this case, prison officials argued that in the past, outbreaks of violence and disruptions would occur because specific prisoners had achieved celebrity-like status among the inmate population, so to counter and prevent those occurrences, they implemented the policy that prohibited the press from face-to-face interviews with inmates. Second, the case does not extend to the press a greater First Amendment right than what is granted to people in the general public. In not extending the First Amendment to the press, the Court granted prison officials more power and autonomy to run prisons in a manner that is free from the press or media's inspections. The Court was particularly impressed by the fact that penal administrators had created prison tours so that the press and others could have access to conditions inside of prisons. The Court was also aware that if the press wanted to learn about what occurs within the context of prisons, its members/employees could speak to newly released inmates, friends, and family members of inmates who were confined, and even clergy members who visited inmates. The Court interpreted this to mean that the press and members in the general public had equal access to information from prisoners and the conditions under which they are confined.

Pollock v. Marshall

843 F. 2d 656 (1988)

Facts

Mark Pollock, appellant inmate, filed a Section 1983 petition that challenged the decision of the U.S. District Court for the Southern District of Ohio that granted summary judgment to the appellee, a correctional superintendent in a civil rights action brought by Pollock. Pollock, a prisoner at the maximum security Southern Ohio Correctional Facility, professed a belief in the religion of the Lakota tribe of American Indians. The Lakotas believed that hair was sacred and should not be cut. Pollock sought an exemption to Ohio's prison regulation that requires all inmates to cut their hair under Ohio Admin.

Code Section 5120-9-25(F), claiming a violation of his civil rights. The appellee claimed that no constitutional violation occurred because valid penal interests outweighed any constitutional amendment right to grow long hair. The District Court agreed and granted the motion. The Sixth Circuit Court of Appeals affirmed the District Court's grant of summary judgment. The court held that the appellee could constitutionally require the appellant to cut his hair. The Circuit Court found that the interests offered by the Superintendent were both legitimate and reasonably related to the regulation limiting the length of appellant's hair.

Issue

Whether a prison may regulate the length of an inmate's hair under a regulation that conflicts with an inmate's religious beliefs.

Holding by the Sixth Circuit Court of Appeals

The Sixth Circuit Court of Appeals affirmed the decision of the District Court holding that after balancing the interests of the appellee (keeping inmates' hair cut) and the appellant (exercising the Lakota religion), the court held that the regulation requiring inmates to cut their hair was not unconstitutional.

Reason

In *Pollock*, the Sixth Circuit Court of Appeals agreed that the District Court was correct in its belief that the plaintiff sincerely and genuinely believed in the Lakota Indian religion. The District Court referred to cases such as *Jihaad v. O'Brien* (645 F.2d 556, 6th Cir. 1981) and *Walker v. Mintzes* (771 F.2d 920 6th Cir. 1985) for established standards on how to evaluate restrictions on inmates in the exercise of their First Amendment rights. The District Court determined that the defendant must prove necessity of any restrictions it imposes and must demonstrate the reasonableness of the restriction. The plaintiff in this case argued that the District Court applied the wrong standard in evaluating his First Amendment claim. He contended that the correct standard is found in *Turner v. Safley*. *Turner* held that when a prison regulation impinges on inmates' constitutional rights, the regulation is valid if it is reasonably related to legitimate penological interests. In reviewing this decision, the U.S. Supreme Court was clear that subjecting the daily judgments of prison officials to an inflexible strict scrutiny analysis would seriously hamper their ability to handle security problems, and would distance the decision-making process. The Court enumerated four factors related under *Turner*. First, the prison regulations must have a valid and rational connection to the legitimate and neutral government objective in question. Second, courts must determine whether there are alternative means of exercising the right that remains open to inmates. Third, courts should consider the impact that accommodating the asserted constitutional right will have on guards, other inmates, and prison resources. Fourth, the court must consider whether there are reasonable alternatives to the prison regulation.

In the current case, the Sixth Circuit Court found merit in the prison's need to identify inmates for purposes such as mail call and roll call, and to ensure that no one has escaped. In addition, excessive hair creates problems with control of contraband, such as pills and handcuff keys. Prison officials believe that increased hair length would require guards to spend more time searching inmates. This would exacerbate tension between inmates and guards. Prison officials also believed that longer hair increased the likelihood of homosexual attacks, because longer hair increased attractiveness. Longer hair was also thought to create sanitation concerns, such as head lice. The circuit court agreed that these concerns were legitimate and reasonably related to the prison regulation that limited the length of prisoners' hair. The court reasoned that limiting hair length for these reasons advanced legitimate penological interests. Moreover, the court held that the plaintiff remained free to exercise the other doctrines of his religion. After balancing the needs of the prison with those of *Pollock*, the court held that the regulation restricting hair length was not unconstitutional.

Case Significance

This case is significant because it further reveals that the Appeals Court is committed to the U.S. Supreme Court decision in *Turner*, in that when it can be demonstrated that penal policies are in place to justify reasonable and legitimate penological interests, officials are likely to prevail even when the issue stems from the First Amendment's freedom of religion right. In *Pollock*, the Sixth Circuit Court reaffirmed *Turner*. This case also shows that on balance, the courts are likely to give more weight to a policy that prevents the flow of contraband, encourages inmate identification, and prevents sanitation problems, homosexual attacks, and tension between guards and inmates compared to the inmates' need to wear longer hair. The case does not prohibit the Lakota religion, it simply prohibits inmate worshippers from growing long hair because other accommodations are available for the practice of religion.

Ponte v. Real

471 U.S. 491 (1985)

Facts

Respondent John Real was an inmate at the Massachusetts Correctional Institution at Wolpole. In December 1981, Real was working in the prison metal shop when he heard a commotion in an adjacent office. He entered the office and observed an inmate fighting with a correctional officer. A second correctional officer attempted to break up the fight and ordered Real out of the office, but Real remained in the office observing the fight. Another correctional officer ended up escorting Real to his cell. A week later, Real received notice that he was charged with three violations of prison regulations as a result of his refusal to leave the room where the brawl took place. He notified prison authorities that he wanted to call four witnesses at a hearing that would be held on these charges: two prisoners, the charging officer, and the officer who was involved in the fight. A hearing was held in February 1982. At the hearing, the charging officer appeared and testified against Real, but the board declined to call any other witnesses and did not indicate on the record of the hearing why they refused to call the other witnesses. Real was found guilty and received 25 days in isolation and the loss of 150 days good time credit. He then sought a writ of habeas corpus in a Massachusetts trial court, which sustained his claim that prison officials had deprived him of his Fourteenth Amendment due process rights because they gave no reasons why he was not allowed to call the requested witnesses at the hearing. On appeal, the Massachusetts Supreme Judicial Court affirmed the holding that prison authorities violated Real's due process rights by not putting in the administrative record the reasons he was denied the opportunity to call witnesses in his defense and declared a Massachusetts statute that governed the presentation of proof in prison disciplinary hearings unconstitutional because it did not require prison officials to record the facts or reasons for denying a prisoner's witness request. The U.S. Supreme Court granted certiorari.

Issue

Whether the Due Process Clause of the Fourteenth Amendment requires prison officials to record reasons for denying a prisoner the opportunity to call witnesses on their behalf in the administrative record of prison disciplinary hearings.

U.S. Supreme Court Holding

The U.S. Supreme Court vacated and remanded the case back to the Massachusetts Supreme Judicial Court, holding that the Due Process Clause of the Fourteenth Amendment does not require reasons for denying an inmate's witness request to appear in the administrative record of the disciplinary hearing. However, the Due Process Clause does require that the officials state their reasons for refusing to call witnesses at some point. They may do so either by making the exploration part of the administrative record or by later presenting testimony in court if the deprivation of a liberty interest, such as that afforded by good time credit, is challenged because of the refusal to call the requested witnesses.

Reason

In reviewing the current case, the U.S. Supreme Court cites its previous decision in *Wolff v. McDonnell*. In *Wolff*, the Court ruled that ordinarily the right to present evidence is basic to a fair hearing, but the inmate's right to present witnesses is necessarily circumscribed by the penological need to provide swift discipline in individual cases. This right is additionally circumscribed by the very real dangers in prison life that may result from violence or intimidation directed at either inmates or staff. Essentially, *Wolff* allowed prisoners the right to call witnesses and present evidence in a disciplinary hearing that could be denied, if granting the request could be "unduly hazardous to institutional safety or correctional goals." The Court maintained that it never required a disciplinary board to explain why it denied a prisoner's request for witnesses in the administrative record. Rather, the Court suggested that prison boards make such denials part of the prison record. The Court noted that it applied due process rights to prison disciplinary hearings to protect the prisoner's liberty interest in good time credit. In *Wolff*, the Court made it clear that allowing prisoners the right would be unduly hazardous to institutional safety or correctional goals, and limited the right of prisoners to call witnesses on their behalf at such hearings. In this case, in answering the question of whether the federal due process requirements impose a duty on the board to explain why witnesses were not allowed to testify, the Court answered, "Yes," but in a limited manner. The board can either make the reasons a part of the administrative record or present testimony in court if the deprivation of a liberty interest is challenged. Moreover, the reasons will satisfy due process requirements established in *Wolff* as long as they can be shown to be logically related to preventing undue hazards to institutional safety or correctional goals.

Case Significance

This case is significant for several reasons. First, it acknowledges that prisoners are entitled to due process in matters related to disciplinary hearings, especially when a liberty interest is at issue. Second, it makes clear what the Supreme Court intended in the *Wolff* decision with respect to what administrators are required to provide to an inmate who was part of a prison disciplinary hearing. In the current case, the Court is clear that due process is satisfied when reasons are given for not allowing an inmate to present witnesses on his behalf. The Court stated that as long as an administrator can provide reasons in the administrative record that are either written or verbal (in court), either will do, especially if the reasons are predicated on the notion that it is logically related to preventing undue hazards to institutional safety or correctional goals. The case gives great power to administrators to protect the interest of their correctional facilities, if calling witnesses means the escalation of violence or retaliation against inmates or correctional officers. It also places the inmate at the mercy of the institution because this case gives administrators permission to decide cases in the manner they see fit.

Procunier v. Martinez
416 U.S. 396 (1974)

Facts

California prisoners brought a class action suit against California penal institutions in the U.S. District Court for the Northern District of California challenging the constitutionality of state prison regulations regarding mail censorship issued by the Director of the California Department of Corrections and the ban against the use of law students and legal paraprofessionals to conduct attorney-client interviews with inmates. The California prison mail regulations prohibited inmate correspondence that "unduly complained, magnified grievances, expressed inflammatory political, racial or religious views or beliefs, or contained matters deemed defamatory or otherwise inappropriate." The District Court ruled that the mail regulations were unconstitutional under the First Amendment because they were "unduly vague" and violated the Fourteenth Amendment guarantee of procedural due process, and it enjoined their continued enforcement. Moreover, the court required that inmates be notified of the rejection of correspondence and that the author of the correspondence be allowed to protest the decision and secure review by a prison official other than the original censor. The District Court also held that the ban against the use of law students and legal paraprofessionals to conduct client-attorney interviews with inmates violated the right of access to the courts and enjoined its continued enforcement. Appellants contended that the District Court should have abstained from deciding the constitutionality of the mail censorship regulation.

Issue

Can a prison director regulate prison mail to suppress political, racial, religious, or adversarial views of prisoners? Does preventing law students or paraprofessionals from working for private attorneys to contact prisoners violate prisoners' constitutional right to access the courts?

U.S. Supreme Court Holding

The Supreme Court affirmed the decision of the District Court, holding that California's prison mail regulations violated the prisoners' First Amendment right to free speech because it did not advance a substantial governmental interest unrelated to the prisoner's right to free speech, and the ban on interviews between law students or paraprofessionals working for private attorneys violated the prisoners' right to access the courts because it was not related to a separate or unrelated security interest.

Reason

In this case, the U.S. Supreme Court was charged with determining the proper standard for deciding whether a particular regulation or practice relating to inmate correspondence constitutes an impermissible restraint of First Amendment liberties. The Court applied a medium-level substantial interest test to weigh California's right to regulate prisoner mail versus the inmates' First Amendment freedom of speech rights. In constitutional law, government regulations frequently conflict with the rights of persons. To resolve such conflicts, the federal courts test the reasoning of the government regulation by "weighing" it against the constitutional right. However, because the federal courts treat certain rights as more important than others, three different levels of tests are used to weigh the government regulations in question. By the time of *Procunier v. Martinez*, there was considerable confusion among the lower federal courts in regard to the level of test to use when considering a prisoner's freedom of speech rights and ability to send mail. Some courts were using the highest level strict scrutiny test, which required the government to show a "compelling interest" before regulating in the area of a prisoner's right to free speech. Under the strict scrutiny test, it is very difficult for the government regulation to pass constitutional muster, and the right in question is treated as fundamental. Other lower courts had been using the lowest level rational relation test, which only requires the government to show that its regulation is rationally related to a separate and unrelated security interest. Under the lowest level rational relations test, the right in question is recognized, but it is relatively easy for the government to regulate in the area. To clear up the confusion, the Court made it clear that the proper constitutional test for prisoners' freedom of speech rights was the minimum-level substantial interest test. Under this test, the government must show that its regulation advances a substantial interest in the least restrictive way. The medium-level test treats the constitutional right in question as important, but is flexible enough to allow for regulation in the area. Using the medium-level case, the Court found the California mail regulations unconstitutional because they were not advancing a substantial government interest unrelated to the freedom of speech. The Court also struck down California's regulations banning law students or paraprofessionals working for private attorneys from meeting with prisoners. The ruling allowed law students and paraprofessionals who worked for law school clinics access to prisoners, because California advanced no security justification for regulating contacts between law students and paraprofessionals and prisoners separate from access to the court reasons.

Case Significance

The case is important because the Supreme Court agreed with the District Court's determination that the prison regulation of mail censorship was unconstitutionally vague, lacked due process, and placed inmates at the mercy of prison employees. The Court also disagreed with the constitutionality of the prison's policy banning inmates from having the right to access the courts by denying them attorney-client interviews with law students and paraprofessionals working for law school clinics. This case reaffirms the Supreme Court's ruling in *Johnson v. Avery*. The case is also important because it requires policy governing the censorship of inmate correspondence to be based on clear policy designed to preserve internal order, discipline, and the maintenance of institutional security against escape. The Court is clear in *Procunier* that prison officials cannot censor inmate correspondence simply to eliminate unflattering or unwelcomed opinions or factually inaccurate statements. Rather, they must show that a regulation authorizing mail censorship furthers one or more of the substantial governmental interests of security, order, and rehabilitation. At the same time, inmates can protest when their correspondence is censored by an independent party. This ensures fairness. The Court was particularly concerned with the regulation because those parties that are not incarcerated also have a liberty interest at issue.

Procunier v. Navarette
434 U.S. 555 (1978)

Facts

Respondent Navarette, a prisoner at California's Soledad prison, brought a Section 1983 claim seeking damages to the U.S. District Court for the Northern District of California, claiming that California prison officials "negligently" interfered with his First and Fourteenth Amendment rights to receive and send mail during the years 1971 and 1972. He alleged that the prison failed to send his outgoing letters to legal assistance groups, law students, the news media, prisoners at other institutions, and personal friends. He also alleged that prison supervisory personnel negligently failed to provide training to subordinates responsible for outgoing mail. More specifically, the respondent claimed the following: (1) Officers in charge of mailing failed to mail various items of correspondence during the fifteen months that he was at Soledad; (2) He sought relief because of wrongful failure to mail the same items. This interference was conducted in "bad faith" and disregarded Navarette's rights; (3) The interference recurred because subordinate officers had "negligently and inadvertently" misapplied the prison mail regulations, and supervisory officers negligently failed to train their subordinates, which directly violated the respondent's constitutional rights.

Prison officials asserted qualified immunity from Navarette's allegations, arguing that prisoner petitioners' rights to send mail did not exist in 1971–72 but were established in 1974 with the *Procunier v. Martinez* decision. The District Court ruled in favor of prison officials by granting summary judgment based on their qualified immunity from liability from damages under Section 1983. The Ninth Circuit Court of Appeals reversed the District Court's ruling that prisoners are entitled to First and Fourteenth Amendment protection for their outgoing mail and the claim in question could be brought under Section 1983. The Appeals Court also claimed that granting summary judgment to the petitioners was improper because the petitioners were not entitled to prevail as a matter of law.

Issue

Whether the Ninth Circuit Court of Appeals correctly reversed the District Court's judgment with respect to Navarette's third claim for relief alleging negligent interference with a claimed constitutional right.

U.S. Supreme Court Holding

The U.S. Supreme Court reversed the decision of the Ninth Circuit Court of Appeals, holding that the circuit court erred in reversing the District Court's summary judgment for petitioners.

Reason

In this case, the U.S. Supreme Court ruled the Ninth Circuit Court of Appeals erred because of the following: (1) The petitioners were entitled to immunity unless they "knew or reasonably should have known" that the action they took with respect to respondent's mail would violate his federal rights, or they took the action with "malicious intervention" to cause a deprivation of constitutional right or other injury to respondent; (2) There was no established First and Fourteenth Amendment rights that protected state prisoners' mail privileges at the time this case was decided. Therefore, as a matter of law, there was no basis for the Appeals Court to reject the immunity defense on the grounds that petitioners knew or should have known that their alleged conduct violated a constitutional right; (3) Neither should petitioners' immunity defense be overruled under the standard authorizing liability where the defendant state official has acted with malicious intent to deprive the plaintiff of a constitutional right or cause him other injury, because the claim in question charged negligent conduct, not intentional injury.

In citing *Wood v. Strickland* (420 U.S. 308, 1975), the U.S. Supreme Court reasoned that the immunity defense would not be available to petitioners because the constitutional right allegedly infringed was clearly established at the time of their challenged conduct, if they knew or should have known of the right, and if they knew or should have known that their conduct violated the constitutional norm. In this case, prison officials argued that in 1971 and 1972, when the action occurred, there was no established First Amendment right that protected the mailing privileges of state prisons, and no federal right existed. Therefore, they asserted there was no way of knowing. The Supreme Court agreed with the petitioners and ruled they were entitled to judgment as a matter of law. The Appeals Court in its decision had ruled on no earlier opinions.

Case Significance

This case is significant for several reasons. First, it defines the degrees of immunity that criminal justice agencies and others are entitled to use as a defense for alleged law violations. For example, the case distinguishes the difference between absolute and qualified immunity. This case is also important because it placed limitations on what Section 1983 claims could be used for with respect to damages sought and the defense of qualified immunity. Another important aspect about the case is that the U.S. Supreme Court did not extend to prison inmates any First and Fourteenth Amendment protection that did not exist at the time the actions in this case occurred, namely, that prisoners have the right to send and receive mail, because there was no state or federal right at the time.

Reed v. Woodruff County

7 F.3d 808 (8th Cir. 1993)

Facts

Plaintiffs, the father and brother of a deceased prisoner, Howard Reed, brought a Section 1983 claim against defendants, Woodruff County, Arkansas, jail officials, charging that they were negligent and violated Reed's constitutional rights and were responsible for his wrongful death. Reed was a trustee prisoner who was incarcerated for failing to appear in municipal court. Prior to his death, when jailer Charlene Smith responded to a jail disturbance, she was told by inmates that they had not seen Reed for some time. Smith checked Reed's cell but could not see him, and he did not answer her verbal calls. Smith returned to the front desk and asked Bobby Bogarth, a City of Augusta police officer and a licensed emergency medical technician, to check Reed's cell. Bogarth found Reed hanging by his neck in the shower stall and determined he was dead. Both officers decided to leave the scene intact pending an investigation into Reed's death. The coroner determined that Reed accidentally killed himself while engaging in autoerotic asphyxiation. The Reeds claimed that Bogarth acted with deliberate indifference to their brother's death and denied him proper medical care by not treating him before determining he was dead. During the course of the litigation, the U.S. District Court for the Eastern District of Arkansas denied the jail officials' motion for summary judgment on the Section 1983 claim and also held that they were not entitled to qualified immunity because the law on deliberate indifference under the Eighth Amendment was already established at the time of the incident. On appeal, the court held that Reed's family failed to point out facts sufficient to show that the officers acted with deliberate indifference to the prisoner's medical needs at the time the officers discovered the prisoner and determined that he was dead. Bogarth, a trained medical technician, testified that he had determined the prisoner was dead.

Issue

Whether the Woodruff County jail officials were entitled to summary judgment in regard to the Eighth Amendment claim that they acted with deliberate indifference to Reed's death by denying him proper medical care before determining he was dead, when they found him hanging in his cell.

Holding for the Eighth Circuit Court of Appeals

The Eighth Circuit Court of Appeals reversed and remanded the case with instructions to grant the county's motion for summary judgment and dismissed the family's claim with prejudice.

Reason

The Eighth Circuit Court in this case reasoned that the District Court erred when it denied summary judgment to the defendant. Accordingly, the Eighth Circuit Court held that for plaintiffs to state a claim for relief under Section 1983, they must allege that the defendant's action amounted to a violation of a right, privilege, or immunity protected by the U.S. Constitution. Essentially, the Reeds contended that the defendants violated Howard Reed's Eighth Amendment right to medical care. To determine such issues, the U.S. Supreme Court has evaluated such matters using the standard of whether custodians or prison officials acted with deliberate indifference to a prisoner's serious medical needs. The Eighth Circuit stated that to survive a summary judgment motion, plaintiffs must point out facts sufficient to show that Bogarth acted with deliberate indifference to Reed's medical needs at the time he was discovered hanging. The family argued that Bogarth should have attempted artificial resuscitation before determining that Reed was dead, and such an attempt may have saved his life. However, the plaintiffs had not met their burden. Finally, the Eighth Circuit Court held that the plaintiffs' evidence was insufficient to overcome a motion for summary judgment.

Case Significance

This case is important to courts in the Eighth Circuit, but not necessarily to other courts because this was not heard by the U.S. Supreme Court. In this case, the Circuit Court stated that if plaintiffs wanted to prevail in their Section 1983 claim, they needed to be able to point to facts sufficient enough to show that an officer allegedly responsible for death or injury of an inmate acted with deliberate indifference to the serious medical needs of an inmate, which they failed to prove. Essentially, the circuit court stated that it is not enough to allege wrongful death at the hands of jails, and the accusing party has the burden of proving that officials charged with custodial duties over inmates have failed to assist or treat and can be shown to have had a responsibility in the prisoner's death. At the same time, the lower court is corrected by having its decision reversed and remanded. The Circuit Court instructs the lower court that the Woodruff County Jail should have been allowed to use the qualified immunity defense.

Rhodes v. Chapman

452 U.S. 337 (1981)

Facts

Respondents, prisoners who were housed in the same cell at the maximum security Southern Ohio Correctional Facility, brought a class action suit under Section 1983 to the U.S. District Court for the Southern District of Ohio alleging that the Ohio prison officials' practice of "double-celling," or housing two prisoners in a single cell, constituted cruel and unusual punishment in violation of the Eighth and Fourteenth Amendments. The District Court found the practice of double-celling at the Ohio facility to constitute cruel and unusual punishment prohibited by the Eighth Amendment for the following reasons: (1) Inmates were serving long prison terms; (2) The prison housed 38 percent more inmates than it was designed for; (3) Several studies indicated that prisoners needed more space for living quarters; (4) The suggestion that double-celled inmates spent most of their time in the cells; and (5) Double-celling was not a temporary condition of the prison. The Sixth Circuit Court of Appeals affirmed the District Court's decision, finding that the District Court reached a constitutionally permissible conclusion. The case was appealed to the U.S. Supreme Court, and it granted certiorari.

Issue

Whether the practice of double-celling at the Ohio facility amounts to cruel and unusual punishment in violation of the Eighth and Fourteenth Amendments to the U.S. Constitution.

U.S. Supreme Court Holding

The Court reversed the decision of the Sixth Circuit Court of Appeals holding that double-celling is not cruel and unusual punishment prohibited by the Eighth and Fourteenth Amendments.

Reason

In this case, the Court cited its ruling in *Estelle v. Gamble,* where it decided that deliberate indifference to a prisoner's medical needs is cruel and unusual punishment in violation of the Eighth Amendment, because inmates depend on prison authorities for meeting those needs, and denial of prisoners' basic medical needs results in the infliction of wanton and unnecessary punishment without penological purpose. In this case, the Court extends its holding in *Gamble* to all conditions of confinement cases, including the practice of double-celling by Ohio officials. The Court restated that because prisoners must rely on prison authorities for basic human needs, depriving inmates of the minimal civilized measure of life's necessities alone, or in combination, results in cruel and unusual punishment when under contemporary standards of decency the deprivation involves wanton and unnecessary pain without penological purpose. At the same time, the Court commented that prison conditions are expected to be harsh and are part of the penalty criminal offenders pay for their offenses against society. However, the pain that a prisoner experiences may not be grossly disproportionate to the severity of the crime warranting imprisonment. Applying their legal reasoning to the practice of double-celling, the Court found that because double-celling; (1) did not lead to deprivations of essential food, medical care or sanitation; (2) increased violence among prisoners; or (3) he infliction of any kind of unnecessary or wanton pain, it did not rise to the level of cruel and unusual punishment within the meaning of the Eighth Amendment. Although the Court did find that the practice of double-celling led to diminished jobs and educational opportunities among inmates, limited work hours, and less personal space, it commented that these kinds of deprivations were not punishments.

Case Significance

This case is important for several reasons. First, by 1981, prisoners across the nation were flooding the federal courts with various complaints and litigation about constitutional rights violations, including the Eighth Amendment conditions of confinement. As the District Court and the Sixth Circuit Court's ruling in this case reveals, federal judges had only a vague idea as to when the deprivation of a condition of confinement rose to the level of an Eighth Amendment violation. With its ruling in this case, the U.S. Supreme Court sets guidelines for determining when any condition of confinement, alone or in combination with others, becomes cruel and unusual punishment. Under the principle of *stare decisis*, the Court binds the lower federal courts to its holding in this case, providing uniformity among the lower courts in regard to conditions of confinement cases. Second, on a more practical level, the case represents a clear belief on the part of the U.S. Supreme Court that prison officials are better suited to understand the daily needs that confront prisons, because double-celling became necessary after the prison population experienced an increase. The situation was exacerbated by the fact that the Southern Ohio Correctional Facility was the only maximum security prison where state inmates could be sentenced, because other prisons offered a lower level of security. This would have placed a heavy burden on other facilities. Third, the Court does not make light of the constitutional guarantee against cruel and unusual punishment since it determined that prisoners' complaints about being inconvenienced or uncomfortable is a consequence of sharing a cell with another prisoner and does not qualify as cruel or unusual punishment within the meaning of the Eighth and Fourteenth Amendments. The protection, where conditions of confinement are concerned, would more appropriately protect against the denial of medical care, food, sanitation, and violence committed by prison guards.

Robert v. U.S. Jaycees
468 U.S. 609 (1984)

Facts

In 1974, the Minneapolis and St. Paul chapters of the U.S. Jaycees began to admit women as regular members so that by the time of the lawsuit a substantial number of its members were female. In 1984, the national organization of the Jaycees revoked the licenses of two Minnesota chapters for violating by-laws that denied admission of women to the Jaycees. The two chapters responded by filing a discrimination lawsuit against the Minnesota Department of Human Rights, arguing that the national organization's actions were in violation of Minnesota's anti-discrimination laws. The Minnesota Department of Human Rights determined that the national organization's by-laws violated the Minnesota Human Rights Act on the basis that the Jaycees organization was a "place of public accommodation." The national Jaycees filed suit in the U.S. District Court for the District of Minnesota, which certified to the Minnesota Supreme Court to answer the question as to whether the Jaycees was a place of public accommodation. The Minnesota Supreme Court found that the Jaycees were a place of public accommodation, and the national organization renewed its suit with the District Court to challenge the constitutionality of the Minnesota Supreme Court's decision. On appeal, the Eighth Circuit Court of Appeals reversed the District Court's decision ruling that by requiring the U.S. Jaycees to admit women as full voting members, the Minnesota Human Rights Act violates the First and Fourteenth Amendment rights of the organization's members. The case was appealed to the U.S. Supreme Court, and it granted certiorari.

Issue

Did Minnesota's attempt to enforce the anti-discrimination law violate the Jaycees' right to free association under the First Amendment?

U.S. Supreme Court Holding

The U.S. Supreme Court reversed the ruling of the Eighth Circuit Court, holding that compelling the U.S. Jaycees to accept women into their organization because of Minnesota's anti-discrimination law did not infringe on the national chapter's First Amendment right to association.

Reason

In this case, the U.S. Supreme Court's decision was based on constitutionally protected freedom of association in two distinct senses. First, the Court concluded that choices to enter into and maintain certain intimate human relationships must be secured against undue intrusion by the state because of the role of such relationships in safeguarding the individual freedom that is central to the Constitution. Second, the Court has recognized a right to associate for the purpose of engaging in those acts protected by the First Amendment—especially speech, assembly, petition for the redress of grievances, and the exercise of religion. The U.S. Constitution guarantees freedom of association of this variety as a means of preserving individual liberties. In reviewing this case, the Court concluded that the Jaycees chapters lack the distinctive characteristics that might afford constitutional protection to the decision of its members to exclude women. In fact, the Court reasoned that the Minnesota Act does not aim at suppression of speech, does not distinguish between prohibited and permitted activity on the basis of viewpoint, and does not license enforcement authorities to administer the statute on the basis of such constitutionally impressionable criteria. Moreover, even the Jaycees do not contend that the Act has been applied in this case to hamper the organization's ability to express its views. The reality is that the Act reflects the state's strong commitment to eliminate discrimination and ensure its citizens equal access to public goods and services. The Court went on to argue that the Act's goal, which is unrelated to the suppression, serves compelling state interests to the highest order.

Case Significance

This case is important because of its First Amendment analysis of the right to association. It has two implications for people in places of confinement. The first implication is the right to maintain family relations. The second is the right to have membership or association in groups within penal settings. In this case, the Court ruled that the Constitution first protects the right of individuals "to enter into and maintain certain intimate human relationships." This may suggest that visitation and the right to send and receive mail are mandatorily protected activities because such access to relatives, friends, clergy, and others is allowed for continued association after conviction. Does this also imply that conjugal visits could be an issue to be litigated since it applies to continued association? The second issue is the right to engage in expressive association. Inmates have a right to peaceably assemble to speak, the right to worship, and the right to petition the government to redress grievances. They also have the right to join groups. These may include those that are constructive and productive, helping rehabilitate offenders. Groups in prison that have been considered constructive are the Jaycees, Alcoholics Anonymous, and the Boy Scouts of America. In contrast, there are some groups that are believed to hinder the rehabilitation process. Such groups typically include those advocating racism, hate, and those that center on unhealthy sexual behavior. Nevertheless, under the First Amendment, prisoners have the right to freely associate with these groups as long as their behavior poses no threat to the smooth functioning of the correctional institutions.

Roe v. Fauver

Cir. A. No. 88-1225 (AET),
1988 WL 106316 (D.N.J. Oct. 11)

Facts

In this case, the defendants asked for summary judgment and the plaintiffs asked to file an amended complaint. This matter was previously before the court on a motion by plaintiff's injunction, which was denied on May 13, 1988. William Fauver, Commissioner of New Jersey Corrections, filed a motion for summary judgment with the U.S. District Court for the District of New Jersey in connection with a lawsuit filed by Jane Roe against the New Jersey Department of Corrections. In filing for summary judgment, Fauver maintained that Roe plead no genuine interests of fact and that he is entitled to summary judgment as a matter of law. Roe, a prisoner within the New Jersey prison system was diagnosed with AIDS and argued that her confinement in continued isolation to a hospital room at St. Francis Medical Center, a hospital for female prisoners with AIDS, without an individual hearing to show she was at a risk to herself or others violated her Fourteenth Amendment due process rights. She argued that illegally segregating her from other inmates and depriving her of all recreation, education, and work program privileges she had as a minimum security prisoner constituted cruel and unusual punishment in violation of the Eighth Amendment. In addition, she argued that her confinement deprived her of adequate legal access, and that the medical care she received for AIDS amounted to deliberate indifference to her serious medical needs, also in violation of her Eighth Amendment rights.

Issue

Whether the segregation itself is proper and whether the treatment plaintiffs received once they were segregated was poor.

Holding by the District Court

The U.S. District Court for the District of New Jersey granted the plaintiff's motion to amend the complaint and denied the defendant's motion for summary judgment.

Reason

Due to the changing nature of AIDS treatment, the District Court distinguished this case from earlier cases when not much was known about AIDS. In earlier cases, the courts often found that segregating AIDS prisoners without a hearing did not violate the Eighth and Fourteenth Amendments to the U.S. Constitution. In this case, the District Court cited *Perez v. Neubert* (611 F.Supp. 830, D.N.J. 1985), a case involving Marielito Cubans who challenged their segregation in state prisons from the general population of inmates as controlling, because the *Perez* court heard arguments to determine whether the wholesale treatment of an entire class of inmates was justified. Using the *Perez* standard, the District Court denied the New Jersey Corrections official's motion for summary judgment, reasoning that genuine issues of material fact remain regarding the procedures and justifications for segregating female prisoners with AIDS or (1) reasons for confining them under conditions that deprive them of recreation, education, work, and legal access without a hearing; (2) whether such conditions of confinement violate Roe's and other female AIDS inmates' equal protection of the law because male inmates diagnosed with AIDS received more privileges in treatment; (3) whether such treatment constitutes cruel and unusual punishment; (4) whether Roe and other inmates (some were male and female hospital patients without AIDS) were being deprived legal access while confined at St. Francis Hospital; and (5) whether the hospital was acting with deliberate indifference to inmates with AIDS regarding their medical care.

Case Significance

This case is primarily about the care, treatment, and rights of prisoners diagnosed with AIDS. Though not decided by an appellate court or even the U.S. Supreme Court, the case is important for several reasons. First, it reveals that the plaintiff's Eighth and Fourteenth Amendment rights were violated. Because of this, the District Court granted the plaintiff's motion to amend the complaint and denied the defendant's motion for summary judgment. More specifically, in this case, the plaintiff alleged a constitutional rights violation. Where the Fourteenth Amendment was concerned, Roe alleged that she received no equal protection under the law. The District Court argued that while *Hewitt v. Helms* provided prison officials authority to transfer prisoners and alter their custody status, it did not allow officials to place inmates in a disciplinary unit without a hearing. Moreover, *Hewitt* requires an informal evidentiary review of reasons for placing inmates in segregated units. Another concern under the Fourteenth Amendment was the comparison treatment received by men at St. Francis who were also diagnosed with AIDS. Inmates with similar status, regardless of gender, must be treated the same or equal protection claims can be established. Where the Eighth Amendment was concerned, the plaintiffs argued that they did not receive adequate medical care, which constituted a violation of deliberate indifference as established in *Estelle v. Gamble*. The District Court was clear in this case when it stated the fact that because inmates have some medical care does not mean they cannot file a claim for inadequate medical care. The women inmates claimed that they were not always given the correct dosage of AZT when needed. In fact, they claimed that when they requested the medicine, it would either be given late or not at all. Finally, the District Court stated it could not grant summary judgment for the defendant because the allegations raised genuine issues of material fact as to whether the Eighth and Fourteenth Amendments had been violated.

Rosada v. Civiletti
621 F.2d 1179 (2d Cir. 1980)

Facts

In 1978, petitioners Efran Caban, Raymond Velez, Pedro Rosada, and Felix Melendez, inmates at the Federal Correctional Institution at Danbury, Connecticut, filed suit with the U.S. District Court for the District of Connecticut seeking release from federal incarceration. The petitioners all were U.S. citizens who had been arrested in Mexico in November 1975, and all were sentenced to nine years' imprisonment by the Mexican courts for violating Mexico's drug laws. In December 1977, the inmates were transferred from Mexican prison to U.S. prisons pursuant to a treaty between the United States and Mexico allowing them to serve out their Mexican penal sentences in U.S. prisons. Under the terms of the treaty, a U.S. citizen convicted of a criminal offense in Mexico may transfer from Mexican custody to American custody provided that (1) the offense committed must be generally punishable in the United States and is neither a political nor immigration offense; (2) the transferring prisoner must be both a national of the United States and not a domiciliary of Mexico; (3) only prisoners with at least six months remaining on their sentence with no appeal or collateral attack pending in Mexican courts are eligible; and (4) Mexico, the United States, and the transferring prisoner must give consent to the change in custody. The treaty also provided that the transferring nation have exclusive jurisdiction over proceedings brought by a transferring offender to challenge, modify, or set aside convictions or sentences handed down by its courts to prevent prisoners from challenging their convictions in the country to which they were being transferred. The petitioners in this case argued that their consent to transfer had been unlawfully coerced and their continued detention by U.S. authorities based on the convictions in Mexico, violated their right to due process of law guaranteed by the Fifth Amendment. The District Court granted the inmates' petition for release from federal incarceration after finding that their consent to transfer had been unlawfully coerced by the brutal conditions in the Mexican prisons they were in and, emphasizing circumstances unique to the petitioners, concluded that they would have signed anything to get out of Mexico. Civiletti, the Attorney General of the United States, appealed to the Second Circuit Court of Appeals.

Issue

Whether prisoners voluntarily and intelligently agreed to forgo their right to challenge their Mexican convictions in the U.S. courts when they agreed to a change in custody from Mexico to the United States.

Holding by the Second Circuit Court of Appeals

The Second Circuit Court of Appeals held that prisoners are estopped from receiving release from incarceration because statutory procedures governing their transfer to U.S. custody are carefully structured to ensure each of them voluntarily and intelligently agreed to forgo due process rights to challenge the Mexican conviction in the U.S. courts.

Reason

While the Court of Appeals thought that the prisoners convicted in Mexico were denied fairness and decency and that the conditions in the Mexican prisons demonstrated insensitivity to their dignity as human beings, the court ruled that the prisoners lawfully gave up their due process rights when they agreed to transfer to U.S. prisons. The Second Circuit Court of Appeals found the prisoners' decision to transfer to be voluntary after finding that representatives from the U.S. Embassy visited the men while they were in Mexican prison, supplying them with a booklet explaining the terms of the treaty. In fact, they were told that under the treaty, "a United States citizen who transferred to American custody would not have any legal remedies available in the United States to challenge, modify, or set aside his conviction or sentence." While in the United States, the men met a federal public defender who explained their rights under the treaty before they appeared in a federal magistrate court where they agreed to forgo challenges to their Mexican convictions in the U.S. courts. Finally, the Court of Appeals noted that the shocking conditions in Mexican prisons motivated the prison transfer treaty, and that permitting the prisoners to violate treaty terms by attacking their Mexican convictions in American courts would jeopardize the interests of Americans currently incarcerated in Mexico and the other countries where the United States had approved of similar treaties.

Case Significance

In 1974, members of Congress and journalists in the United States began to investigate outrageous conditions that U.S. citizens were subjected to in Mexican jails and prisons. This led to the 1976 treaty between Mexico and the United States, allowing citizens of either country who had been convicted of criminal offenses to serve out their terms in their native land. The United States entered into similar treaties with several other countries. This case is one of the first to challenge the provisions of the treaties. In the case at hand, even though both the District Court and the Second Circuit Court of Appeals sympathized with the defendants, the Court of Appeals finally determined that granting the prisoners relief in U.S. courts in violation of the treaty would jeopardize the ability of current prisoners to transfer from any county with such a treaty back to the United States, and denied the prisoners relief.

Ruiz v. Estelle
503 F.Supp 1265 (1980)

Facts

This Section 1983 lawsuit began in 1972 when Texas prisoner David Ruiz alleged a violation of his constitutional rights against W. J. Estelle, Jr., the Director of the Texas Department of Corrections (TDC). In 1974, Ruiz's lawsuit was joined with seven other TDC inmates into a single class action, and additional members of the TDC were named as defendants. From 1974 through 1977, the parties engaged in discovery efforts, and from October 1978 to September 1979, a trial was held with the U.S. District Court for the Southern District of Texas to determine the merits of the case. The trial involved the testimony of 349 inmates and the admission of 1,565 exhibits into evidence. At the time of the trial, the plaintiffs became the class of all past, present, and future TDC inmates and the defendants became all the members of the TDC. A "Totality of

Conditions of Confinement" case, the plaintiffs alleged that the conditions of confinement in the TDC, which included overcrowding, security and supervision problems, an inadequate health care system, discipline procedure problems, insufficient access to the courts, and other general issues, amounted to cruel and unusual punishment prohibited by the Eighth and Fourteenth Amendments of the U.S. Constitution. The District Court first found that overcrowding in the TDC had reached crisis proportions and was at the root of most of the other violations. More than 1,000 inmates were sleeping on the floors, and inmates often slept with the knowledge that they could be attacked at any time. They were also unduly exposed to disease and infection from others. In sum, the District Court found overcrowding to be so bad in the TDC that it caused severe psychological harm and physical discomfort amounting to cruel and unusual punishment in violation of the Eighth and Fourteenth Amendments. The District Court also found that the TDC was in violation of the Eighth Amendment because its staff could not ensure the personal safety of inmates due to severe inadequacies, which included understaffing, a lack of training, and the use of armed inmate-guards (building tenders), which often resulted in the brutal treatment of inmates. Furthermore, the District Court found the health care system so inadequate that inmates, especially those with psychiatric problems and the disabled, suffered without penological purpose. The District Court also determined that disciplinary procedures in the TDC lacked ample due process procedures, that conditions in both administrative and disciplinary segregation were constitutionally deficient, that inmates did not have reasonable access to the courts, and that other conditions such as fire safety, sanitation, work safety, and hygiene were below constitutional standards because they exposed inmates to undue risks. In all, the court concluded that the "totality of conditions of confinement rendered the TDC unconstitutional" and authorized that a "Special Master" be appointed to oversee operations at the TDC to ensure that remedies would be formulated so that prison conditions would be brought into compliance with constitutional standards.

Issue

Whether conditions in the TDC were so severe that they violated the Texas prisoners' Eighth and Fourteenth Amendment rights to be free from cruel and unusual punishment.

Holding by the U.S. District Court

The District Court ordered that TDC reduce the inmate population at each unit, increase security and support staff, furnish adequate medical and mental health care, and bring living and working environments into compliance with state health and safety standards. The court further required that TDC abate staff brutality, the use of building tenders, abuse of the disciplinary process, and further violations of the inmates' rights to access to the courts.

Reason

By the time this case was decided, the federal courts had ruled on several "totality of conditions of confinement" cases in Alabama, Georgia, Louisiana, and Mississippi. Referring to these cases, the Texas District Court determined that overcrowding itself could cause prison conditions to fall below the Eighth Amendment standards when they resulted in cruel and unusual punishment or punishment without penological purpose. Referring to past conditions of confinement cases, the District Court also determined that deficiencies in ensuring inmates' personal safety, nutrition, health, and sanitation alone or in conjunction with one another also cause a prison system to fall below constitutional standards. Since the U.S. Supreme Court ruled on the medical conditions of confinement cases in *Estelle v. Gamble*, the District Court relied on it to determine that the medical system at the TDC denied inmates their constitutional rights to adequate medical treatment in a prison setting. A commononality between the federal totality of conditions of confinement cases and the Supreme Court's ruling in *Estelle* was that because prisoners had to rely on the prison system to meet basic human needs, such as providing adequate living space, personal protection, nutrition, health care, and sanitation, the system had a constitutional duty to ensure that those needs were in accord with minimal standards of decency. Indecent prison conditions were those that caused the inmate to suffer as a result of unmet basic human needs, and as such, amounted to cruel and unusual punishment or punishment without penological purpose. Ruling on other matters, the District Court utilized most of the U.S. Supreme Court cases decided by the time of trial to make rulings on the discipline procedure in the TDC and other relevant issues. In all, this case is considered the most important federal court ruling to date in determining that conditions in the TDC were unconstitutional.

Case Significance

This case is important for several reasons. First, the District Court ruled on the totality of confinement conditions that went largely ignored prior to this time. Essentially, the court ruled that inmates were subjected to and exposed to conditions that ran counter to the Eighth and Fourteenth Amendment prohibitions against cruel and unusual punishment. More particularly, the court found that TDC prisons: (1) were overcrowded; (2) had security and supervision problems, which often meant more inmates were subjected to violence, in many cases by "elite inmates" or building tenders; (3) had discipline procedure problems; (4) offered insufficient access to the courts; and (5) suffered from other problems that do not mark the progress of a humane and progressive society. The court reasoned that because prisoners were in the custody of the TDC, the state violated the Constitution by treating inmates as less than humane. This case is a clear victory for inmate rights, in general, and for the total conditions of confinement in particular. The case also signals that the judiciary moved to intervene and encroach in the area of corrections by appointing a special master to ensure that the TDC would comply and operate its prisons in a constitutionally correct manner.

Sandin v. Conner
515 U.S. 472 (1995)

Facts

DeMont Conner was a Hawaii state prisoner serving thirty years to life for murder, kidnapping, robbery, and burglary at the Halawa Correctional Facility, a maximum security prison in central Oahu. In August 1987, he violated prison rules by directing foul and abusive language at a correctional officer after he was subjected to a strip search that included inspection of the rectal area. Eleven days later, Conner received notice that he had been charged with disciplinary infractions and was scheduled to appear before the prison disciplinary committee for a hearing on August 28. After refusing to allow Conner to call witnesses on his behalf—because the witnesses were unavailable due to their transfer within the Halawa Correctional Center to the medium security module, and the fact that the prison was short-staffed—the prison disciplinary committee found Conner guilty of misconduct and sentenced him to thirty days in solitary confinement in a special holding unit. Conner sought administrative review of the committee's decision within fourteen days after receiving the sentence. Nine months later, the Deputy Administrator found the misconduct charge unsupported and expunged Conner's record. However, before the Deputy Administrator decided on the appeal, Conner had filed suit with the U.S. District Court for the District of Hawaii claiming that Hawaiian prison officials deprived him of his Fourteenth Amendment procedural due process rights in connection with the disciplinary hearing. He sought injunctive relief, declaratory relief, and damages. The District Court granted summary judgment for the prison officials. The Ninth Circuit Court of Appeals reversed, finding that Conner had a liberty interest to be free from disciplinary segregation and had not received all of his due process rights at the disciplinary hearing. The state petitioned the case to the U.S. Supreme Court, and it granted certiorari.

Issue

Whether Hawaii state prisoners had a liberty interest to be free from disciplinary segregation providing them with Fourteenth Amendment due process rights at disciplinary hearings to decide whether they should be placed in solitary confinement.

U.S. Supreme Court Holding

The U.S. Supreme Court reversed the Ninth Circuit Court of Appeals, holding that neither the Hawaii prison regulation in question nor the Due Process Clause of the Fourteenth Amendment afforded Conner a protected liberty interest that would entitle him to the procedural protection established in *Wolff v. McDonnell*.

Reason

In this case, the Ninth Circuit Court of Appeals looked to the language of Hawaii's prison regulations, finding that they created a liberty interest for prisoners to remain free from disciplinary segregation because the regulation mandated that the disciplinary committee impose disciplinary segregation only on a substantial finding of evidence against the accused, limiting the discretion of prison officials in making such decisions. The Court of Appeals holding was consistent with the U.S. Supreme Court's leading Fourteenth Amendment case in this area, *Hewitt v. Helms*, where the Court found that mandatory state prison regulations that limited state officials' discretion before they could discipline prisoners created a liberty interest for the prisoners that was protected by the Due Process Clause. The U.S. Supreme Court, however, found fault with its ruling in *Hewitt* and reversed the Court of Appeals, announcing that it was reverting to decisions made in *Wolff v. McDonnell* and *Meachum v. Fano* to determine if state regulations create liberty interests for prisoners that are protected by the Fourteenth Amendment. The U.S. Supreme Court thought that the *Hewitt* decision was creating disincentives for states to codify prison management procedure to provide the uniform treatment of prisoners and that it was leading to the involvement of the federal courts in the day-to-day management of the prisons, thus wasting valuable court resources. In reversing the Ninth Circuit Court of Appeals, the U.S. Supreme Court abandoned the practice of looking to the language of the regulations at stake to determine if they created a liberty interest for prisoners. It reinstated its *Wolff* and *Meachum* policy of examining whether the punishment or restraint imposed by prison officials resulted in unexpected situations for prisoners, such as a transfer to a mental hospital, or whether they added length to prison sentences, such as loss of good time, to determine if the (prisoner) punishment created a liberty interest protected by the Due Process Clause. In the present case, the Supreme Court found that placing Hawaii prisoners in disciplinary segregation did not cause a longer sentence in such an unexpected manner as to invoke due process protections.

Case Significance

This case is important for several reasons. First, it demonstrates the U.S. Supreme Court's attempt to limit the number of claims that prisoners file in the federal court system. Second, the Court departs from its ruling in *Hewitt* (decided in 1983) where it held that mandatory state prison regulations that limit state officials' discretion before they can discipline prisoners created a liberty interest for prisoners. If the Court had followed *Hewitt*, this case would have favored Conner. Rather, the Court retreated from its ruling in *Hewitt*, and cited *Wolff v. McDonnell* and *Meachum v. Fano*, where it favored examining whether punishment imposed on the prisoner by the prison official resulted in unexpected or adverse situations for prisoners. Essentially, this case created a standard that required a prisoner to demonstrate that authorities had imposed an atypical hardship rather than carrying out daily operations of prisons. The Court reasoned that being placed in solitary confinement did not meet the new standard.

Saxbe v. Washington Post

417 U.S. 843 (1974)

Facts

The Washington Post and one of its reporters brought suit in the U.S. District Court for the District of Columbia challenging the constitutionality of 4b(6) of

Policy Statement 12201A of Federal Bureau of Prisons regulations prohibiting interviews between journalists and individually designated prisoners of the federal prisons. The Federal Bureau of Prisons supported their ban on interviews between the press and specific individual prisoners based on the "big wheel" theory, where prison officials argued that special attention by the press greatly enhanced the status of such inmates among other inmates and induced such inmates to become behavior problems by continually challenging prison rules. The District Court ruled that the prison regulation violated the prisoners' First Amendment rights. The case was appealed to the Court of Appeals for the District of Columbia Circuit, and it reversed the decision of the District Court. The case was petitioned to the U.S. Supreme Court, and it granted certiorari.

Issue

Whether a federal prison policy prohibiting newspaper interviews of individually designated inmates of federal prisons abridges the First Amendment's freedom of the press.

U.S. Supreme Court Holding

The Supreme Court reversed the Court of Appeals for the District of Columbia Circuit, holding that the prison regulation does not violate First Amendment freedom of the press rights of the journalists because it does not deny newsmen access to prisoners that is afforded to the general public. The case was remanded back to the District Court.

Reason

The U.S. Supreme Court decided *Saxbe* and *Pell v. Procunier* on the same day and in *Saxbe*, the Court commented that the cases were constitutionally indistinguishable. In both cases, the Court ruled that journalists had no constitutional rights to access prisons that went beyond those of the general public. Moreover, the Court noticed that Policy Statement 12201A provided members of the press substantial access to the federal prisons to observe and report prison conditions. Journalists were also given access to the prisons and to prison inmates that in many ways exceeded what is afforded members of the general public since the policy allowed them to tour the prisons and photograph any prison facility. Moreover, journalists could briefly interview any inmate they encountered. Journalists and inmates were allowed unlimited written correspondence with each other. Furthermore, the Court was aware that because of the high turnover in the prison population, it was clear that journalists could talk to newly released prisoners. The Supreme Court ruled that these avenues to access prisons and prisoners were viable approaches.

Case Significance

This case is important for several reasons. First, it does not extend to the press a greater First Amendment protection than that enjoyed by other citizens. It treats them equally, since members of the press are not permitted to demand personal interviews with any inmate they choose. However, the press can visit prisons, correspond with specific inmates, and communicate with an inmate's family members, friends, and clergy. These viable avenues of access allow the press to learn about prison conditions and inmate treatment in a way that is consistent with the level of First Amendment protection guaranteed to all Americans. It does not place prison officials at the mercy of the press's request for visitation. Second, this case is important because it helps prison officials curb levels of violence by ensuring that select prisoners will not attain the status of "celebrity" inmates. In this case, prison administrators reported that the experience of the California Department of Corrections was that a small number of inmates became "public figures" within the prison society after contact with journalists, which led to disciplinary problems that had the potential to engulf a large portion of the prison population. Thus, this decision helps protect a security interest because prohibiting the press from giving certain inmates media coverage will prevent these inmates from becoming "big wheels" in the prison population.

Smith v. Coughlin
748 F.2d 783 (1984)

Facts

Lemuel Smith appealed the ruling of the U.S. District Court for the Southern Division of New York upholding prison regulations that restricted his First Amendment freedoms. Smith was convicted of killing a correctional officer, was given the death sentence, and was awaiting his execution at a special Unit of Condemned Persons (UCP) at Green Haven Correctional Facility in New York. In the interests of avoiding prison disruption and to prevent contraband from being smuggled into the prison, Smith was allowed contact visits only with his priest, lawyer, and doctor. Furthermore, because prison officials did not think anything would deter him from future acts of violence, and due to his notoriety, could be a target of violence from other prisoners, Smith was not allowed to attend prison congregation church services. Smith was claiming a violation of his First, Fifth, Sixth, Eighth, and Fourteenth Amendment rights. More specifically, he argued that his confinement to the UCP and the many associated restrictions (1) deprived him of a liberty interest without due process; (2) subjected him to cruel and unusual punishment; (3) denied him equal protection of the laws; (4) denied him freedom of speech and religion; and (5) deprived him of access to court. He moved for a preliminary injunction. The case was appealed to the U.S. Second Circuit Court of Appeals.

Issue

Whether confinement to the UCP violates the prisoner's First, Fifth, Sixth, Eighth, and Fourteenth Amendment rights.

Holding by the U.S. Second Circuit Court of Appeals

The Second Circuit Court of Appeals affirmed the decision of the District Court, holding that restrictions on visits by nonlawyers in the employ of his attorney violated the appellant's constitutional rights and that the appellant's confinement and limitations imposed on him pursuant to state law are not otherwise unconstitutional. The case was remanded to allow an award for nominal damages.

Reason

In deciding this case, the Second Circuit Court of Appeals considered several issues. First, it considered the due process argument. The court reasoned that although Smith argued that his confinement to the UCP was made without a prior hearing and violated his Fifth Amendment right to due process, the court disagreed, finding the argument without merit stating that the Constitution does not create any protected liberty interest in a prisoner remaining in the general prison population. The court agreed that N.Y. Corrections Law Section 650 expressly mandated his confinement. Thus, there was no Fifth Amendment violation. Where the issue of the Eighth Amendment was argued claiming cruel and unusual punishment, the court disagreed with Smith when he alleged that the totality of his conditions of confinement violated his rights. The court reasoned that this argument was without merit because discomforts compelled by conditions of confinement do not constitute a violation of the Amendment. Moreover, the court stated that restraints on an inmate do not violate the Amendment unless they are "totally without penological justification," "grossly disproportionate," or "involve the unnecessary and wanton infliction of pain." The Second Circuit Court drew this conclusion after reviewing reports from the District Court that found that Smith's "physical and mental discomforts were minimized to the extent permitted by security requirements" and that "Smith was not suffering from any psychological damage as a result of the condition of his incarceration."

In Smith's equal protection argument under the Fourteenth Amendment, he claims that his incarceration was more onerous than those of other inmates convicted of murder and other crimes of violence. The Second Circuit Court reasoned that administrators, when making classifications, need only demonstrate a rational basis for their distinctions. The court saw where the appellees provided several reasons that demonstrated a rational basis for the appellant's treatment. In Smith's First Amendment claim of freedom of speech and free exercise of religion, he argued that limits on visitation rights restricted his freedom of speech, and the prison officials refused to allow him to congregate for religious services, depriving him of the right to freely exercise his religion. The court disagreed that the prison could not restrict these freedoms. Accordingly, the court stated that freedoms that are challenges to prison restrictions that are argued to inhibit First Amendment interests must be analyzed in terms of the legitimate policies and goals of the corrections system. The court also stated that courts should defer to the expertise of prison officials unless there is evidence showing that officials have exaggerated the need for their restrictions. In the present case, prison officials argued that to allow Smith to have contact visits with persons other than his priest, lawyer, and doctor would have (1) interfered with proper prison administration; (2) created security risks; and (3) increased the likelihood that contraband would have been introduced into prison. Where the claim of free exercise of religion is made, the court found that a compelling security interest justified the denial to participate in congregated religious services.

Smith had two Sixth Amendment claims: (1) UCP's conditions of incarceration would weaken his will to live over time, which would force him to surrender his right to appeal, and (2) The ban on visits by non-lawyers employed by his attorney denied him effective assistance of counsel. The Circuit Court agreed with the District Court's finding that Smith was denied effective counsel because he was not permitted to have paralegal personnel. The Circuit Court also argued that Smith should have been allowed to have an award of damages for this violation. Finally, the Second Circuit Court concluded that with the exception of the ban on paralegal visits, the confinement conditions at UCP were constitutional. The court affirmed and remanded the case back to the District Court to award nominal damages for the Sixth Amendment violation.

Case Significance

This case is important because it is consistent with many of the previous decisions that the U.S. Supreme Court has ruled. In this case, the Second Circuit Court of Appeals did not attempt to engage in judicial activism in its ruling; rather, it commented that its decision was based on the premise that prison officials, and not the federal courts, were to run prisons based on legitimate penological interests and their expertise, which dictates what prisons need to operate in a safe manner. The court also noted that the task of the court was to rule on whether prison regulations of prisoners on matters normally protected by the First Amendment and others were legitimately connected to security interests.

Smith v. Wade

461 U.S. 30 (1983)

Facts

Respondent Daniel Wade was an inmate at Algoa Reformatory, a unit of the Missouri Department of Corrections for youthful first offenders. In the summer of 1976, Wade placed himself in Algoa's protective custody unit because of attacks against him by other inmates. Because of disciplinary violations while in protective custody, Wade was given a short term in punitive segregation and then transferred to administrative segregation. Petitioner William H. Smith was a guard who worked in Algoa's administrative segregation unit. On Wade's first night in administrative segregation, he was assigned a cell with another inmate. Later that night, when Smith came on duty, Smith placed a third inmate in Wade's cell. That night Wade's cellmates harassed, beat, and sexually assaulted him. As a result of the attacks, Wade brought a Section 1983 suit to the U.S. District Court for the Western District of Missouri against Smith and four other correctional officials, alleging that his Eighth Amendment rights had been violated. Wade testified that the third prisoner who had been added to his cell had been placed in administrative segregation for fighting, and Smith made no effort to find the prisoner another cell when in fact there was another in the same unit with only one inmate. Wade asserted that Smith should have known that an assault against him was likely given the circumstances. At the trial, the District Court judge instructed the jury that a respondent could recover only if the petitioner was guilty of "gross negligence" or "egregious failure to protect" the respondent. The judge also charged the jury that it could award punitive damages in addition to the compensatory damages if it found the conduct of one of the defendants to be a reckless or callous disregard of, or indifference to, the rights and safety of others. The jury found Smith liable and awarded Wade $25,000 in compensatory damages and $5,000 in punitive damages. The Court of Appeals for the Eighth Circuit affirmed the District Court's decision, and Smith appealed only the punitive damage award to the U.S. Supreme Court. The Court granted certiorari.

Issue

Whether the District Court for the Western district of Missouri applied the correct legal standard in instructing the jury it might award punitive damages under Section 1983.

U.S. Supreme Court Holding

The U.S. Supreme Court affirmed the judgment of the Eighth Circuit Court of Appeals, holding that a jury may be permitted to assess punitive damages in a Section 1983 lawsuit when the defendant's conduct is shown to be motivated by evil motive or intent, or when it involves reckless or callous indifference to the federally protected rights of others. The Court also held that this threshold applies when the underlying standard of liability for compensatory damages is based on recklessness.

Reason

In the current case, Smith contended that punitive damages could not be awarded in a Section 1983 lawsuit unless actual intent to injure was shown and that the jury should have been instructed that there must be a finding of "ill will, spite, or intent to injure" before punitive damages could be awarded. The Court reasoned that punitive damages are awarded to punish transgressors for outrageous conduct and to deter the transgressors and others from similar conduct in the future, and that society has an interest in deterring and punishing all intentional and reckless invasions of the rights of others. The Court then found that a jury could award punitive damages if the defendant acted with ill will, spite, or intent to injure or with reckless or callous indifference to the rights of others, and the Court affirmed the Eighth Circuit Court of Appeals ruling.

Case Significance

This case is important for several reasons. First, the U.S. Supreme Court upholds an inmate's right to be free from cruel and unusual punishment that is perpetuated by inmates and correctional guards, by holding that the guard at Algoa Reformatory had an affirmative duty to protect the inmate from violent attacks, especially in areas of a prison that had previously experienced a violent assault that resulted in one death. Even if there was no malice or intent on the part of the officer, he should have known that the potential for harm or violence against Wade existed. Second, this case is important because it shows that despite having qualified immunity, a correctional official can still be held liable for compensatory and punitive damages as a result of an Eighth Amendment violation. Third, the case should send a clear message to prison officials that they must do a better job of protecting inmates and consider the plight of prisoners. If officials are found to be reckless or show callous indifference to a federally protected right, they could be sued, and punitive damages will attach, especially if the case is brought under a Section 1983 claim. This case signals that the Eighth Amendment right against being subjected to cruel and unusual punishment applies in prison and not only to conditions of confinement, but also to prison safety.

Stone v. Powell
428 U.S. 465 (1976)

Facts

Respondent Lloyd Powell was convicted of homicide in a California state court in 1968, and a California Court of Appeals affirmed his conviction. Respondent David Rice was convicted of murder in a Nebraska state court in 1971, and the Nebraska Supreme Court affirmed his conviction. In separate proceedings, both sought federal habeas corpus relief on the grounds that evidence was introduced at their state trials in violation of their Fourth Amendment protection against unreasonable search and seizure. In each case, the Fourth Amendment issues were presented to the state courts. Powell submitted a petition for federal habeas corpus contending that testimonial evidence should have been excluded from introduction at his trial because it violated his Fourth Amendment rights. However, the District Court disagreed, stating that if any error occurred during the trial in admitting the testimony, it constituted harmless error beyond a reasonable doubt. The Ninth Circuit Court of Appeals reversed, citing the state ordinance was unconstitutional and the arrest was illegal and the admission of evidence was not harmless error. In the matter of Rice, before convicting him of murder, the trial court denied his motion to suppress evidence police obtained from a warrant to search his home. The evidence was in plain view. On appeal, the Supreme Court of Nebraska affirmed the conviction, holding that the search of Rice's home was valid. Rice filed an appeal for habeas corpus in the U.S. District Court for Nebraska contending his incarceration was illegal because the evidence used to convict him was derived from an unlawful search of his home. The District Court concluded that the search was invalid. The Court of Appeals for the Eighth Circuit affirmed. In the matter of Powell, he claimed he was convicted of murder on the basis of evidence seized pursuant to a search warrant that he claimed was invalid. Because of this, he contended the evidence should have been suppressed. The trial court denied the motion of suppression. Powell filed a habeas corpus petition in federal District Court. The court concluded the warrant was invalid and rejected the state's argument that even if the warrant was invalid, probable cause justified the search. The Ninth Circuit Court of Appeals reversed, citing the ordinance as unconstitutionally vague. Petitioners Stone and Wolf, the wardens of the respective state prisons where the defendants were incarcerated, petitioned the U.S. Supreme Court for a review of the scope of federal habeas corpus petitions, raising the question concerning the scope and the role of the exclusionary rule on collateral review of cases involving Fourth Amendment claims.

Issue

Whether a federal court, in ruling on a petition for habeas corpus filed by a state prisoner, should consider a claim that evidence obtained by an unconstitutional search or seizure was introduced at the trial, when he has previously been afforded an opportunity for full and fair litigation of his claim in the state court.

U.S. Supreme Court Holding

The U.S. Supreme Court reversed the judgment of both Courts of Appeals, holding that where the state has provided a full opportunity for full and fair review of a Fourth Amendment claim in state court, a prisoner may not be granted federal habeas corpus review on the grounds that evidence obtained in an unconstitutional search or seizure was introduced at his or her state trial.

Reason

Historically, the federal judiciary believed it was inappropriate to review a state search and seizure claim. The U.S. Supreme Court changed this policy with its decision in *Kauffman v. United States* (394 U.S. 217, 1969). In *Kauffman*, the Court commented that federal habeas corpus review was available for state prisoners alleging that unconstitutional evidence was introduced against them at trial. In this case, the Court noted that since *Kauffman*, state courts were becoming more experienced in interpreting Fourth Amendment claims, which had been made available to state departments only since 1961, when the Court incorporated the Fourth Amendment to apply to the states with its decision in *Mapp v. Ohio* (367 U.S. 643, 1961). The Court also commented that state judges were just as competent to rule on Fourth Amendment issues as federal judges, and that allowing habeas corpus review would inevitably lead to the uneven application of the Fourth Amendment in the state courts. Thus, in this case, the Court reverted back to the traditional rule, making state unconstitutional search and seizure claims unavailable for federal habeas corpus review.

Case Significance

This case is important because it reveals that the U.S. Supreme Court is unwilling to allow prisoners to have their cases retried or to be released on a technicality. In this case, the Court is clear when it states that when issues of the Fourth Amendment are provided a full opportunity to be addressed in a state court or trial, the Constitution does not provide prisoners a right to federal habeas corpus to have the matter reexamined. Rather, the Exclusionary Rule, though judge-made, must be relied on and used as the mechanism to safeguard and protect against unreasonable searches and seizures that violate the Fourth Amendment. The writ of habeas corpus is a mechanism that requires the wardens to bring those who are illegally detained before the court and to show just cause as to why they are imprisoned. However, both defendants in this case were offered a trial, and motions were made to suppress either physical or testimonial evidence to gain a criminal conviction. The motions were denied by the hearing court, and the prisoners were not automatically entitled to a federal habeas corpus. The petition does not and should not represent a second opportunity to have one's case heard. The case is also important because it represents the Court's attempt to restrict federal habeas corpus review. This is used to reduce the flow of such cases at the federal level.

Superintendent v. Hill

472 U.S. 445 (1985)

Facts

In May 1982, Sergeant Maguire, who worked at a state prison in Walpole, Massachusetts, opened the door to a walkway and found an inmate named

Stephens bleeding from the mouth and suffering from a swollen eye. Dirt was strewn about the walkway, indicating that a struggle had taken place. Maguire saw inmates Gerald Hill, Joseph Crawford, and one other inmate jogging away together down the walkway. He concluded that the three inmates assaulted Stephens. Hill and Crawford each received disciplinary reports charging them with assault of another inmate. At separate hearings, the only evidence used against them was Maguire's testimony and a written report. Hill and Crawford maintained their innocence, and Stephens testified that Hill and Crawford did not cause his injuries. The prison disciplinary board found the inmates guilty of assaulting another inmate and revoked their good time credit, which cost them 100 days and confinement in isolation for 15 days. After unsuccessfully appealing to the prison superintendent, Hill and Crawford filed suit in a Massachusetts Superior Court alleging that the disciplinary committee's action violated their Fourteenth Amendment due process rights because there was no evidence to support the board's decision. The Superior Court granted summary judgment for Hill and Crawford, holding that the disciplinary committee's finding of guilt rested on no evidence constitutionally adequate to support its findings, and ordered the loss of good time to be restored. The Massachusetts Supreme Judicial Court affirmed. The Massachusetts Attorney General filed a petition for a writ of certiorari, and the U.S. Supreme Court granted review.

Issue

Whether revocation of an inmate's good time credits violates the Due Process Clause of the Fourteenth Amendment if the decision of the prison disciplinary board is not supported by a certain amount of evidence in the record.

U.S. Supreme Court Holding

The U.S. Supreme Court reversed and remanded the case, holding that the revocation of good time does not comport with the minimal constitutional requirements for due process unless the findings of the prison disciplinary board are supported by some evidence in the record. It held that the evidence before the disciplinary board in this case was sufficient to meet the requirements imposed by the Due Process Clause of the Fourteenth Amendment.

Reason

In *Wolff v. McDonnell*, the Supreme Court handed down the minimum constitutional due process requirements for prison disciplinary hearings involving the loss of good time. However, the Court in *Wolff* never specified the amount of evidence necessary to support the fact finders' decision, whether it should be "some evidence" or the stricter test of "substantial evidence." Recognizing that the loss of good time credits represented an important liberty interest for inmates, the Court weighed the prisoners' liberty interests against the security needs of prison officials and their need to maintain a set of rules to ensure the safety of prisoners. The Court thought that a stringent evidence requirement at disciplinary hearings would impose burdensome administrative requirements that would be susceptible to manipulation and jeopardize the disciplinary process as a means of rehabilitation. Considering the interests of both prisoners and officials, the Court decided that the evidence standard for prison disciplinary decisions involving the loss of good time is that the decisions must be supported by any evidence, even if minimal, to prevent arbitrary decision making and still maintain prison discipline. Setting the evidence standard low, the Court then decided that Massachusetts prison officials met that standard in the case at hand and reversed the decision of the Massachusetts Supreme Judicial Court. In the current case, the Court found nothing in the Constitution that requires evidence that logically precluded any conclusion other than that reached by the disciplinary board. It also highlighted that due process in this case requires only that there be some evidence to support this finding made in the hearing, which relied on the testimony and written report of Maguire.

Case Significance

This case is significant for several reasons. First, it supports the Court's decision in *Wolff*, the leading case regarding due process requirements of prison disciplinary hearings by setting an evidence standard for a disciplinary committee's decisions involving the loss of a prisoner's good time. Second, it is important because in the prison culture of no snitching, it is unlikely that inmates either involved or witnesses to crimes or infractions will come forward to provide evidence against a fellow inmates. Because of this, disciplinary hearing boards must often rely solely on testimony that comes from the correctional guard.

Talley v. Stephens
247 F. Supp. 683 (1965)

Facts

Arkansas State Penitentiary prisoners Warren Harsh, Vernon Sloan, and Winston Talley brought suit in equity to the U.S. District Court for the East-

ern District of Arkansas against Dan Stephens, Superintendent of that institution, for restraining the respondents from continuing certain prison practices that petitioners claimed were in violation of their Fourteenth Amendment
rights. They claimed that they had been unconstitutionally subjected to cruel
and unusual punishment by prison officials and other inmates, and have been
unconstitutionally denied access to the courts to secure redress of their grievances. Harsh and Sloan claimed they had been forced to perform heavy manual labor on the penitentiary farm beyond what they were capable of
performing. Harsh and Sloan also claimed they had been denied needed medical assistance and that attendance at "sick calls" had been unreasonably restricted.
Prisoner Talley claimed that prison staff and inmate "trustee guards" had been
whipping him with a leather strap five feet in length, four inches wide, and a
quarter of an inch thick attached to a wooden shaft about six inches long, for
violations of prison rules and failure to work hard, and that this amounts to
cruel and unusual punishment.

Issue

Whether forcing prisoners to perform heavy manual labor beyond their
strength, denying prisoners needed medical assistances, restricting prisoner attendance at sick calls, denying prisoners access to court, and punishing the prisoners by whipping them with a strap constitutes cruel and unusual punishment
in violation of the Eighth and Fourteenth Amendments to the U.S. Constitution.

Holding by the U.S. District Court

It is cruel and unusual punishment for prison officials to (1) knowingly compel prisoners to perform physical labor beyond their strength, which constitutes
a danger to their lives or health or is unduly painful; (2) withhold needed medical assistance or restrict attendance at sick calls; and (3) impose any punishments on prisoners, including whipping with a strap, without reference to
recognizable standards where a prisoner will know what caused him to be whipped
or punished and how much punishment a given conduct will produce.

Reason

The District Court argued that while persons convicted of crimes lose many
of the rights and privileges enjoyed by law-abiding citizens, they do not lose all
of their civil rights, and due process and equal protection of the Fourteenth
Amendment follow them into the prison and protect them from unconstitutional administrative action. The court further stated that (1) Prison authorities
are not permitted to inflict cruel and unusual punishments for violations of

prison rules; (2) They may not discriminate against a prisoner or class of prisoners; and (3) They may not deny a prisoner reasonable access to the courts to test the validity of his confinement or secure judicial protection of his constitutional rights. More specifically, in this case, the court addressed the first claim by petitioners Harsh and Sloan, where they claimed they were required to do field work in excess of their physical capabilities. The court held that both men were working under serious physical handicaps and assigned work that they were unable to do. The court provided injunctive relief, and the respondents agreed. The court reasoned that via physical labor, the inmates were being subjected to cruel and unusual punishment in violation of the Eighth Amendment.

The District Court also examined the issue of the infliction of corporal punishment when petitioners alleged to have received whippings with a leather strap five feet in length. In this case, the court was unwilling to say that the Constitution forbids the use of corporal punishment. However, the court indicated that this punishment must not be excessive. It must be inflicted as dispassionately as possible and by reasonable people. Moreover, corporal punishment must be applied in reference to recognizable standards whereby a prisoner knows what conduct will cause him to receive a whipping and how much punishment will be given from the conduct. The court held that no standards existed with respect to corporal punishment at the Arkansas Penitentiary. The court was also troubled by the fact that a prisoner could be whipped if he did not produce "sufficient work." This subjective judgment was left to the Assistant Warden and elite inmate guards.

The District Court also considered the issue of the prisoners' complaint about being denied the right to access the courts. In this case, the court discovered that Talley experienced reprisal when he provided testimony in his complaints. Despite this, the court recognized the importance of giving "wide latitude and discretion to the judgment" of prison officials on matters involving running prisons without being bound to do so by a higher court. The judge in this case had "no difficulty" finding that it was cruel and unusual punishment for officials to compel prisoners to perform physical labor that is beyond their strength, constitutes a danger to their lives or health, or is unduly painful. The judge gave no reason for his finding other than that the prisoners who made the complaint, Harsh and Sloan, were judged by a prison physician as being in poor physical condition. Harsh and Sloan were assigned lighter duties at the prison farm. The judge gave no reason for finding that denying prisoners needed medical assistance or restricting their attendance at sick calls also constituted cruel and unusual punishment.

Regarding Talley's whipping claim, the judge refused to consider whipping in itself as cruel and unusual punishment, noting that the Arkansas criminal code did not ban the punishment of whipping. However, the judge found that prison officials had no written rules delegating why prisoners would receive whippings or any other punishment, and officials whipped and punished prisoners at whim. Also, Arkansas had no rules regarding how punishment was to be administered for particular rule infractions. The judge found that the Arkansas practices were cruel and unusual punishment, because they were administered without safeguards against "excessive" or "passionate" punishments, and the prisoners had no way of ascertaining what kind of conduct produced punishment, and in what amounts. The judge enjoined Arkansas prison officials from punishing prisoners until they developed a "punishment schedule" recognizable by the prisoners.

Case Significance

This case is significant for several reasons. First, it is the first Eighth Amendment cruel and unusual punishment prisoner rights case, so the U.S. District Court was breaking new ground in this case. Second, at the time of the case (1965), prison conditions were far worse in Southern prisons than in Northern prisons, and this case preceded a series of prisoner rights cases that resulted in the federal courts declaring all the Southern states' prison systems unconstitutional. Third, though the ruling was not applicable to the entire U.S. penal system or even the circuit that included the Arkansas prison system, since the District Court ruled on the matter, the case was very instructive in highlighting the conditions under which many prison inmates were confined. In the 1960s, prior to the time the federal court system began to entertain inmate litigation, penal administrators routinely ruled places of confinement as they saw fit, with total disregard for issues of cruel and unusual punishment or denying inmates' access to court. This case was the first where the courts became involved in prison affairs.

Theriault v. Carlson
353 F. Supp 1061(1973)

Facts

While serving a prison sentence in the U.S. Penitentiary in Atlanta, Harry W. Theriault, a convicted thief and self-proclaimed escapee, created a new faith or church known as the Church of the New Song (CONS). Declaring as its source certain obscure passages from the Book of Revelations in the New Testament, CONS concerned itself with a supreme spirit known as Eclat and espoused, in general, a doctrine of brotherhood and love. When he was thwarted in his attempts to arrange commercial services for his church, Theriault filed an action seeking equal religious rights for the members of CONS. The original petition was co-signed by 165 inmates at the Atlanta federal penitentiary. At court, the evidence revealed that Theriault's idea for a new religion began as a joke, but, after some reflection, his inspiration became real. A prison official from the federal penitentiary in Marion, Illinois, to which Theriault was transferred as soon as the class action was filed, admitted on the stand that the religious activities were serious. Theriault had received a "degree" from a mail-order house in California. From the beginning, prison officials took a dim view of Theriault and his followers, branding his religion as fake because it was supported by a group of the most hardened criminals in federal custody. They refused to allow him to conduct religious services in the prison solely because his religion was not recognized. When he asked for equal time given to other religions, he was placed in punitive segregation. Theriault filed a class action suit in the U.S. District Court for the Northern District of Georgia, Atlanta Division, claiming that federal prison authorities violated his First Amendment right to religious freedom when he was denied the right to hold religious services.

Issue

Whether Theriault and his followers established a legitimate church in CONS that required federal prison authorities to recognize their free exercise rights to practice religion.

Holding by the U.S. District Court

The District Court held that under the Establishment Clause of the First Amendment, CONS had to be recognized as a legitimate religion, requiring federal authorities to allow its followers to freely exercise their right to practice religion without punishment.

Reason

The District Court reasoned that even though Theriault and his followers could still be playing a game and perpetrating a fraud on prison authorities, it could not declare CONS unconstitutional, because such a ruling would violate government neutrality toward religion and involve the government in favoring the worth of one religion over another in violation of the First

Amendment's Establishment Clause. After finding that CONS was an established religion, the District Court then reasoned that the Free Exercise Clause of the First Amendment required prison authorities to grant its followers similar religious privileges as those of more conventional faiths.

Case Significance

The case is important for several reasons. First, the District Court recognized that the First Amendment protects individuals' (including prisoners') rights to religious freedom and to worship in a manner consistent with their beliefs. Moreover, the case is anchored in the free exercise of one's religion and the Establishment Clause. Essentially, the court ruled that prison officials had to recognize CONS as a legitimate religion and allow followers to freely exercise their fundamental right to worship to the same extent as that afforded other inmates who may believe in more traditional religions. Second, in this case, the District Court made its establishment clause ruling by importing broad First Amendment law principles from general rulings that required government neutrality toward the recognition of a religion. Prison officials had argued that the establishment of prison religions should be treated similarly to the way it is treated in the military, which is considered an exception to general First Amendment law rulings, and allows for denying servicemen their right to worship at places of their choice, but substitutes neutral religious services to allow them their free exercise rights to practice religion. Third, the case is a victory for prisoners, not simply members of CONS, because it requires prison authorities to recognize that newly created religions with a following legally allow them to freely practice their beliefs to the extent as other conventional religions. However, because this case was decided by a District Court, its ruling would not be regionally or nationally followed.

Theriault v. Silber

391 F. Supp 578 (1978)

Facts

Federal prison officials appealed Theriault's victory in *Theriault v. Carlson* with the federal District Court in Atlanta that established the Church of the New Song (CONS) as a legitimate religion to the Fifth Circuit Court of Appeals.

The cause before the court was for a full evidentiary hearing concerning the petitioner's claims that the defendants had punished him because of his religious views and activities, that the prison chaplains at the Federal Corrections Institute at La Tuna, Texas, had illegally reported on his religious activities, and that they have denied him the free exercise of his religion. The court received into evidence without objection, the entire multivolume transcript of the proceedings in the U.S. District Court for the Northern District of Georgia concerning the same issues and controversies and involving the same parties. The Fifth Circuit Court of Appeals also received into evidence and considered, where pertinent and for whatever value they may prove, those portions of the record and exhibits in the petitioner's criminal trial that concerned his religious views as collectivized and expressed by his faith in CONS.

Issue

Whether the beliefs professed by petitioners are sincerely held and whether they are, in their own way or manner, religious.

Holding by the District Court

The U.S. District Court for the Western District of Texas vacated and remanded the case, holding that CONS appeared not to be a religion, but a masquerade designed to obtain First Amendment protection for acts that otherwise would be unlawful and disallowed by prison authorities. Since it was determined that it was not a religion, its members were not entitled to First Amendment protection.

Reason

In this case, the Fifth Circuit Court of Appeals discovered that instead of urging its followers to accept any particular theology or philosophy of life, CONS encouraged them to have a relatively nonstructured, free-form, do-as-you-please philosophy, with the sole purpose of causing or encouraging disruptive behavior that created disciplinary problems in prison. In fact, the Fifth Circuit Court of Appeals found that the church existed to cause disruption to penal authority. For example, the "church" requested that the prison accept the need of the religion to provide inmates with a steak and wine feast. Prison officials also reported that CONS used many of its services to hold "gripe sessions" designed to gain advantage over other inmates who were not members of CONS. The officials reported that the services completely lacked religious content. The Circuit Court also found that the members of CONS created their organization for the purpose of improving the position of their members by attempting to gain leverage over prison administrators. Moreover, the court stated that because of the political and nonreligious nature of the doctrine of CONS developed by its founder over the past three years, along with the violent and vicious tone of its services at the Atlanta Penitentiary, the court believed that the "church" had failed the legitimacy test and was not a religion in the scope of the First Amendment.

Case Significance

This case is significant for several reasons. First, this case overturns the decisions made in *Theriault I* where the District Court found CONS to be a legitimate religion. However, three years later on appeal by the Fifth Circuit Court, CONS was held as not a legitimate religion but a group that was a masquerade designed to falsely obtain First Amendment protection for acts that otherwise would be unlawful and disallowed by prison authorities. Second, the case demonstrates the care used by the Fifth Circuit Court in its evidentiary hearing to determine if CONS was a legitimate religion entitled to the same rights as the more traditionally recognized religions. This case shows that the federal court officially broke away from its policy of maintaining government neutrality in referring to judge the merits of a religion for Establishment Clause cases and establishes guidelines for judging whether prisoner-led religions are legitimate. Third, the case suggests that just because inmates proclaim a practice as a religion, it does not always meet muster, especially where there are competing interests. For example, providing or accommodating for a religion that requires steak and wine could create an undue financial burden on prisons, especially if every religious group in prison argues that they want the same accommodation, or they are being denied the First Amendment right to the free exercise of their faith or an equal protection violation.

Thongvanh v. Thalacker
17 F.3d 256 (1994)

Facts

Iowa prison officials appealed the U.S. District Court for the Northern District of Iowa's ruling that prison regulations forbidding Thongvanh, a Laotian prisoner at Iowa Men's Reformatory (IMR), to correspond by mail in his native language violated his First Amendment rights to free speech. Prior to the District Court's decision, prison officials allowed Thongvanh to correspond by mail in Laotian with his parents and grandparents because they spoke no English. Though he spoke English poorly, Thongvanh was forced to correspond with all others by mail in English. Prison officials argued that, because security interests required the monitoring of prison mail and the fact that they had no Laotian interpreters on their staff, they could not monitor most of Thongvanh's mail if he was allowed to use his native language. At the same time, Iowa prison officials denied Thongvanh the right to correspond with others in his native language. However, officials at IMR allowed Spanish-speaking prisoners and a German-speaking prisoner the right to correspond by mail with anyone in their native language, because they had bilingual staff members who monitored such mail. Prison officials at IMR filed a motion for judgment as a matter of law, which the District Court denied.

Issue

Whether the prison officials' ban on allowing Thongvanh to correspond in Laotian by mail with all persons other than his parents and grandparents violates Thongvanh's First and Fourteenth Amendment rights to free speech and equal protection.

Holding by the Eighth Circuit Court of Appeals

The Eighth Circuit Court of Appeals affirmed the District Court's decision in part and reversed it in part, holding that although inconvenient for the IMR, the defendant's letters could have been translated at a refugee service center cost-free, and hence there was no reason the correspondence could not have been sent there. Moreover, the IMR failed to preserve the issue of the inmate's brother presenting a special security risk, and the verdict was not against the weight of the evidence.

Reason

The Eighth Circuit Court of Appeals weighed Thongvanh's First Amendment right to correspond by mail in his native language against IMR's security interests. In this case, the Circuit Court cited the standard set in *Turner v. Safley*. In *Turner*, the U.S. Supreme Court listed four factors that must be considered: (1) whether there is a valid rational connection between the regulation and the legitimate government interest it purports to further; (2) whether the inmate has an alternative means of exercising his constitutional right; (3) the impact that accommodation of the inmate's right would have on others; and (4) the absence of a ready alternative to the regulation. While the Eighth Circuit Court of Appeals found that prison officials had reasonable security interests in monitoring prisoners' mail, they also found that a local Refugee Service Center agreed to provide Iowa prison officials with a no-cost Laotian-to-English translation service to monitor Thongvanh's letters, providing prison officials with a reasonable alternative to not having staff members to decipher the mail. Ultimately, the Circuit Court found that (1) The prison regulations abridged Thongvanh's First Amendment rights; (2) The reason to limit Thongvanh to correspond in Laotian with his parents and grandparents only was not reasonably related to a valid security interest (prison officials gave no reason why he should not correspond in his native language other than the lack of interpreters); and (3) Thongvanh was not treated the same as similarly situated Spanish- and German-speaking prisoners.

Case Significance

This case is important for several reasons. First, a similar trend running through this case (and several others where the courts granted a prisoner his or her rights) is that prison officials recognized similar rights to similarly situated prisoners when denying the respondent his rights. In this case, the Circuit Court protects the inmate's First Amendment right to free speech, or specifically the right to send and receive mail, even when the prison created a policy requiring all communication to be in English. With noted exceptions extended to Spanish- and German-speaking prisoners, the Circuit Court's ruling, in part, is based on equal protection under the law established in the Fourteenth Amendment. Second, this case is important because it preserves the right of foreign prisoners in America's custody to communicate through mail with friends and family in their respective homelands. Corrections has always viewed the exercise of sending and receiving mail as part of rehabilitation, because it increases the likelihood that they will be upbeat instead of depressed. This was not a difficult case for the Eighth Circuit Court of Appeals to decide by weighing the *Turner* test against the prison's security interests and the inmate's interest, since accommodations had been given to other inmates, and a translation service existed that offered free assistance to IMR. Moreover, prison officials' arguments justifying security interests were weakened considerably when evidence of granting of similar rights and privileges to similarly situated prisoners was presented.

Thornbaugh v. Abbott
490 U.S. 401 (1989)

Facts

Respondents, federal prison inmates and certain publishers, filed a class action suit in the U.S. District Court for the District of Columbia Circuit. They alleged that federal prison regulations allowing prison officials to reject forty-six publications sent to the inmates from outside the prison violated their First Amendment rights. The federal regulations in question allowed the wardens to reject books, single issues of magazines, newspapers, and other materials sent to prisoners from outside the prison if the publication was determined to be detrimental to security interests. Publications could be rejected if they described (among other things) the making of weapons, alcoholic beverages, and drugs or generally encouraged violent and disruptive activities within the prison. If the publication was a magazine or a newspaper, only the single issue determined to be detrimental to security interests was rejected. For example, regarding sexual material, most heterosexual material was admitted, whereas publications depicting homosexuality, sadomasochism, bestiality, and sexual material involving children were rejected. The inmates and publishers sought injunctive relief. The District Court upheld the prison regulations using the lowest level "reasonable relation" test from *Turner v. Safley* to judge the prison regulations against the prisoners' First Amendment interest, which required only that regulations be reasonably related to a significant security interest. The Court of Appeals for the District of Columbia reversed the District Court's ruling, finding that the regulations were unconstitutional when it used the middle-level and heightened scrutiny "least restrictive" test articulated in *Procunier v. Martinez,* which required that the regulations be the least restrictive way of advancing an important or substantial government interest. The petitioner prison officials sought certiorari, and the U.S. Supreme Court granted it.

Issue

Whether courts should use the *Turner* "reasonable relations" test or *Martinez* "least restrictive" test to weigh prisoners' First Amendment right to receive publications against prison regulations deemed to protect security interests.

U.S. Supreme Court Holding

The U.S. Supreme Court vacated and remanded the judgment of the appellate court for further proceeding, holding that regulations, such as those that affect the sending of publications to prisoners, must be analyzed under the standard set forth in *Turner v. Safley*. Under the *Turner* reasonableness test, such regulations are valid if they are reasonably related to legitimate penological interests. The Court also held that the *Martinez* analysis used by the Court of Appeals for the District of Columbia was limited to regulations concerning outgoing correspondence.

Reason

In this case, the U.S. Supreme Court distinguished *Turner* from *Martinez* reasoning that *Martinez* involved outgoing mail, which did not pose a threat to internal prison order, whereas *Turner* involved incoming correspondence from other inmates, which greatly impacted the internal prison environment. The Court thought that the present case was more like *Turner* because the incoming publications significantly affected the internal prison environment. The Court favored *Turner*'s reasonable relation standard requiring only that prison regulations be rationally related to legitimate security interests over *Martinez*'s least restrictive test on matters involving internal prison relations, because the *Turner* standard allowed prison officials greater discretion in the running of the prisons, which the Court thought was necessary in the volatile prison environment. The Supreme Court also overruled using the *Martinez* standard in favor of the *Turner* standard in any case involving incoming mail. Under the four-part reasonable relation test as articulated in *Turner*, the Court found that the regulations in question were rationally related to security interests and allowed prisoners alternative means of exercising their First Amendment rights. The Court also found that accommodating the prisoners' rights could negatively impact the prison environment, and that the restrictive practices articulated in the regulations were reasonably necessary.

Case Significance

This case is significant for several reasons. First, it defers to the wisdom and authority of prison administrators to run their facilities in a manner that will ensure their safety. The Court held that only the warden may reject publications, "only if it is determined detrimental to the security, good order, or discipline of the institution or if it might facilitate criminal activity." At the same time, the warden may not reject a publication "solely because its content is religious, philosophical, political, social, or sexual or because its content is unpopular or re-pugnant." For example, in places of confinement, the threat of violence and dis-order always exists, especially where publications are concerned. For example, prisoners who may have gang ties or connections with separatist groups should not be allowed to receive publications on how to start a race war or how to build bombs or make other weapons. Moreover, offenders who are homosexual or sexually attracted to children could offend the sensibilities of other inmates who may have children of their own or who are homophobic, if such materials are not screened and prohibited. Some prison officials may enforce policies that prohibit prisoners from having nude photos of a significant other, such as a spouse, girl-friend, or boyfriend, if the possibility exists that the photos will be stolen and circulated within the correctional facilities. These incidents could threaten secu-rity, discipline, and order that are needed in places of confinement. Second, the case is important because there are conditions attached to the regulation. The Court stated that wardens cannot prohibit publications because of personal dis-like; there must exist a legitimate penological interest, established in *Turner v. Safley*. This serves as the standard to balance the interest of prison administra-tors and the constitutional rights of inmates.

Turner v. Safley
482 U.S. 78 (1987)

Facts

Prisoners housed at the Renz Correctional Institute, a Missouri prison lo-cated in Cedar City that housed medium and maximum security female pris-oners and minimum security male prisoners, brought suit against the Missouri Department of Corrections in the U.S. District Court for the Western District of Missouri. The Renz prisoners challenged the constitutionality of two prison regulations as practiced at Renz: (1) a prohibition with some exceptions on correspondence between inmates at different state prisons, and (2) an almost complete ban on inmate marriages. Prisoners contended that the policies vi-olated their First Amendment rights to freedom of expression and marriage. The District Court applied the highest level strict scrutiny test to judge the prison regulations, which burdens the government with the difficult task of providing compelling reasons to justify regulating the areas protected by con-stitutional rights. Under the strict scrutiny test, the District Court ruled in favor of the prisoners' findings that both regulations violated their First Amendment rights. The Eighth Circuit Court of Appeals affirmed the District Court's ruling. The prison system appealed the case to the U.S. Supreme Court, and it granted certiorari.

Issue

What is the proper test that a federal court should use in weighing prisoners' First Amendment rights against prison regulations, and can prison officials ban inmate marriages and prohibit prisoners from corresponding with prisoners housed in other state prisons?

U.S. Supreme Court Holding

The Supreme Court stated that the District Court erred in applying the highest level of strict scrutiny standard of review to the prison regulations in cases involving the constitutional rights of prisoners and prison officials that do not involve the rights of nonprisoners. The Court also held that the lowest level reasonableness test is to be used when weighing prison regulations against the constitutional rights of prisoners. In the case at hand, under the reasonableness test, the prison mail regulations are valid because there is a rational connection between the regulations and prison security. The ban on inmate marriages, however, was found not to be reasonably related to a legitimate security interest, and the U.S. Supreme Court remanded the case back to the Eighth Circuit Court of Appeals for further proceedings.

Reason

In this case, to clear up confusion in the lower federal courts, the U.S. Supreme Court made it clear that the proper test to use in weighing any prison regulation against a prisoner's constitutional right is the lowest level reasonableness test. The Court noted that the reasonableness test gives proper deference to the judgment of prison officials on matters concerning the running of prisons, and also protects prisoner rights by preventing exaggerated prison security claims. The Court detailed how the reasonableness test was to be applied in prisoner rights cases by identifying four considerations: (1) whether there is a valid, rational connection between the prisoner regulation and the government security interests involved; (2) whether the prisoners have alternative means open to express the right involved; (3) the impact the accommodation the prisoner right will have on guards, other inmates, and the general allocation of resources; and (4) the absence of ready alternatives. Under the reasonableness test, the Court first found that the mail regulations were valid because (1) They were rationally related to security concerns to prevent escapes, arrange assaults and other violent acts, and control prison gangs; (2) The inmates could still express themselves through the mail; (3) The regulations ensured institutional order, an important consideration in regard to guards and other inmates; and (4) No reasonable alternatives existed by which to regulate inmate correspondence. Applying the same test to the marriage ban (unless the birth of a child was involved), the Court reached a different conclusion, ruling that the regulation was an exaggerated security response to a security interest and remanded the case back to the Eighth Circuit Court of Appeals for further hearings. The U.S. Supreme Court reasoned that (1) The prison officials' claim that marriages supported love triangles that might lead to violent confrontations and that such violent confrontations would interfere with the women's rehabilitation plans was an exaggerated response to inmate marriage and not reasonably related to valid security interests, because allowing marriages did not necessarily mean a dangerous love triangle would result; and (2) Alternatives to the Missouri regulation existed that would accommodate inmate marriages that presented *de minimus* security concerns such as denying marriage only if they presented a threat to the order of the prison.

Case Significance

This case is significant for several reasons. First, it is arguably the most important case decided by the Supreme Court in the area of prisoners' rights. More specifically, it gives prison officials the right or authority to implement policies that can be justified on the basis of being reasonably related to legitimate penological interests, especially safety, security, and rehabilitation. As such, when prisoners claim that a regulation infringes on a fundamental or constitutional right, the courts will likely cite *Turner,* using the lowest level reasonableness test. Second, the decision should limit the number of challenges that have flooded the federal courts. Third, in setting the lowest level reasonableness test as the standard to weigh a prisoner's right against a regulation, the Court almost ensures that the regulation will survive. This case represents the emphasis that the Rehnquist Court placed on letting prison officials run the prisons and the desire to move away from judicial activism or having the courts dictate correctional policy to prison officials, which was a practice more common in the first four years of the prisoner rights movement. The Court also notes that the medium-level substantial interest test as expressed in *Procunier v. Martinez* still applies in cases involving prison regulations and the rights of those who are not prisoners.

Udey v. Kastner

805 F.2d 1218 (1986)

Facts

Petitioner, Edwin Udey, a prisoner in the Federal Correctional Institution in Texarkana, Texas, filed suit in the U.S. District Court for the Eastern District of Texas, alleging that when prison officials refused his special list of organically grown produce washed in distilled water, they denied his religious beliefs in violation of the free exercise clause of the First Amendment. At the time of the lawsuit, Udey refused to eat regular prison food and was being force-fed through nasal tubes. The District Court found that Udey's religious beliefs were insincere, and therefore the right to partake of his specific diet was not protected by the First Amendment. Subsequently, the District Court ruled that the First Amendment did not require prison officials to provide Udey a special diet. Moreover, the court reversed and remanded the case for an evidentiary hearing to determine whether meeting Udey's religious and dietary requirements would place an undue burden on the prison system and whether there was any good reason not to provide him with food that complies with his religious diet. Prison officials argued that additional security costs of $15,000 each year would be needed to prevent the theft or pilferage of the special foods by other prisoners and allowing Udey his special diet would disrupt the system by fostering a proliferation of similar claims, forcing prison officials to administer an undue number of special diets. Udey appealed to the Fifth Circuit Court of Appeals.

Issue

Does Udey's First Amendment free exercise of religion rights require prison officials to provide him a special diet of organically grown food washed in distilled water?

Holding by the Fifth Circuit Court

The Fifth Circuit Court of Appeals affirmed the District Court's decision that Udey's special diet request was not protected by the First Amendment because administering it would place an undue burden on prison officials.

Reason

In this case, the Court of Appeals rejected the District Court's reasoning that Udey's diet request could be denied because of the undue burden of additional security costs, since inadequate resources could not be used as a reason to deny a person his constitutional rights. However, the Fifth Circuit Court of Appeals agreed with the District Court that allowing Udey his dietary request could dramatically increase lawsuits related to individual special diets and would involve an entanglement with religion that government should seek to avoid. More specifically, the Fifth Circuit Court reasoned that an undue burden would be imposed on the prison system by the diet cost of $15,000 a year to honor Udey's request, hostility would come from other inmates, theft of specialty food could occur, and a black market would form. These consequences would invariably lead to security problems. The Circuit Court found the most compelling argument was the fact that the probable proliferation of claims for specific individual religious dietary requirements would emerge.

Case Significance

The case is important for a number of reasons. First, the decision reveals that the federal court is unwilling to allow prison officials to deny claims of religious dietary needs when it is believed that accommodating the needs of some prisoners will give rise to fraudulent and exaggerated claims made by other prisoners that will create problems for prison administrators. Second, the decision speaks to the court's unwillingness to force prison officials to administer an undue number of religious diets resulting in the excessive entanglement of religion and government prohibited by the First Amendment. This ruling reflects the Court of Appeals' view regarding prison security at a time when prisoner's were flooding the federal courts with all forms of litigation. On a practical level, if the case had been decided for the petitioner, prison officials would be required to hire more employees to prevent the theft of special foods for religious worship at the whim of prisoners, even if it could not be demonstrated that the prisoners' religious beliefs and practices were sincere.

United States v. Bailey

444 U.S. 394 (1980)

Facts

On the morning of August 26, 1976, respondents Clifford Bailey, James T. Cogdell, Ronald C. Cosley, and Ralph Walker, federal prisoners, escaped from a District of Columbia jail by crawling through a window from which a bar had been removed and sliding down a knotted bed sheet. They remained at-large for periods ranging from one month to three and a half months before authorities recaptured them. Each of the prisoners was charged with violating 18 U.S.C. Section 751(a), which governs escape from federal custody. At their District Court trials, each of the four prisoners asserted duress or necessity as a defense to their escapes. They alleged that they escaped to free themselves from inhumane conditions at the jail. The District Court ruled that to plea duress as a defense, the prisoners would have to introduce evidence demonstrating (1) oppressive jail conditions, and (2) that they attempted to surrender once they freed themselves from the oppressive jail conditions. One trial involving three of the prisoners resulted in the jury convicting the prisoners after the District Court told the jury to disregard evidence presented by the prisoners of oppressive jail conditions and refused to instruct the jury on the duress defense because more of the prisoners could show that they attempted to surrender once they freed themselves from the jail. A second trial involving another prisoner also resulted in a conviction after the District Court ruled that the prisoner failed to present evidence of oppressive jail conditions. The Court of Appeals for the District Court of Columbia Circuit reversed, holding that the District Court had improperly precluded consideration by the respective juries of respondents' evidence. The Court of Appeals ruled that because 751(a) required the government to prove that the prisoner left federal custody voluntarily with an intent to avoid confinement, the District Court should have allowed evidence of oppressive jail conditions for the following reasons: (1) to determine if the prisoners had the requisite level of intent for a conviction under 751(a), and (2) because 751(a) is a continuing offense, to determine if the prisoners were justified in not returning to the jail at a later date. The U.S. Supreme Court granted certiorari.

Issue

Whether the prisoners are allowed to present evidence of oppressive prison and jail conditions to a jury when asserting a defense of duress or necessity to a 751(a) violation, even though they failed to show that they turned themselves in voluntarily after escaping from federal custody, which is a necessary element of the duress or necessity defense to an escape from custody charge.

U.S. Supreme Court Holding

The U.S. Supreme Court reversed the decision of the Court of Appeals for the District Court of Columbia, holding that an escape is not entitled to a defense of duress or necessity unless he or she made a bona fide effort to surrender once free from custody and that evidence of improper prison conditions had been properly barred from the juries' consideration because the prisoners offered insufficient evidence that they surrendered immediately after they left federal custody.

Reason

The U.S. Supreme Court found that the District Court properly instructed the jury to disregard evidence of oppressive jail conditions because the prisoners did not have the right to introduce such evidence. However, the Court disagreed with the Court of Appeals imposing the added burden of the government having to prove that respondents acted "with an intent to avoid confinement." The Court further reasoned that the word "intent" is ambiguous, but the majority of the Court of Appeals left little doubt that it was a responsibility of the prosecutor to prove that the respondents acted with the purpose of leaving the jail without authorization. The Court went on to say that it does not agree with the position of the Appeals Court because there is nothing in the language of 751(a) that indicated that Congress intended to require such a heightened standard of culpability or a narrow definition of confinement. Moreover, the Court ruled that in pleading the defense of duress or necessity in regard to prison and jail escapes, a prisoner must first show that he or she made a bona fide attempt to voluntarily turn him or herself in before evidence of oppressive jail prison conditions would be presented. The Court thought allowing evidence of oppressive jail conditions without first requiring that the defendant show he voluntarily turned himself in when pleading the defense of duress or necessity would result into wasting valuable trial time in 751(a) cases, and such cases would turn the courtroom into a floor for unnecessarily hearing every unpleasant aspect of prisons and jails.

Case Significance

The case is significant because the U.S. Supreme Court found that when prisoners escape from custody, the government is not required to prove that escapees acted with the intent to flee custody under Section 751(a).

United States v. Gouveia et al.

467 U.S. 180 (1984)

Facts

In November 1978, an inmate at the Federal Correctional Institution in Lompoc, California, was found dead from forty-five stab wounds to the chest. Four indigent prisoners were placed in administrative detention during the investigation of their fellow inmate's death, and remained there for nineteen months before they were indicted and arraigned in federal District Court for murder, at which time counsel was appointed for them. While in detention, the prisoners were allowed regular visitation privileges, access to legal materials, exercise, and unmonitored phone calls. Before trial, the prisoners filed a motion to dismiss the case against them, claiming that their Sixth Amendment right to counsel was violated when they were placed in administrative detention without the benefit of counsel. The U.S. District Court for the Central District of California denied their motion, and they went to trial. The proceeding lasted for a week, ending in a mistrial. On retrial, the respondents were eventually convicted of first-degree murder and conspiracy to commit murder.

In August 1979, another inmate was stabbed to death at the same institution. This time, two other prisoners were suspected of the murder and placed in administrative detention, where they remained for eight months. In March 1980, the two inmates were indicted by a federal grand jury for murder, and in April 1980 both prisoners were appointed an attorney and released from detention. Before trial, both prisoners filed a motion to dismiss the indictments against them on the grounds that their confinement in detention without appointed counsel violated their due process right of the Fifth Amendment and their Sixth Amendment right to a speedy trial and the right to counsel. This time, the U.S. District Court for the Central District of California dismissed the two prisoners' lawsuits, but a panel of the U.S. Court of Appeals for the Ninth Circuit reversed. The Court of Appeals for the Ninth Circuit, *en banc*, joined the appeals of the six prisoners and reversed, holding that denying the prisoners counsel while they were held in administrative detention before the indictments were handed down violated their Sixth Amendment right to counsel and overturned all six murder convictions. The case was appealed to the U.S. Supreme Court, and it granted certiorari.

Issue

Whether the Sixth Amendment requires the appointment of counsel to indigent inmates during their preindictment segregation.

U.S. Supreme Court Holding

The U.S. Supreme Court reversed and remanded the decision of the Ninth Circuit Court of Appeals, holding that the Sixth Amendment does not require the appointment of counsel to inmates in segregation before any judicial proceedings are initiated against them.

Reason

The U.S. Supreme Court reasoned that the Court of Appeals for the Ninth Circuit, *en banc*, misinterpreted its ruling in *Kirby v. Illinois* (406 U.S. 682, 1972) and departed from its interpretation of the Sixth Amendment right to counsel guarantee. While citing a long line of past cases such as *Kirby*, *Powell v. Alabama* (287 U.S. 45, 1932), *Hamilton v. Alabama* (368 U.S. 52, 1961), *Gideon v. Wainwright* (372 U.S. 335, 1963), *White v. Maryland* (373 U.S. 59, 1963), *Massiah v. United States* (377 U.S. 201, 1964), *United States v. Wade* (388 U.S. 218, 1967), and *Gilbert v. California* (388 U.S. 263, 1967), the Court made it clear that the Sixth Amendment right to counsel attaches only after judicial proceedings are initiated against the defendant by way of indictment, information, arraignment, or preliminary hearings. The Court noted that the reason for the Sixth Amendment right to counsel was to protect the accused at trial when confronted with both the intricacies of law and the prosecution. The Court thought that in ruling that the right to counsel for segregated prisoners attached prior to the time of indictment, the Court of Appeals was legitimately trying to protect the prisoners in segregation from the possibility that the government might delay the initiation of formal charges against them while it developed its case, which could leave the unaided inmate at a severe disadvantage as witnesses' memories fade, alibi witnesses are transferred, and physical evidence deteriorates. However, the Court noted that the Fifth Amendment protects prisoners in segregation by requiring the dismissal of an indictment if the defendant can prove that the government delayed bringing the indictment, to gain an advantage over the defendant, and that the delay caused the defendant actual prejudice in presenting his defense.

Case Significance

The case is important for a number of reasons. First, the U.S. Supreme Court reiterates several previous rulings, namely *Kirby v. Illinois,* but recognizes that *Kirby* was not a prison case. Nevertheless, the decision also applies to inmates. That is, the case holds that there is no constitutional entitlement or guarantee of counsel to inmates in administrative segregation prior to the initiation of an adversarial judicial proceeding. As such, there is no legal right for inmates in segregation to be appointed an attorney until indictments are handed down to them in their involvement of new crimes. However, as noted by the Court in this case, there is nothing that prevents the opportunity for respondents to retain their own private counsel while in administrative segregation. Second, the criminal justice system cannot afford to offer the assistance of an attorney for indefinite periods postconviction. The Constitution makes no special provisions that guarantee an attorney after a defendant has been convicted. Such a practice would create a devastating economic hardship on the justice system. Third, the Constitution only intended for citizens to have legal representation during the period of confrontation between the citizens and the government's resources, including the complexities of the law and the state prosecutor. The wisdom is that laypersons need someone versed in the law to protect their legal interests, and the threat does not exist prior to judicial proceedings.

United States v. Hearst

563 F. 2d 1331 (1977)

Facts

Patricia Hearst, a member of the Symbionese Liberation Army, was arrested in September 1975 for involvement in bank robbery. While in custody at the San Mateo, California, jail, she made incriminating statements to her friend Patricia Tobin, which were recorded by jail officials. More specifically, officials electronically recorded the conversations between the two that took place in the jail visiting room over a telephone-like intercom system, because Hearst and Tobin were separated by bullet-proof glass. The jail supervisor then delivered the tape to the FBI and to the prosecution to be used at the Hearst trial. The government introduced photographs and testimony descriptive of the appellant's role in the robbery. The appellant raised the defense of duress, contending that her co-participants compelled her to engage in the criminal activity. In this case, defense attorneys F. Lee Bailey and Albert Johnson argued that jail officials violated Hearst's Fourth Amendment rights when they (1) electronically monitored her conversation with Tobin in the jail visiting room without her knowledge, and (2) delivered the tape to the government. Despite the case receiving great media attention, the defense did not move for a change of venue or for a continuance on the grounds of pretrial publicity. Instead, the defense relied on the *voir dire* of the prospective jurors. The defense motioned for a suppression of the Tobin tape, and the motion was denied. At trial, which started in February 1976, Bailey put Hearst on the witness stand; she took the Fifth Amendment right not to self-incriminate in the presence of the jury. Hearst was convicted on March 20. She put forth a motion for a new trial, and it was denied. She unsuccessfully appealed to the U.S. Supreme Court, and it denied certiorari.

Issue

Does the Fourth Amendment protect pretrial detainees from jail officials electronically monitoring their conversations with visitors in the jail visiting room without their knowledge, and can jail officials deliver tapes and transcripts of the intercepted conversations to prosecutors and other interested government officials without violating the pretrial detainee's Fourth Amendment rights?

Holding by the Ninth Circuit Court of Appeals

The Ninth Circuit Court of Appeals held that monitoring and recording prisoner-visitor conversations without their knowledge in the interest of maintaining jail security are reasonable and do not violate the Fourth Amendment, and lawful seizures of the conversation may be transferred to other governmental agencies. The Circuit Court concluded that no reversible error occurred and that the judgment of the District Court was affirmed.

Reason

In this case, the Ninth Circuit Court quoted several cases that were decided by the U.S. Supreme Court. The Appeals Court adopted the reasoning that jail inmates and pretrial detainees have no reasonable expectation of privacy in a jail setting that would invoke the Fourth Amendment protection if the searches were related to reasonable security goals. In regard to pretrial detainees, previous U.S. Supreme Court decisions implied that unreasonable searches may be assumed to be punishment, and it is unconstitutional to punish pretrial detainees. The tapes could have been excluded from Hearst's trial on this basis. However, the Ninth Circuit Court of Appeals dismissed the punishment issue, finding that it was reasonable for jail and prison authorities to search jail inmates by electronically monitoring conversations between occupants in visiting rooms to maintain security. Finally, the Circuit Court determined that if the conversations were lawfully seized, they could be lawfully transferred to other governmental agencies.

Case Significance

This case is important for several reasons. First, it reveals that the Court of Appeals did not give deference to Patricia Hearst or her father's celebrity status or wealth when it refused to exclude incriminating evidence. Second, this case affirms the U.S. Supreme Court's previous rulings that pretrial detainees have no reasonable expectations of privacy in jails that could invoke Fourth Amendment protections, because jails are traditionally places of heavy surveillance. However, because it is unconstitutional to punish pretrial detainees, the case law at the time was still unclear regarding the suppression of evidence seized in searches of pretrial detainees deemed not reasonably related to security interests.

United States v. Hitchcock
467 F.2d 1107 (1972)

Facts

Hitchcock, an Arizona state prisoner serving a life sentence for murder, appealed his criminal conviction for filing fraudulent income tax refund claims to the Internal Revenue Service. He was given six concurrent five-year sentences to run consecutively with his life sentence. The main evidence used against him was found during a warrantless search of his prison cell. Hitchcock claims that the evidence found during the search was in violation of his Fourth Amendment right to be free from unreasonable searches and seizures. The Ninth Circuit Court of Appeals reviewed the case.

Issue

Whether prisoners have reasonable expectations of privacy in their prison cells that would invoke the Fourth Amendment protection from unreasonable search and seizure.

Holding by the Ninth Circuit Court of Appeals

The Ninth Circuit Court of Appeals affirmed the conviction, holding that prisoners do not have reasonable expectations of privacy or Fourth Amendment protection against unreasonable searches and seizures in their prison cells.

Reason

In this case, the Ninth Circuit Court of Appeals cited the U.S. Supreme Court's decision in *Katz v. United States* (389 U.S. 347, 1967), where the Court ruled that the Fourth Amendment no longer depended on "constitutionally protected places." Rather, the Court contended that now it considers whether the person has exhibited an expectation of privacy and, second, whether society views the expectation reasonable. Moreover, the Circuit Court reasoned that since the Fourth Amendment requires the person to have a reasonable expectation of privacy when searched, it concluded that the Amendment does not protect prisoners against unreasonable searches of their cells. In this case, the Circuit Court of Appeals did not dispute whether Hitchcock intended to keep the documents private. The court, however, found the expectation to be unreasonable because a jail or prison is not the equivalent of a man's house. The Circuit Court argued that within the context of confinement, surveillance is the order of the day; therefore, there is no reasonable expectation of privacy.

Case Significance

This case is important for several reasons. First, the Ninth Circuit Court of Appeals applies or interprets the U.S. Supreme Court decision in *Kirby v. Illinois* (406 U.S. 682, 1972) to a prison setting. Second, the Circuit Court is clear that prisoners do not enjoy Fourth Amendment protection from cell searches. On a practical level, jails and prisons are places where criminals are sentenced after they are convicted of criminal behavior. Therefore, the offenders who occupy prison space are not known as safe and trustworthy individuals. It is not considered likely that they will abstain from criminal behavior while incarcerated. Therefore, jail and correctional guards must be able to search their cells for a variety of items that could pose a threat to security and the safety of others. The decision is this case is clear; jail inmates and prisoners do not enjoy constitutional protection from searches. Moreover, in *Katz*, the U.S. Supreme Court declared that the Fourth Amendment protects persons and not places, and modified its Fourth Amendment analysis to determine whether the person has a reasonable expectation of privacy when being searched. In *Lanza v.*

New York, decided in 1962, the Court used the older Fourth Amendment analysis when it determined whether a person had a reasonable expectation of privacy in the place searched. *Lanza* is important because it is one of the first prisoner rights cases, and the federal courts still refer to its holding because of the ruling that prisoners and jail inmates do not have reasonable expectations of privacy during confinement. When the federal courts use *Lanza*, they usually note that the same result in regard to Fourth Amendment protections is reached whether using the "person" or "place" analysis.

Vitek v. Jones
445 U.S. 480 (1980)

Facts

Appellee Jones, a convicted Nebraska prisoner, was transferred to a mental hospital pursuant to a statute that stated if a designated physician or psychologist finds that a prisoner "suffers from a mental disease or defect" that "cannot be given proper treatment" in prison, the Director of Correctional Services may transfer the prisoner to a mental hospital. Jones challenged the actions of the prison officials by bringing suit to the U.S. District Court for the District of Nebraska, claiming that his transfer to a mental hospital violated his Fourteenth Amendment due process rights. The District Court declared the Nebraska statute unconstitutional, holding that transferring a prisoner to a mental hospital without adequate notice and opportunity for a hearing deprived him of his liberty without due process of law, which violates the Fourteenth Amendment. The District Court ruled that such transfers must be accompanied by adequate notice and an adversary hearing before an independent decision maker, a written statement by the fact-finder of the evidence relied on and reasons for the decision, and the availability of counsel for indigent prisoners. The court permanently enjoined the State from transferring the appellee to the mental hospital without following the prescribed procedures. Subsequently, Jones was paroled on conditions that he accept mental treatment, but he violated that parole and was returned to prison. Relying on the appellee's history of mental illness and the state's representation that he was a serious threat to his own and others' safety, the District Court held that the parole and revocation therefore did not render the case moot because Jones was still subject to being transferred to the mental hospital.

Issue

Whether the Due Process Clause of the Fourteenth Amendment entitles a prisoner convicted and incarcerated in the state of Nebraska to certain procedural protections, including notice, an adversary hearing, and provision of counsel, before he is transferred involuntarily to a state mental hospital for treatment of a mental disease or defect.

U.S. Supreme Court Holding

The Supreme Court affirmed the decision of the District Court, holding that the court was correct in finding that the case is not moot because the appellee was back in prison and a transfer could reoccur. Moreover, the involuntary transfer of appellee to a mental hospital implicates a liberty interest that is protected by the Due Process Clause of the Fourteenth Amendment.

Reason

The Supreme Court reasoned that the Nebraska statute created a liberty interest in which due process protection should attach because the law determined conditions that warranted Jones's transfer to a mental hospital. The law created due process rights that entitled Jones to procedural protections in connection with his transfer because it prescribed the objective condition that he could only be transferred to a mental hospital after determining he had a mental disease or defect that could not be properly treated in a prison. In other words, Jones was allowed to challenge how prison officials determined he was suffering from a mental disease or defect that could not be treated in a prison because those were the only circumstances under which he could be involuntarily transferred to a mental hospital. The Court agreed with the District Court in that there is a stigmatizing consequence attached to a prisoner being transferred to a mental health facility for involuntary treatment and also with the mandatory behavior modification program that Jones would have been subjected to in Nebraska. The transfer would amount to a major change in conditions of confinement and a "grievous loss" that should not be imposed without an adequate hearing. More specifically, the Court thought the transfer constituted the kind of deprivation that warrants procedural safeguards. The Court did not agree entirely with the District Court's ruling that all indigent prisoners should be appointed counsel at such hearings and modified the District Court's order to mandate counsel only in situations involving indigent prisoners who are unable to understand or exercise their rights.

Case Significance

This case is significant for several reasons. First, it is the leading case governing the transfer of prisoners to state mental hospitals. Second, prior to this decision, prison officials could indiscriminately transfer prisoners to mental facilities. After the *Vitek* decision, the U.S. Supreme Court upheld the District Court's minimum procedural due process requirements that must be afforded a prisoner before he is transferred to a mental hospital. These procedural safeguards include (1) written notice to the prisoner that a transfer to a mental hospital is being considered; (2) a hearing sufficiently after the notice to permit the prisoner to prepare; (3) an opportunity at the hearing to present testimony of witnesses by the defense and to confront and cross-examine witnesses called by the state; (4) an independent decision maker; (5) a written statement by the fact-finder as to the evidence relied on and the reasons for transferring the inmate; (6) availability of legal counsel, furnished by the state, if the inmate is financially unable to afford one; and (7) effective and timely notice of all the foregoing rights. These rights are in place to protect the prisoner from unwelcomed treatment. Third, the U.S. Supreme Court, in this case requires that if an inmate is to be determined "mentally ill," it must be determined by an expert psychiatrist or psychologist and not a correctional guard, fellow inmate, or prison warden.

Washington v. Harper

494 U.S. 210 (1990)

Facts

Walter Harper was sentenced to the Washington State Penitentiary in 1976 for robbery. While incarcerated from 1976 to 1980, he spent most of his time in the prison's mental health unit, where he consented to the administration of psychotropic drugs. Harper was paroled in 1980, but violated parole in December 1981 and was sent to Washington's Special Offender Center (SOC), a treatment center to diagnose and treat offenders with serious mental disorders. At first, he voluntarily consented to take prescribed antipsychotic medications, but in November 1982 he refused to continue taking these medications. Pursuant to SOC Policy 600.30, the treating physician sought to require Harper to involuntarily take the prescribed medication. SOC Policy 600.30 allowed a prisoner who refused to take antipsychotic medication a hearing before a special committee consisting of a psychiatrist, a psychologist, and the Associate Superintendent of the Center, none of whom may be involved in the prisoner's treatment and diagnosis. If the committee determined by majority vote that the prisoner suffered from a mental disorder and was gravely ill or gravely disabled or dangerous, the prisoner could be medicated against his will, provided the psychiatrist was in the majority. At the hearing, the prisoner had a right to attend, present evidence, including witnesses, to cross-examine staff witnesses, and to have a lay advisor who is not involved and understands the psychiatric issues at hand. At the end of the hearing, if the prisoner was required to take antipsychotic medication, the treating psychiatrist was required to submit bi-weekly reports to the Department of Corrections medical director. At the end of 180 days, a new hearing was required to consider further treatment. Such a hearing was held in November 1982, and in accordance with SOC Policy 600.30 and periodic review, Harper was required to take antipsychotic medications for one year. In November 1983, Harper was transferred to the Washington State Reformatory, where he took no medication. In one month, his condition deteriorated and he was sent back to the SOC, where another Policy 600.30 hearing was held. Again, the committee approved that the respondent take antipsychotic medication against his will. Subject to periodic review, Harper was forced to take medication involuntarily until June 1986, when he was transferred to the Washington State Penitentiary. However, in February 1985, Harper filed suit in state court, claiming that the failure to provide him with a judicial hearing before he was involuntarily administered antipsychotic medication violated his due process constitutional rights. After a trial, the state court held that the procedures in Policy 600.30 met the constitutional requirements of due process. On appeal, the Washington State Supreme Court reversed the lower court, holding that under the Due Process Clause of the U.S. Constitution, the State could only administer antipsychotic medications to a nonconsenting prisoner if at a judicial hearing, where the prisoner had full adversarial protections, the State could show the medication was necessary and effective for advancing a compelling state interest.

Issue

Whether the Due Process Clause of the Fourteenth Amendment requires a judicial hearing before the State may treat a mentally ill prisoner with antipsychotic drugs against his will.

U.S. Supreme Court Holding

The U.S. Supreme Court held that given the requirements of the prison environment, the Due Process Clause permits the State to treat a prisoner who has a serious mental illness with antipsychotic drugs against his will if the inmate is dangerous to himself or others and the treatment is in the inmate's medical interest. SOC Policy 600.30 comports with these requirements, and the Court rejected the contention that the policy's substantive standards are deficient under the U.S. Constitution. A judicial hearing is not required before a state may treat a mentally ill prisoner with antipsychotic drugs against his will.

Reason

Before addressing the issue of whether the Due Process Clause required a judicial hearing before a prisoner could involuntarily be administered antipsychotic medication, the U.S. Supreme Court found fault with the Washington Supreme Court's ruling that the state must show it had a "compelling interest" in administering the medication if the prisoner is gravely disabled or presents a serious likelihood of harm to himself or others. The Court asserted that ever since its decision in *Turner v. Safley,* the standard of review for determining the validity of a prison regulation that infringed on an inmate's right was whether the regulation is "reasonably related to legitimate penological objectives." The Court then found that the state had a reasonable and legitimate penological interest in controlling prisoners with mental disabilities who pose a threat to both staff and other inmates by providing them with antipsychotic medication for their illness. The Court then determined that SOC Policy 600.30 was a rational means of furthering the state's legitimate penological objectives, because its exclusive application was to inmates who were gravely disabled or represented a significant danger to themselves or others, and that the drugs were to be administered for no purpose other than treatment. In their analysis of whether a judicial hearing was required, the Court could find no advantage in giving the mentally ill prisoner a formal judicial hearing before a judge with no experience in treating the mentally ill, over an informal hearing between the prisoner and those experienced in treating the mentally ill. In holding that SOC Policy 600.30 satisfied constitutional due process requirements, the Court commented that a judicial hearing requirement would be a waste of judicial resources. In the end, the Court was satisfied that the prisoner's constitutional due process rights were not violated in a SOC Policy 600.30 hearing, which allowed sufficient due process safeguards for the prisoner, such as the ability to present witnesses, cross-examine staff witnesses, and have lay help.

Case Significance

Forcing antipsychotic medication on anyone presents serious constitutional rights issues. Determining that it is within the realm of rational and legitimate penological objectives for prison staff to force a severely mentally ill prisoner to take antipsychotic medication creates constitutional due process rights for the prisoner because the treatment is involuntary. The medication cannot be administered for purposes other than treating the prisoner, who must be determined to be severely mentally ill. As the Supreme Court observed, the antipsychotic medication has severe and even lethal side effects, and could be improperly used to punish the prisoner, which would be a violation of the Eighth Amendment's ban against cruel and unusual punishment.

Watson v. Jones

980 F. 2d 1165

Facts

Missouri Eastern Correctional Center inmates Joseph Watson and Bill Harris brought suit to the U.S. District Court for the Eastern District of Missouri alleging that Correctional Officer Marie Jones violated their Fourth Amendment rights by sexually harassing them for almost two months in 1990 while she performed daily routine pat-down searches. Watson and Harris contended that Jones tickled them while performing searches; deliberately examined genital, anus, lower stomach, and thigh areas routinely; and that Jones's searches often included prolonged rubbing and fondling of the genitals and anus area. Watson and Harris also alleged that when they informed Jones that they wished to be searched by male guards, she retaliated by citing them for false disciplinary violations. If they refused to be searched, they would be put in the "hole." Jones responded by noting that she only patted down the defendants six to seven times during the two-month period, and in accordance with Missouri correctional procedures, she never patted an inmate in the crotch unless she knew something was there. Jones denied touching the inmates' genital, anal, and upper thigh areas; she claims she touched the inmates' lower stomachs with the back of her hands in accordance with Missouri search procedures. The District Court dismissed Watson and Harris's suit by granting summary judgment to Jones, because the inmates presented only broad and conclusory allegations that Jones denied. Watson and Harris appealed.

Issue

Did Watson and Harris present enough specific evidence of sexual harassment in their favor to allow the District Court to find that Jones's pat-down searches of them violated their Fourth Amendment privacy rights?

Eighth Circuit Court of Appeals Holding

The Eighth Circuit Court of Appeals reversed the District Court's summary judgment order and remanded the case for further proceedings after finding that the evidence produced by Watson and Harris was more than broad and conclusory, and could entitle the inmates to a legal judgment in their favor.

Reason

In this case, the first issue for the Eighth Circuit Court of Appeals to decide was whether the District Court's summary judgment order was based on the inmates presenting only broad and conclusory evidence. The Circuit Court found it was proper. After finding that Watson and Harris presented evidence in their allegations substantiating that they were subjected to improper routine searches for over a two-month period that included a record of the complaints they made to prison officials about those searches in the conduct violation they attached to the report, the Court of Appeals overruled the District Court's summary judgment order, stating that while the evidence lacked detail it was not broad and conclusory. A second issue the Circuit Court addressed was whether Watson and Harris's Fourth Amendment rights were violated because of the routine search procedures used by Jones. Whereas a Fourth Amendment violation could possibly occur if the inmates had to involuntarily expose their genital areas to a correctional officer of the opposite sex during a search, in an earlier case the Court of Appeals ruled that female correctional officers could conduct pat-down searches of male inmates in Missouri state prisons. However, in this case, the Eighth Circuit Court of Appeals decided a Fourth Amendment violation could have occurred because Watson and Harris were alleging that the pat-down searches violated their constitutional rights because of the manner in which Jones conducted them, and not solely because they were searched by a female correctional officer following correctional procedures.

Case Significance

The case is important because the Eighth Circuit Court of Appeals ruled in an earlier case that pat-down searches of male inmates by female correctional officers do not violate the male inmates' Fourth Amendment rights solely because the searches were conducted by female officers. The Court of Appeals implied that Watson and Harris's suit would have been dismissed if it had been based solely on officer Jones's routine search practices. The court, however, distinguished this case, admitting that if Watson and Harris's fondling and exposure of genital area allegations were true, then a Fourth Amendment violation occurred.

West v. Atkins

487 U.S. 42 (1988)

Facts

Quincy West, a prisoner at Odom Correctional Center in Jackson, North Carolina, tore his left Achilles tendon while playing volleyball. A physician at Odom examined West and recommended that he be transferred for orthopedic services to the Central Prison Hospital in Raleigh, an acute medical care facility for all of North Carolina's prisoners. While at Central Prison Hospital, West saw Dr. Samuel Atkins, a private physician who provided part-time orthopedic services to inmates on a contract basis with the State of North Carolina. Over the next several months, Atkins treated West's injury by placing his leg in a series of casts. West alleged that although Atkins told him that surgery would be necessary, he refused to schedule it, and discharged West while his ankle was still swollen and painful and his movement impeded. Since West was a prisoner in close custody, he was not free to employ or see another physician of his choosing. West brought a Section 1983 lawsuit to the U.S. District Court for the Eastern District of North Carolina against Atkins, claiming that the doctor acted with deliberate indifference to his medical needs by refusing to schedule surgery for him, thus subjecting him to cruel and unusual punishment in violation of the Eighth Amendment. The District Court ruled that because the "contract physician" was not acting "under color of state law," a judicial prerequisite for a Section 1983 lawsuit, West could not sue Atkins. The Fourth Circuit Court of Appeals affirmed the District Court ruling. The case was appealed to the U.S. Supreme Court, and it granted certiorari.

Issue

Whether a physician who is under contract with the state to provide medical services to inmates at a state-prison hospital on a part-time basis acts "under color of state law" within the meaning of Section 1983 when he treats an inmate.

U.S. Supreme Court Holding

The Supreme Court held that a physician who is under state contract to provide medical services to inmates at a state-prison hospital on a part-time basis acts under color of state law within the meaning of Section 1983 when he treats an inmate. The Court reversed the judgment of the Fourth Circuit Court of Appeals and remanded the case back to the District Court to determine if Atkins acted with deliberate indifference to West's basic medical needs in violation of the Eighth Amendment.

Reason

In determining whether Atkins was acting under the color of state law, the U.S. Supreme Court reasoned that it is the physician's function within the state system, and not the terms of his employment, that determines whether his actions can be attributed to the state. The main issue regarding liability is determined by the relationship between the state, the physician, and the prisoner. The Court also reasoned that contracting out for medical care does not relieve the state of its constitutional duty to provide medical care to those in custody and does not deprive the prisoners of a means to exercise their Eighth Amendment right to be free from cruel and unusual punishment. The Court held that the state had an affirmative duty to provide adequate medical care to West, and because the state delegated that function to Atkins, who voluntarily assumed that obligation by contract, liability ensued.

Case Significance

This case is important because it is not uncommon for states to contract out for medical and other services it provides for prisoners. This case makes it clear that contracting out for private services does not relieve a state from its affirmative obligations to provide prisoners with basic needs, nor does it prevent prisoners from exercising their constitutional rights.

Whitley v. Albers
475 U.S. 312 (1986)

Facts

Prisoners of the Oregon State Penitentiary rioted by taking control of Cell-block A, which consisted of two tiers of barred cells and a stairway that connected the upper and lower cellblocks. During the course of the riot, the prisoners took a correctional officer hostage and placed him in an upper tier cell. After attempts to negotiate with the prisoners broke down, Captain Harol Whitley, the prison security manager, devised a plan to rescue the hostage and take control of the cellblock by force. The plan called for Whitley to enter the cellblock unarmed, but followed by three correctional officers with shotguns, who were to fire a warning shot as Whitley entered the cellblock. Whitley was to go up the stairwell to rescue the hostage, and the guards were to shoot low at anybody who attempted to follow him up the stairs. In executing the plan, one of the officers fired the warning shot as Whitley entered the cellblock. Whitley then chased one of the inmate leaders up the stairs, and prisoner Albers followed Whitley up the stairs. To protect Whitley, one of the correctional officers seriously injured Albers by shooting him in the knee to prevent him from following Whitley up the stairs. Whitley subdued the inmate leader that he chased up the stairs and freed the hostage, thus quelling the riot. Albers brought suit to the U.S. District Court for the District of Oregon alleging a violation of his Eighth Amendment rights, but the District Court directed a verdict for the correctional officials after finding that their use of force was necessary to protect Whitley, secure the release of the hostage, and quell the prison disturbance. The Ninth Circuit Court of Appeals reversed the District Court and ordered a new trial, ruling that Albers had a valid Eighth Amendment claim if he could show that the emergency plan adopted by correctional officers was carried out with deliberate indifference to his right to be free from cruel and unusual punishment. The case was appealed to the U.S. Supreme Court, and it granted certiorari.

Issue

What standard governs a prison inmate's claim that officials subjected him to cruel and unusual punishment by shooting him during the course of their attempt to quell a prison riot?

U.S. Supreme Court Holding

The U.S. Supreme Court held that the shooting of the respondent does not violate his Eighth Amendment right to be free from cruel and unusual punishment. Where a prison security measure is undertaken to resolve a disturbance that poses significant risks to the safety of inmates and prison staff, the question of whether the measure inflicted unnecessary and wanton pain and suffering ultimately turns on whether force was applied in a good-faith effort to maintain or restore discipline, or maliciously and sadistically for the purpose of causing harm.

Viewing the evidence in the most favorable light to the respondent, it does not appear that the evidence supports a reliable inference or wantonness in the infliction of pain under this standard.

Reason

The Court decided that the deliberate indifference standard it announced in *Estelle v. Gamble* was appropriate in cases involving the State's responsibility to provide prisoners with medical needs or other important responsibilities, but did not adequately capture the competing interests in cases involving the use of force by correctional authorities to restore order in the face of a prison disturbance. Distinguishing Eighth Amendment claims involving state responsibility to meet the basic needs of prisoners from Eighth Amendment claims involving the use of force to quell prison disturbances, the Court announced a new standard. The Court reasoned that in claims involving the use of force by correctional authorities to quell prison disturbances, officials must take into account the very real threats the disturbance presents to other inmates and officials themselves, in addition to possible harms to inmates against whom the force might be used. For the Court, the question of whether the correctional officials' response to quell the disturbance amounted to the wanton and unnecessary infliction of pain and suffering, or cruel and unusual punishment, turns on whether the force applied was done in good faith to maintain or restore discipline or whether the force used was for the purpose of maliciously and sadistically causing harm to the inmates. Applying the new standard to the present case, the U.S. Supreme Court thought that the shooting of Albers was necessary to protect Whitley and ultimately restore order to the cellblock.

Case Significance

The U.S. Supreme Court clears up confusion among the lower federal courts regarding the standard to use in judging prisoners' claims involving the excessive use of force by correctional officials to maintain order and quell disturbances by distinguishing such cases from those involving prison officials not providing inmates with basic needs. In distinguishing the two types of cases, the Court also announced a new and more appropriate standard for reviewing excessive use of force claims. After *Whitley,* the lower federal courts began using both the deliberate indifference standard and the malicious and sadistic standard for deciding prisoner Eighth Amendment claims, depending on the nature of the claim.

Wilson v. Seiter

501 U.S. 294 (1991)

Facts

Petitioner Pearly Wilson, an Ohio state prisoner at Hocking Correctional Facility (HCF) in Nelsonville, brought a Section 1983 claim against respondent Richard P. Seiter, then Director of the Ohio Department of Rehabilitation and Corrections, alleging conditions of overcrowding, excessive noise, insufficient locker storage space, inadequate heating and cooling, and improper ventilation. The claim also alleged that restrooms were inadequate and dirty, and dining facilities and food preparation were unsanitary. In addition, housing healthy inmates with mentally and physically ill inmates resulted in cruel and unusual punishment in violation of the Eighth and Fourteenth Amendments to the U.S. Constitution. Wilson's affidavit described the challenged conditions and charged that the authorities, after notification, had failed to take remedial action. The respondent's affidavit denied that some of the alleged conditions existed and described efforts by prison officials to improve the others. The petitioner sought declaratory relief as well as $900,000 in compensatory and punitive damages. The District Court dismissed the lawsuit by granting summary judgment for Ohio prison officials after Seiter described efforts to improve conditions, and the Sixth Circuit Court of Appeals affirmed on the grounds that the affidavit failed to establish the requisite culpable state of mind on the part of the respondents. The U.S. Supreme Court granted certiorari.

Issue

Whether a prisoner claiming that conditions of confinement constitute cruel and unusual punishment must show a culpable state of mind on the part of correctional officials and, if so, what state of mind is required.

U.S. Supreme Court Holding

In this case, the Supreme Court vacated the judgment of the Sixth Circuit Court of Appeals and remanded the case for reconsideration under the appropriate standard.

Reason

The Court first reviewed its decision in *Estelle v. Gamble*, noting that in that case, it rejected the inmate's claim that prison doctors inflicted cruel and unusual punishment on him because the inmate failed to establish that the prison doctor possessed a sufficiently culpable state of mind to inflict punishment, or that doctors were deliberately indifferent to his serious medical needs. In this case, the Court held that only the unnecessary and wanton infliction of pain implicated the Eighth Amendment, and to advance such a claim, the inmate must show that the doctor's state of mind was that he was "deliberately indifferent" to the inmate's serious medical needs. A showing of negligence alone on the part of prison doctors was not enough to advance an Eighth Amendment claim because it did not establish the state of mind necessary on the part of correctional officers to inflict wanton and unnecessary punishment on inmates. The Court then reviewed its decision in *Rhodes v. Chapman,* in which it held that only those deprivations denying the "minimal civilized measure of life's necessities" are sufficiently grave to form the basis for an Eighth Amendment claim.

Distinguishing its holding in *Rhodes* from its holding in *Estelle,* the Court commented that in *Rhodes,* it pointed out an objective component to an Eighth Amendment claim that referred to the nature of the condition of confinement, whereas in *Estelle,* it addressed a subjective component to an Eighth Amendment claim that referred to the prison officials' state of mind. The Court then extended its holding in *Estelle* to apply to any kind of conditions of confinement case, whether it be inhumane conditions of confinement, failure to attend to medical needs, or both, making it necessary for a prisoner challenging any condition of confinement alone or in combination to show that prison officials had the culpable state of mind that they were deliberately indifferent to the needs of the prisoners. The Court then joined its holding in *Rhodes* with its holding in *Estelle,* and declared that to be successful in a conditions of confinement claim, a prisoner must first show an objective component, or that an inhumane condition of confinement or a combination of conditions of confinement (such as medical care, overcrowding, the food he is feed, cell temperature, the clothes he is issued, or the protection he receives) falls below minimal civilized standards, and then the prisoner must also show a subjective component, or that officials were of the state of mind that they were deliberately indifferent to the prisoner's needs. The Court then distinguished its holding in *Whitley v. Albers* from its holding in *Estelle* and *Rhodes.* In *Whitley,* the Court held that prison officials must have the culpable state of mind of acting maliciously and sadistically for the purposes of causing harm in situations involving prison officials' responses to a prison disturbance. The Court commented that the subjective "malicious and sadistic" standard it expressed in *Whitley* only applies to use of force cases involving prison officials responding to a disturbance and is not an appropriate standard to use in judging the prison officials' state of mind in conditions of confinement cases. The Court then vacated the judgment of the Sixth Circuit Court of Appeals dismissal of Wilson's condition of confinement case. The Sixth Circuit Court ruled that because prison officials did not act maliciously and sadistically with the intent of causing harm to the prisoners in maintaining prison conditions at HCF, there were no Eighth Amendment violations. The U.S. Supreme Court remanded the case back to the Sixth Circuit Court of Appeals for reconsideration of Wilson's condition of confinement claim under the appropriate deliberate indifference standard.

Case Significance

The case is important for several reasons. It is seen as one of the most significant Eighth Amendment prison law cases heard by the U.S. Supreme Court because the Court synthesized its past Eighth Amendment ruling to forge a basic outline for deciding Eighth Amendment cruel and unusual punishment cases. With its holding in this case, the Court first applied its holdings in *Estelle* and *Rhodes* to apply to all conditions of confinement cases, requiring that a successful conditions of confinement claim consists of both an objective and a subjective component; a prisoner must show that conditions of confinement fell below the minimum standard of civility, and that prison officials acted with deliberate indifference to correcting the conditions. In this case, the suit was rejected by the U.S. Supreme Court, which declared that prison officials must exhibit deliberate indifference to prisoners' needs and living conditions before inmates will successfully prevail in their suits. In essence, the Court said that deliberate indifference to the needs of the inmate must be found to constitute cruel and unusual punishment. The Court also rejected the argument that a court must look at the overall conditions to decide whether there was cruel and unusual punishment. While this process had been practiced by many federal courts in deciding that prisoners' conditions were unconstitutional, this ruling changed that common practice. The case makes it more difficult for inmates to prevail in conditions of confinement cases, unless they can establish that a correctional administrator is operating in a deliberately indifferent manner.

Wolff v. McDonnell
418 U.S. 539 (1974)

Facts

Respondent Wolff filed a Section 1983 claim on behalf of himself and other inmates at the Nebraska Penal and Correctional Complex in Lincoln for damages and injunctive relief, alleging that disciplinary proceedings involving the loss of inmate good time violated the Due Process Clause of the Fourteenth Amendment to the U.S. Constitution, that inmate legal assistance during these proceedings did not meet constitutional standards, and that regulations allowing prison officials to open inmate mail to and from attorneys in the inmates' presence was unconstitutionally restrictive. The District Court refused to hear Wolff's due process claim and ruled in favor of Nebraska correctional officials on the other two complaints. The Eighth Circuit Court of Appeals reversed the District Court holding with respect to the due process claim, and held that procedural requirements applicable in parole revocation hearings that included advance notice to the inmate of the charges against him; disclosure of evidence to be used against the inmate; the opportunity to be heard in person and present witnesses and documentary evidence; a right to cross-examine adverse witnesses; a neutral and detached hearing body; and the possible appointment of an attorney to represent the inmate in certain circumstances should be followed in prison hearings involving the loss of good time. The Eighth Circuit Court also affirmed the District Court's ruling with regard to the opening of inmate mail, and ordered further proceedings to determine if the state met its burden in providing legal assistance to inmates during the disciplinary hearing. The case was petitioned to the U.S. Supreme Court, and it granted certiorari.

Issue

Whether Nebraska's prison disciplinary hearing complied with the Due Process Clause of the Fourteenth Amendment. Whether the inmate legal assistance program for these hearings met constitutional standards. Whether restrictions governing the opening of inmate mail to and from attorneys was unduly restrictive.

U.S. Supreme Court Holding

The Court affirmed in part, reversed in part, and remanded the case, holding that in inmate disciplinary hearings involving the loss of good time, there should be written notice of charges given to the inmate, a written statement as to the evidence relied on and reasons for disciplinary action, and the inmate should be allowed to call witnesses and present documentary evidence on his behalf, when doing so would not jeopardize institutional safety or correctional goals, but that due process does not require confrontation and cross-examination procedures and does not require the inmate to have a right to counsel. Unless the state provides some alternative to assist inmates at these hearings, inmates cannot be barred from assisting one another. No federal constitutional right was violated by the opening of inmate mail to and from attorneys by correctional officials in the presence of the inmate receiving the mail.

Reason

At the time of litigation, Nebraska's disciplinary hearing procedures involving the loss of inmate good time involved (1) a preliminary conference between the Chief Corrections Supervisor and the charging party where the inmate was informed of the conduct violation and engages in a discussion on its merits; (2) the preparation of a conduct report to be read to the inmate at a hearing before the Adjustment Committee composed of Associate Warden Custody, the Correctional Industries Superintendent, and the Reception Center Director; and (3) the opportunity to ask questions of the charging party.

The Court of Appeals suggested wholesale changes in the process similar to those used in parole revocation hearings that included (1) advance notice to the inmate of the charges against him; (2) disclosure of evidence to be used against the inmate; (3) the opportunity to be heard in person and present witnesses and documentary evidence; (4) a right to cross-examine adverse witnesses; (5) a neutral and detached hearing body; and (6) the possible appointment of an attorney to represent the inmate in certain circumstances. Despite this, the U.S. Supreme Court held that the Due Process Clause of the Fourteenth Amendment required (1) written notice of charges given to the inmate, (2) a written statement as to the evidence relied on and reasons for disciplinary action, and (3) that the inmate should be allowed to call witnesses and present documentary evidence on his behalf when doing so would not be unduly hazardous to institutional safety or correctional goals, but that due process does not require confrontation and cross-examination procedure and does not require the inmate to have a right to counsel.

In making its determination, the Court first noted that "the touchstone of due process is protection of the individual against arbitrary actions of the government," but that every case of government impairment of a private interest does not require a hearing. However, the Court found that Nebraska created a liberty interest for its inmates through the accumulation of good time, and that the loss of good time, because of disciplinary actions to a prisoner was serious enough to warrant minimal due process protections. In finding that each due process issue is different, the Court rejected using the "parole violation" procedural requirements ordered by the Court of Appeals in favor of the above requirements, which were fashioned by the Court to protect the specific due process rights of prisoners at disciplinary hearings involving the loss of good time, taking into consideration the security needs of corrections officials.

In total, the U.S. Supreme Court found no constitutional problems in allowing the Adjustment Committee to conduct the disciplinary hearings, limited the right to call witnesses on their behalf to situations the committee found that would not involve prison disturbances, and thought that injecting the attorney into such proceedings would not further correctional goals. The Court was concerned about the ability of illiterate inmates to understand the proceedings and further ordered that illiterate and all other inmates at such proceedings should be able to enlist the aid of other inmates in their defense, or receive substitute aid from the staff or competent inmates designated by the staff. The Court found no fault with the mail-opening procedures used by correctional officials.

Case Significance

This case is important for several reasons. First, it creates a procedure to be used when due process issues arise regarding the loss of good time earned by an inmate or where major prison disciplinary proceedings are concerned. Due process requires that written notice of the charges be given to the inmate; the factfinder makes written statements of the evidence relied on and reasons for the disciplinary action taken; and the inmate be allowed to call witnesses and present documentary evidence, except when doing so would be unduly hazardous to institutional security or correctional goals. Second, the case is important because it does not require that correctional institutions bear the expense of providing inmates with an attorney while they are processed through disciplinary hearings. In fact, the Court articulated that due process does not require confrontation and cross-examination of adverse witnesses or the right to counsel. What is important is that inmates be allowed a representative to assist, especially in cases where they may be illiterate. Third, the case allows correctional guards to open inmates' mail as long as the inmate is present. This decision it may serve to reduce claims from inmates that items were stolen, and it protects their right to privacy because they are present as mail is opened by prison officials.

Woods v. White
689 F. Supp. 874 (1988)

Facts

Plaintiff Donald Woods, a prisoner at Wisconsin's Waupun Correctional Institution, filed a Section 1983 lawsuit with the U.S. District Court for the Western District of Wisconsin against Nancy White and Sidney Smith, medical services personnel at the institution's Health Service Unit, claiming that his constitutional rights to privacy were violated in 1986, when White and Smith discussed with nonmedical staff and other inmates that Woods had tested positive for the AIDS virus. The defendants, White and Smith, moved the District Court for a judgment on the pleadings, contending that they were entitled to qualified immunity from any judgment for damages Woods may be entitled to because they could not have known in 1986 that Woods had a right to privacy in his medical records.

Issue

Whether Woods has constitutional rights to privacy in his medical records, and if so, are White and Smith entitled to qualified immunity from any damages Woods may be entitled to for violating his right to privacy.

Holding by the District Court

The District Court judge denied the defendants' motion, holding that as a prisoner, Woods retained his constitutional right to privacy in his medical records and the defense of qualified immunity is not available to the defendants because their unjustified dissemination of confidential medical information to nonmedical staff and other inmates cannot be said to be within their sphere of discretionary functions.

Reason

The District Court determined that a citizen has a constitutional right to privacy in his or her medical records and in the doctor-patient relationship, and that this right is not automatically relinquished when a person becomes incarcerated. In reviewing other constitutional rights to privacy cases, the court determined that privacy rights determinations were made on a case-by-case basis, and the main issue was to weigh the individual's right to confidentiality against the government's reason for disclosure. However, with this case, the court could not find any legitimate countervailing governing interest in the disclosure that Woods tested positive for AIDS. After finding that Woods had privacy rights in his medical records regarding any information relating to AIDS, the court continued to determine if White and Smith were entitled to qualified immunity in 1986 because Woods's right to privacy in his medical records was not clearly established by then, and White and Smith could not have known he had such a right.

The court noted that to have qualified immunity, government officials must show that their "conduct did not violate clearly established statutory or constitutional rights of which a reasonable person would have known," and that the argument for qualified immunity turns on the issue of whether a reasonable person would have known in 1986 that Woods had an expectation of privacy in his medical records. The court resolved the qualified immunity issue by finding that it should have been clear in 1986 to any government official that individual prisoners had a constitutional right to privacy in their medical records for information relating to AIDS. Calling White and Smith's disclosure of Woods's testing positive for AIDS to nonmedical staff and other inmates an unjustified dissemination of information not within the defendant's spheres of discretionary functions, the court denied the motion for a judgment on the pleadings.

Case Significance

The case is important for two reasons. First, it serves to provide AIDS-infected inmates with a degree of protection. More specifically, the court ruled that prisoners' HIV/AIDS status cannot be shared or revealed to other inmates or anyone who is not connected with the medical records in places of confinement. The court stated that while inmates forgo degrees of privacy while incarcerated, they retain privacy where their medical records are concerned. Public disclosure of an inmate's HIV/AIDS status could lead to disparate treatment, violence, or even segregation by others in the institution. Second, the case also clarifies that the defense of qualified immunity cannot be used to justify disseminating confidential medical information to nonmedical staff and other prisoners. This seems to suggest that an inmate could prevail with a legal claim.

Index